RELIGION IN
ANCIENT EGYPT

RELIGION IN ANCIENT EGYPT

Gods, Myths, and Personal Practice

Edited by BYRON E. SHAFER

Authors

JOHN BAINES

LEONARD H. LESKO

DAVID P. SILVERMAN

Cornell University Press ITHACA AND LONDON

First published 1991 by Cornell University Press.
First printing, Cornell Paperbacks, 1991.

Library of Congress Cataloging-in-Publication Data

Religion in ancient Egypt : gods, myths, and personal practice /
    edited by Byron E. Shafer : contributors, John Baines, Leonard H.
  Lesko, David P. Silverman.
        p. cm.
    Lectures given at a symposium held in 1987, sponsored by Fordham
  University
    Includes bibliographical references and index.
    ISBN 0-8014-2550-6 (alk. paper). — ISBN 0-8014-9786-8 (pbk. :
  alk. paper)
    1. Egypt—Religion—Congresses. 2. Cosmogony, Egyptian—
  Congresses. I. Shafer, Byron E. (Byron Esely), 1938– .
  II. Baines, John, 1946– . III. Lesko, Leonard H. IV. Silverman,
  David P. V. Fordham University.
  BL2441.2.R35 1991
  299'.31–dc20   90-40874

Printed in the United States of America

Cloth printing   10 9 8 7 6 5 4 3 2 1

Paperback printing   10 9 8 7 6 5 4

Dedicated to
Charles and Elizabeth Holman

CONTENTS

MAPS

PREFACE

Egyptology is a dynamic field. Ongoing archaeological and epigraphical investigations continuously produce fresh data, some of which point the way to reformulations of previously held hypotheses about ancient Egyptian life, thought, and history. North American and British scholars have contributed significantly to Egyptology. Yet most studies of ancient Egyptian religion have been written by German, Swiss, Dutch, and French scholars. Since 1960 only one book written originally in English has surveyed broad areas of ancient Egyptian religion for a general as well as a scholarly audience.[1]

Charles and Elizabeth Holman, retired business people and lay scholars of ancient Egypt, are the founders and patrons of an annual Egyptological symposium sponsored by Fordham University in New York City. Fascinated by the role of religion in humankind's quest for meaning, the Holmans chose "Ancient Egyptian Religion" as the topic for the 1987 symposium. As co-director of Fordham's Middle East Studies Program and its teacher of the ancient Near East, I began planning the symposium with the Holmans. We were of course aware that the magisterial works on Egyptian religion by Siegfried Morenz and Erik Hornung had become available in English translation in 1973 and 1982,

---

1. A. Rosalie David, *The Ancient Egyptians: Religious Beliefs and Practices* (London: Routledge & Kegan Paul, 1982).

respectively.[2] As we reflected on the symposium's subject and on the available literature, however, we noted a need for an up-to-date, English-language survey of major aspects of ancient Egyptian religion written for the nonspecialist reader. We invited two Egyptologists from the United States, Leonard Lesko of Brown University and David Silverman of the University of Pennsylvania, and one from England, John Baines of the University of Oxford, to give lectures at the symposium, and asked them to commit themselves to the development of their lectures into chapters with accompanying notes for the book that I would undertake to edit. They accepted the assignments and fulfilled their tasks.

Would that Egyptologists could agree on matters of chronology and the spelling of ancient names! The authors of this volume could not always do so. Egyptologists' differences of opinion are based on variant readings of the evidence and are legitimately held. Yet I felt it necessary to standardize chronology and spelling throughout this volume. Some of my choices go against the preference of one author or another. Leonard Lesko disagrees with the dating adopted for the Predynastic and Early Dynastic Periods and with the inclusion of the Third Dynasty in the Early Dynastic Period. He therefore disagrees with one or two of the dates that I have placed in his chapter. John Baines prefers to assign Narmer to the Late Predynastic Period and to exclude the possibility that he was Menes. For these and other disputable editorial decisions, each of the authors has, I believe, forgiven me.

BYRON E. SHAFER

New York, New York

---

2. Siegfried Morenz, *Egyptian Religion*, trans. Ann E. Keep (Ithaca: Cornell University Press; London: Methuen, 1973); Erik Hornung, *Conceptions of God in Ancient Egypt: The One and the Many*, trans. John Baines (Ithaca: Cornell University Press, 1982; London: Routledge & Kegan Paul, 1983).

ABBREVIATIONS

ADAIK   Abhandlungen des Deutschen Archäologischen Instituts, Abteilung Kairo, Ägyptologische Reihe (Glückstadt: Augustin).

AEL   Miriam Lichtheim, *Ancient Egyptian Literature*, 3 vols. (Berkeley: University of California Press, 1973–1980).

ÄgAbh   Ägyptologische Abhandlungen (Wiesbaden: Harrassowitz).

ANET   *Ancient Near Eastern Texts Relating to the Old Testament*, ed. James B. Pritchard, 3d ed. with supplement (Princeton: Princeton University Press, 1969).

AVDAIK   Archäologische Veröffentlichungen des Deutschen Archäologischen Instituts, Abteilung Kairo (Mainz: von Zabern).

BdÉ   Bibliothèque d'Étude (Cairo: Imprimerie de l'Institut français d'Archéologie orientale).

BiAe   Bibliotheca Aegyptiaca (Brussels: Fondation Égyptologique Reine Élisabeth).

BIFAO   *Bulletin de l'Institut français d'Archéologie orientale.*

JARCE   *Journal of the American Research Center in Egypt.*

JEA   *Journal of Egyptian Archaeology.*

JNES   *Journal of Near Eastern Studies.*

LÄ   *Lexikon der Ägyptologie*, ed. Wolfgang Helck, Eberhard Otto, and Wolfhart Westendorf, 7 vols. (Wiesbaden: Harrassowitz, 1972–).

LAE   *The Literature of Ancient Egypt*, ed. William Kelly Simpson (New Haven: Yale University Press, 1972).

MÄS   Münchner Ägyptologische Studien.

MDAIK   *Mitteilungen des Deutschen Archäologischen Instituts, Abteilung Kairo.*

OBO   Orbis biblicus et orientalis (Freiburg, Switzerland: Universitätsverlag; Göttingen: Vandenhoeck & Ruprecht).

OMRO	*Oudheidkundige Mededelingen uit het Rijksmuseum van Oudheden te Leiden.*
PÄ	Probleme der Ägyptologie (Leiden: Brill).
RdÉ	*Revue d'Égyptologie.*
SAK	*Studien zur Altägyptischen Kultur.*
SDAIK	Sonderschriften des Deutschen Archäologischen Instituts, Abteilung Kairo (Mainz: von Zabern).
Urk.	Urkunden des ägyptischen Altertums.
ZÄS	*Zeitschrift für Ägyptische Sprache und Altertumskunde.*

INTRODUCTION

Byron E. Shafer

Ancient Egyptian civilization flourished for the better part of three thousand years before fading from existence nearly two millennia ago, during the Roman Empire. In our time, important elements of that civilization have come to life again, if only in museums and books. Nineteenth- and twentieth-century scholars have labored to recover and interpret artifacts of ancient Egypt. The results have enthralled the modern Western world. Headlines and news reports arising from Howard Carter's excavations during the 1920s made "King Tut" a household name, and the public's enthusiasm for the beauty produced by the artisans of Tutankhamun and other Egyptian kings has steadily increased since then. Western tourists stream to Egypt. The Egyptian galleries in such places as London's British Museum, New York City's Metropolitan and Brooklyn museums, and Boston's Museum of Fine Arts teem with avid visitors. And artifacts from excavations in Egypt are a particular focus in the museums of such universities as Chicago, Pennsylvania, Oxford, and Cambridge.

What is it about the ruins and remains of ancient Egypt that captures a Western heart and fascinates a Western mind? Two factors, no doubt, are the artifacts' scope and scale. We are impressed by the big and the bountiful. Two additional factors are their opulence and refinement. We are drawn to what is rich and elegant. But once our interest is whetted by these qualities, what *holds* us is more profound. The artifacts' symmetry and orderedness project a balance and harmony that we seek for

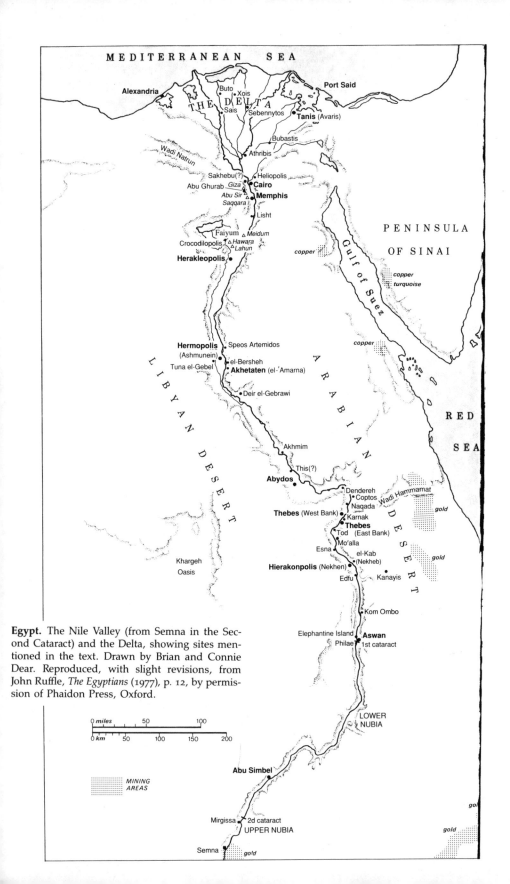

Egypt. The Nile Valley (from Semna in the Second Cataract) and the Delta, showing sites mentioned in the text. Drawn by Brian and Connie Dear. Reproduced, with slight revisions, from John Ruffle, *The Egyptians* (1977), p. 12, by permission of Phaidon Press, Oxford.

ourselves; their homogeneity and stability of form project a congruence and repose that contrast with the pluralism and change that threaten to overwhelm us; and their serene air of confidence projects the kind of tranquil surety for which we long. The artifacts also provide us with inexhaustible images of the triumph of good over evil.

Our aesthetic empathy with ancient Egypt gives rise to questions that probe for a deeper understanding of its culture. What balance did Egyptians strike between picturing life as it *was* and portraying life as it was *hoped to be?* Did images and symbols express the world view of the elite alone, or did they also convey concepts held by peasants? And what world of thought and action lay behind the myriad representations of religious subjects and themes?

As ancient Egyptian artistry is immediately satisfying to modern Western observers, so ancient Egyptian religion is immediately puzzling. Many people today, though undoubtedly concerned with the problem of life's meaning, are agnostics or atheists; very few such people could be found among the ancient Egyptians. Many people today find life's meaning outside of religion and view religion as incidental or tangential to life; very few ancient Egyptians saw it this way. Of today's devout, all but a very few are monotheists; of ancient Egypt's, all but a very few were polytheists. We read theology and value abstraction; they recited myths and preferred concreteness. We demand consistency in religious thought; they did not. We hold omnipotence and omniscience to be necessary attributes of divinity; they did not. We have a canon of scripture; they did not. We reject magic; they did not. We view government as secular and rulers as all too human; they saw government as sacred and kings as somehow divine. We believe that the world needs to be improved, and therefore (if we are religious) to be transformed by communal obedience to God's revealed will; they believed that the world needs to be maintained, and therefore to be stabilized by governmental imposition of order from above.

Egyptian artifacts signal to us in unmistakable ways that religion not only suffused the culture but also shaped it. In order to understand the ancient Egyptians, it is crucial to surmount the apparent "foreignness" of their religion and to attain both a comprehension of their beliefs and practices and an appreciation of them. We can begin the process by recognizing that despite our differences from ancient Egyptians in religious experience, belief, and ritual, the quest for life's meaning has taken us through common territory.

Humans are, as Clifford Geertz tells us, "symbolizing, conceptualizing, meaning-seeking" creatures, and we possess what the ancient Egyptians and all humanity have possessed—a drive "to make sense out of experience, to give it form and order," a drive that is "evidently as real and as pressing as the more familiar biological needs." Simply put, we humans cannot live in a world that we do not understand, so we are driven to establish meaning.[1] Across time, space, and culture, in all of humanity's wrestlings with life and its meaning, the issues have been the same; the questions have been the same. Recognition of this bond with peoples of the past can give rise within us to an empathy capable of transcending our theological and liturgical particularities, an empathy that permits us to value another people's answers, another people's religion.

Some of the questions that today's meaning-seekers share with the meaning-seekers of ancient Egypt are the following:[2]

- Is there something "greater than us" that we identify as deity? If there is, who or what is this divine entity? Is it uncreated or created? Is it singular or plural? Is it shrouded in mystery, or has it been significantly revealed? If revealed, in what or in whom or by what or by whom, and how? Is it within us, among us, or beyond us? Does it have attributes of personhood? What are its powers, and where and how are they manifest?
- What is the nature of the world and the heavens? Did they emanate from the divine, were they created by the divine, or are they unrelated to anything divine? If created, by what process? Are the world and the heavens eternal, or will they come to an end? Are they ordered or chaotic, or both? Are they places of good or of evil, or of both? What are space and time? Do various spaces differ from one another in quality? Do various times differ in quality?
- What is humanity's place both within the world and in relation to the divine? Were we created by the divine? If so, by what process and in what relation to the rest of creation? From what were we made? Of what are we composed? Are we in any way like the divine? Are we in any way like the animals? Are humans meant to

1. Clifford Geertz, *The Interpretation of Cultures: Selected Essays* (New York: Basic Books, 1973), pp. 140, 141.
2. See Joachim Wach, *The Comparative Study of Religions* (New York: Columbia University Press, 1961), pp. 76–95.

be equal, or are we meant to differ from one another in status and rank? What is happiness? How is it found and maintained? What is suffering—its causes, its purposes, its meanings? How can it be overcome? Why does what happens to us happen to us? Is it by fate, by our own choice, or by divine determination? What does the divine expect of us or demand of us? What actions are good, and what actions are bad? Is there life beyond death? If there is, how is it gained or received? What will it be like? Where will it happen? How shall we get there?

The chapters that follow deal with many of these questions.

When we study ancient Egyptian approaches to such questions, it is important to focus on the religious concepts and practices of priests and other members of the intellectual and economic elite, for it is specifically to these concepts and practices that the great preponderance of artifacts testify. It is also important, however, to search out the religious concepts and practices of the common people, insofar as they are accessible to us. In our own world, we recognize that the religious beliefs and actions of a cleric or professional theologian may differ from those of a tenant farmer, assembly-line worker, or homemaker. So, too, in ancient Egypt the religious beliefs and actions of a king, priest, or erudite author might differ from those of a peasant, stonecutter, or serving woman. Concern for presenting the religion of both elite and ordinary people has guided the preparation and organization of this volume.

David Silverman delineates and analyzes ancient Egyptian concepts of the divine and then categorizes and discusses specific gods, their associations, their powers, and their positions in the divine hierarchy. He also treats a subject that has become one of the most disputed in Egyptology—the divinity of the king. In that context, Silverman comments extensively on the pharaoh Akhenaten.

Leonard Lesko explores ancient Egyptian mythology and offers his own translations of key passages. First, he focuses on cosmogonies—myths of the origins of the gods and of the creation of the cosmos, myths that grounded the power of the divine king in his connection to the creator. Lesko then traces major changes and developments in cosmogonical thought over the course of Egyptian history, including a treatment of the Aten and Akhenaten. Lastly, Lesko offers a brief description of cosmological thought—understandings of the nature, structure, and layout of the cosmos.

John Baines seeks to uncover religious practices of the common people as they confronted the reality of widespread suffering and misfortune, a reality at odds with the decorous images of life that dominated elite art and literature. As integral parts of his project, Baines offers hypotheses about social conditions among the masses; the decorum of elite art and literature; the interplay between the concepts of freedom and determination; the bonds between the living and the dead; the deification of individuals; the place of magic, divination, dream interpretation, and other religious rites in the pious practices of individuals; the phenomenon of personal religious experience; and the evolution of people's conception of the creator god.

Nor will these subjects be the only ones. To quote an Egyptian scribe:

> I'll tell you also other things,
> So as to teach you knowledge.[3]

3. From The Satire of the Trades, trans. Miriam Lichtheim, *AEL* 1:190.

1 DIVINITY AND DEITIES IN ANCIENT EGYPT

David P. Silverman

For many people, the religion of ancient Egypt conjures up images of hybrid creatures, bearing animal heads and human bodies. Surely the material culture of Egypt has left countless examples of such figures in painting and in both two- and three-dimensional sculpture. These deities had identities and associations, and they figure prominently in the religious texts during the recorded history of the country and are part of a very complicated and sophisticated set of religious beliefs. It is not possible simply to label one deity a god of one thing and another the god of something else. There were many identifications and interrelations among the members of the pantheon, but underlying this complex network of deities was a highly developed concept of the divine, one that came into being during the early stages of the ancient civilization and evolved into the doctrines upon which the religion of ancient Egypt would be based for more than three thousand years.

My gratitude is extended to Charles and Elizabeth Holman, whose enthusiastic interest and support were responsible for the original symposium and for this volume. I greatly appreciate the efforts of Byron Shafer of Fordham University in organizing the symposium and editing this book. This chapter would not have been possible without the research and editing assistance provided by Melissa Robinson of the University of Pennsylvania. My fellow Egyptologists John Baines and Leonard Lesko were generous with ideas and helpful comments. Janet Richards also made several valuable suggestions with regard to anthropology. *LÄ* is referred to in the notes frequently and is a convenient source of up-to-date references. Entries are often abbreviated, and interested readers are urged to consult the sources quoted therein for detailed studies.

1. Spells on the walls of the pyramid of King Merenre (Sixth Dynasty). South Saqqara. Photo © 1991 by David P. Silverman.

CONCEPTS OF THE DIVINE

To determine what the early Egyptians understood as divine is not a simple task. The developmental stages of their prehistoric records have provided few material remains and even less context. Such concepts are easier to discern in the historical period, a time when the ideas could find expression in form and substance. It is then that religious inscriptions came into frequent use. One set, first recorded during the Old Kingdom on the interior chambers of several of the pyramids at Saqqara, is known as the Pyramid Texts (fig. 1). These funerary inscriptions contain enough descriptive, narrative, and conversational data to allow scholars to form theories about the concepts of divinity during pharaonic times and to offer hypotheses about the concepts in use in the even more distant past. The abundant complementary artifactual and archaeological evidence that was produced during this and later periods is the visible manifestation of those concepts.

As the Egyptians' civilization developed, they recorded more and more, and they documented their beliefs in other collections of spells. Eventually decoration was associated with the texts on the walls of tombs, coffins, and temples. The Egyptians also produced related religious artifacts and illustrated papyri that can provide modern scholars with additional information. Other texts, scenes, and objects facilitate the study of Egyptian concepts of the divine. The wealth of available material increases as one moves from the earlier to the later periods of Egyptian civilization. The material more greatly benefits the study of the religion of well-represented periods than that of the religion of periods less well documented.

Many modern examinations of godhood in the earlier periods of Egyptian civilization have been based primarily on theories developed from materials of the later time periods. In view of the conservative nature of the Egyptians in general and the archaic style of religious texts in particular, such analyses have much merit. One must not forget, however, that these late sources, although more abundant than earlier ones, were far removed from the time the original ideas were formulated and may contain errors or misconceptions that were compounded as they were handed down.

During dynastic times, the Egyptians composed and recorded many theologies detailing the creation of their universe and the origin of the deities and humankind. The theologies were sophisticated, well formulated, and well developed, and in the recent past they have attracted much commentary and interpretation. The formative stages of ancient Egypt's religion have received less investigation, probably because of the ambiguity of prehistoric and archaic remains. Yet scholars are paying increasing attention to these periods. One thinks first of the ground-breaking theoretical essays collected in *The Intellectual Adventure of Ancient Man;* the insightful interpretations of prehistoric and archaic artifactual material by William Hayes, Walther Wolf, Peter Ucko, and Winifred Needler; and studies by Siegfried Morenz, Erik Hornung, and Jan Assmann.[1]

Archaeological evidence from the time before the invention of writing may possibly suggest the existence of developed concepts of the divine.[2] The people of that period venerated animals; they had cult objects; they made sacred burials; and they had places devoted to rituals. All are indications of a sophisticated set of beliefs that may well imply the presence of a divine being or beings. One notes in particular the care taken with human burials in the time before 3000 B.C.E. (fig. 2). Such care clearly implies developed funerary beliefs then existed.

We have no textual evidence, before the introduction of writing, to explicate the meanings of these practices and of the rituals and objects associated with them. Thus we must rely on observation to interpret objects as divine and to infer the underlying concepts. Consider an enigmatic statue of a falcon in the Brooklyn Museum.[3] It has no archaeological or inscriptional context, yet the specific shape of the object and later contextualized parallels suggest that this falcon may have been one of the earliest images used for oracles. Thus, while written contexts and archaeological settings are extremely important for the analysis of re-

---

1. Henri Frankfort et al., *The Intellectual Adventure of Ancient Man* (Chicago: University of Chicago Press, 1946); William C. Hayes, *Most Ancient Egypt* (Chicago: University of Chicago Press, 1965); Walther Wolf, *Die Kunst Ägyptens: Gestalt und Geschichte* (Stuttgart: Kohlhammer, 1957); Peter J. Ucko, *Anthropomorphic Figurines of Predynastic Egypt and Neolithic Crete with Comparative Material from the Prehistoric Near East and Mainland Greece* (London: Szmidla, 1968); Winifred Needler, *Predynastic and Archaic Egypt in the Brooklyn Museum* (New York: Brooklyn Museum, 1984); Siegfried Morenz, *Egyptian Religion,* trans. Ann E. Keep (London: Methuen; Ithaca: Cornell University Press, 1973); Erik Hornung, *Conceptions of God in Ancient Egypt: The One and the Many,* trans. John Baines (Ithaca: Cornell University Press, 1982; London: Routledge & Kegan Paul, 1983). Works by Jan Assmann are listed in Hornung's bibliography and in the selected bibliography in this volume.

2. Hornung, *Conceptions of God,* pp. 100–103.

3. "The Nodding Falcon of the Guennol Collection at The Brooklyn Museum," *Brooklyn Museum Annual* 9 (1967–68): 69–87 (several useful references to other archaic animal figures appear in the notes). See also Needler, *Predynastic and Archaic Egypt,* pp. 368–69.

2. Reconstruction of a Predynastic burial in Egypt, c. 3500 B.C.E. Artifacts are from the Naqada II phase. University Museum, University of Pennsylvania, Philadelphia. Photo (neg. #134562) courtesy of the University Museum, University of Pennsylvania.

ligious beliefs, they are not the only means to determine the religious significance of an object and the concepts underlying its creation.

Still, the difficulty of determining the original concepts of the divine must not be underestimated, for in order to examine them properly one has to project back even further in time. Opinions vary as to just how and when the concept of the divine developed and what form it took. Anthropologists have offered theories about the development of such ideas in the early phases of civilization; historians of religion and Egyptologists have made suggestions as well.[4] But Egyptian beliefs were fluid even during the historic period, and they were never consolidated into a single source that remained constant throughout history. Because the Egyptians had no one "sacred book," scholars do not have a standard theological text on which to rely for information about the relatively well-documented periods. Therefore, the formative stages are extremely difficult to interpret accurately.

Nevertheless, it seems appropriate to speculate that the divine was originally conceived of rather amorphously and that it gradually came to be envisioned in its relation to the world, that is, in relation to natural phenomena. By moving the divine from a more abstract level, or perhaps even a transcendent one, to a more concrete stage, humans could make it more recognizable.[5] It would seem, however, that people could engage in such thought processes only when they had become sophisticated enough to exercise some control over their environment. Then they would have had the time and energy to think about issues beyond their own immediate situation and to formulate concepts involved with long-term survival.

Some scholars have suggested that it was only after writing was introduced that the ancient Egyptians became sophisticated enough intellectually to conceive of god as a person.[6] It is more likely, however, that Egyptians were "advanced" enough to conceive of a higher power or

4. In *Reader in Comparative Religion,* ed. William A. Lessa and Evon Z. Vogt, 4th ed. (New York: Harper & Row, 1979), see Edward B. Tylor, "Animism," pp. 9–19; Sherry B. Ortner, "On Key Symbols," pp. 92–98; and James G. Frazer, "Sympathetic Magic," pp. 337–52. And see the bibliographies in Morenz, *Egyptian Religion,* and in Hornung, *Conceptions of God,* and the works of Morenz, Hornung, and Hans Bonnet cited therein. C. J. Bleeker has also provided a useful bibliography in *Hathor and Thoth,* Studies in the History of Religions 26 (Leiden: Brill, 1973), pp. 161–66, which includes references to his own important studies.

5. For interpretations of "transcendent," see Hornung, *Conceptions of God,* pp. 190–96, and the books and articles of Assmann (see n. 1).

6. See, e.g., Morenz, *Egyptian Religion,* p. 17.

force in human terms before the introduction of writing, for as early as the Predynastic Period they were creating images that may well have represented manifestations of power. Such artifacts, both human and animal in form, occur in various sizes, and the provenances of these artifacts, especially of those from funerary contexts, tend to support the idea of their association with a powerful being or source of veneration.[7] Moreover, the very fact that these images were already being produced in the Predynastic Period suggests that images and decorative motifs deriving from even earlier periods may anticipate or represent the developmental stages of a belief in divine power.[8] Certainly the care with which the dead were buried before 3000 B.C.E. and the developed funerary belief implied by that care suggest sufficient sophistication for such a concept.

Whether conceptualizing the divine in human images rather than in natural or animal images is more advanced and therefore later in date has been much debated.[9] The art of the earliest part of the Predynastic Period has virtually no representations of either human or animal forms, nor have burials of "sacred" animals been found. We do have evidence, however, that humans were interred at that time, an indication of a belief in an afterlife. Figures in what appear to be human form do occur slightly later, and while some of them may be images of fertility and others images of divinity, such interpretations are not universally accepted. Later in the Predynastic Period, animals were buried in what may have been ritual circumstances, and such burials are found in association with contemporary objects that may well represent the divine in animal form.

Yet what appears most significant is not the form the concept of the divine took but the fact that the concept could be manifest in an image. For even when the power/force was represented as an animal, it was possible that the believer also attributed to it human behaviors and traits. Perhaps animal and human elements were fused, as often appears

7. Predynastic figures of human females, birds, turtles, hippopotami, and other animals have been discovered in the excavations of Sir W. M. Flinders Petrie, Walter B. Emery, and others. Needler illustrates several of them in *Predynastic and Archaic Egypt* [n. 1], pp. 335 and 337. She notes that "little is known about their meaning," but that "it has been plausibly suggested that they are symbols of resurrection."

8. Even earlier figures and rock drawings exist. See the comments on and the references to works on this subject in Hayes, *Most Ancient Egypt* [n. 1], pp. 89–90.

9. Morenz, *Egyptian Religion*, p. 17; Hornung, *Conceptions of God*, pp. 101–9 (particularly 105).

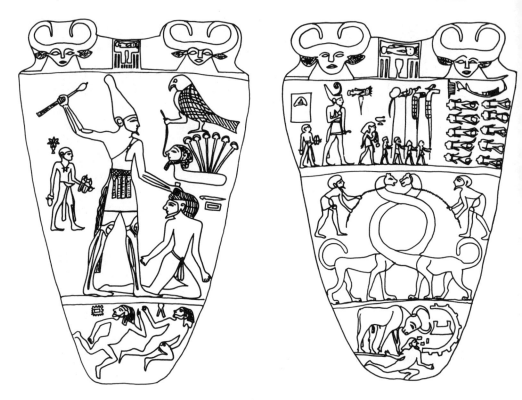

3. Ceremonial palette of King Narmer (First Dynasty). Drawing by Jennifer Houser, after Walter Emery, *Archaic Egypt* (Baltimore: Penguin, 1961), fig. 4.

to have been the case in pharaonic times.[10] Divinities of the Predynastic Period often took the forms of animals, and the animal was frequently shown engaged in a human activity, such as conquering enemies. Such representations occur on the ceremonial palette of King Narmer (fig. 3) and the Libyan Booty Palette. In the same period, one can even find the motif of animal-topped standards with human arms.

Later pictorial and written evidence seems to support the idea of a fusion of animal and human elements. Many deities in the Egyptian

10. Examples of the gods' human behavior and expressions of emotion abound in the religious texts of all periods and are found also in the popular literature. No less frequent are the visual examples, such as the falcon-headed human figure representing Horus depicted on the walls of his temple at Edfu and the Hathoric capitals, such as those in the Temple of Hathor at Dendereh, where the goddess is represented as a human female with bovine ears.

4. Painted scene of Prince Amenherkhopeshef (Twentieth Dynasty) and the god Khnum, in the prince's tomb. Valley of the Queens, Thebes. Photo © 1991 by Byron E. Shafer.

pantheon have animal forms but manifest human behavior, and some can even be represented in a combination of animal and human forms. The god Khnum has the head of a ram and the body of a human (fig. 4); Hathor can be pictured as fully bovine (figs. 5 and 6) or as a human female with the ears of a cow (fig. 7); and the sun god Re-Horakhty can appear as a falcon or as a falcon-headed human (fig. 8).

The religious and literary texts describe the gods as possessing mainly human characteristics: they thought; they spoke; they dined; and they had emotions. Furthermore, they went into battle and traveled by boat. Some even drank to excess, as illustrated by the behavior of the goddess Hathor in The Destruction of Mankind.[11] In The Contendings of Horus

11. For a selection of texts, see *AEL*. The Destruction of Mankind is in *AEL* 2:197–99. See also The Contendings of Horus and Seth, trans. Edward F. Wente, in *LAE* 108–26.

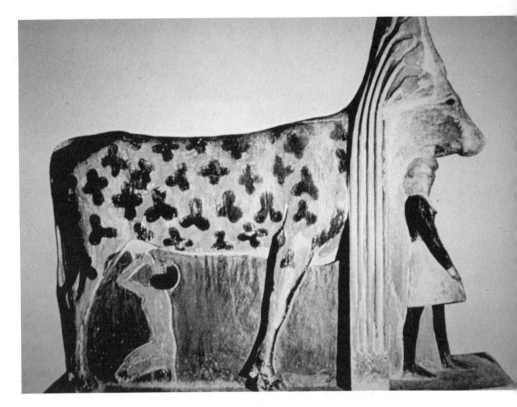

5. Bovine figure of the goddess Hathor protecting and suckling the king, from the Shrine of Hathor, Deir el-Bahri, western Thebes. Egyptian Museum, Cairo. Photo © 1991 by Leonard H. Lesko.

and Seth, a literary text of the New Kingdom with roots in the earliest religious literature, the gods had a sense of humor: in many episodes the antagonist, Seth, is shown as a fool and a frequent butt of jokes. In the same story Hathor exposes herself in a ribald effort to cheer her father out of a bad mood.[12]

These depictions, whether visual or literary, represent a recognizable conceptualization of what was perhaps originally a more abstract divine power or force. The characteristics possessed by these concretizations were those the Egyptians envisioned the supreme power or force to have. The images were not meant to represent actual forms; they were

12. *LAE* 108, 112. For further study of this text, see the bibliographical items cited in *LAE* 108–9.

6. Scene of the deities Taweret (center), Hathor (right), and Sokar-Osiris (left), from the funerary papyrus (Book of the Dead) belonging to the Royal Scribe Ani (Nineteenth Dynasty). British Museum, London, 10470. Photo © Byron E. Shafer.

references to a higher idea of the divine. For that reason a particular force could have multiple images, traits, and descriptions, each of which referred to any or all of its numerous mysterious aspects.[13] The image that the individual saw or read about was only the essence of the actual power it represented; the power, however, could be manifest in the image.

The recognition of some sort of supreme force was the first step in an attempt to distinguish between the individual and the world in which that individual lived.[14] Moreover, that step was taken to gain some control over the phenomena of nature. The many examples of deities

13. Cf. Hornung, *Conceptions of God*, p. 117.
14. Morenz, *Egyptian Religion*, p. 17, uses "power" rather than "force."

7. Hathor capital on a column in the Shrine of Hathor. The mortuary temple of Hatshepsut (Eighteenth Dynasty), Deir el-Bahri, western Thebes. Photo © 1991 by Byron E. Shafer.

associated with cosmic elements during the historic period attest to the importance of this stage in the early phases of the development of the beliefs. At first the supreme force would seem awesome and mysterious, but once it could be comprehended as an entity, it could be recognized, understood, and then reinterpreted in a familiar and recurrent form. In a way, the force could be harnessed. It became humanized. That is, it was put in terms the individual could understand.

If recognition of a supreme force was to develop into a set of religious beliefs, the anthropomorphized concepts had to be organized in such a way that they were comprehensible to most of the population. The ancient Egyptians chose to express them in a variety of concrete visual and written images. Thus the people could envision them in the decoration that covered the walls of the public parts of the temples and tombs, they could read of them in the religious literature, or they could hear of them in popular stories or oral legends.

8. Painted figure of Re-Horakhty and Hathor, Mistress of the West, in the tomb of Queen Nefertari (Nineteenth Dynasty). Valley of the Queens, Thebes. Photo © 1991 by David P. Silverman.

Each culture determines in its own way the form or forms that the supreme being or beings eventually take, but almost all cultures relate the form in some fashion to that of the person.[15] In Egypt the forms were numerous. They could be human (such as the gods Amun and Ptah [fig. 9]) or animal (such as the gods Anubis, pictured as a jackal, and Sobek, as a crocodile). They could also combine human and animal forms in one image (such as the gods Horus, often shown as a falcon-headed man, and Sekhmet, as a lioness-headed woman [fig. 10]). The

15. See Hornung, *Conceptions of God*, p. 105.

9. Relief depicting (left to right) Ptah, Amun, pharaoh, Thoth, and Seshat. Medinet Habu, the mortuary temple of King Ramesses III (Twentieth Dynasty), Thebes. Photo © 1991 by Byron E. Shafer.

form could even vary with the situation (the god Thoth could take the form of an ibis, a baboon, or an ibis-headed human [figs. 11, 12]).[16] A few deities appeared in the forms of creatures not known in the Egyptian environment, but such images were usually composed of parts of animals that ordinarily did appear there (the goddess Taweret embodied parts of a hippopotamus, a crocodile, and a lioness [fig. 6]). The origins of some deities, such as Seth, are not so obvious to us, but their appearance seems naturalistic.[17] Totally fantastic images were unusual in the repertoire, but griffins, sphinxes, and bandy-legged leonine dwarfs did occur.

When elements of the cosmos and environment were rendered in

16. For further discussion of this deity, see Bleeker, *Hathor and Thoth* [n. 4], pp. 106–60.
17. Just what animal(s) Seth represents is debatable. See Herman te Velde, "Seth," *LÄ* 5:908–11.

10. Triad depicting Ptah (left), Sekhmet (right), and King Ramesses II (center) (Nineteenth Dynasty), presumably as a manifestation of Nefertem. Egyptian Museum, Cairo. Photo © 1991 by David P. Silverman.

concrete form, they usually took human shape. Geb (the earth) and Nut (the sky), for example, were pictured respectively as a man and a woman (fig. 13), and the inundation of the Nile, Hapy, was represented as a corpulent man (fig. 14).[18] Even Amun, who may originally have been associated with air and whose name means "the hidden one," took the form of a man. Often the same deity was depicted in animal, human, and combination forms, but the first two predominated. Gender was almost always indicated; hermaphroditic or androgynous images were rare, though fecundity figures were sometimes portrayed as such.

The sort of form that was first used to concretize a supreme power/force is debatable. Again, archaeological evidence is ambiguous.

18. For a full discussion of the significance of these images, see John Baines, *Fecundity Figures: Egyptian Personification and the Iconology of a Genre* (Chicago: Bolchazy-Carducci, 1985).

11. Relief depicting (left to right) the god Thoth, King Ramesses II (Nineteenth Dynasty), and the triad of Thebes—the gods Amun, Mut, and Khonsu. The Ramesseum, the king's mortuary temple, Thebes. Photo © 1991 by Byron E. Shafer.

Something that may confuse the issue is the very early appearance of what seems to be a divine fetish, an emblem that is usually an inanimate, apparently symbolic object. Its often enigmatic form is not always recognizable today as human, animal, or natural.

Regardless of which image came first, the simple recognition of the individual and therefore of the separation of the individual from the elemental forces was in reality a humanization of the world.[19] This development obviated any need for separate concretizations of particular human emotions, for when a deity was formulated and then anthropomorphized, it took on human attributes, whatever its image.

19. Morenz, *Egyptian Religion*, pp. 19–20, and the discussion there of Kurt Sethe, *Urgeschichte und älteste Religion der Ägypter*, Abhandlungen für die Kunde des Morgenlandes 18/4 (Leipzig: Deutsche Morgenländische Gesellschaft, 1930), sec. 31, pp. 24–25.

12. Late Period statuette of the god Thoth, found in the area of Hermopolis. Mallawi Museum, Egypt. Photo © 1991 by David P. Silverman.

Thus these human qualities were evident in most deities and ordinarily could not identify a specific god and were not meant to do so. This understanding allowed for a certain flexibility in divine roles and accounts for the multifaceted nature of Egyptian divinities. Isis could be the conniving female who attempts to learn the secret name of the sun god, the loving sister and wife of the god of the underworld (fig. 15), and the protective mother of Horus. The Egyptian deities were more fluid than those of Greece and Rome, who tended to have static roles and to be identified more with specific human emotions.

Once the form of the deity had been developed, a legend, myth, or story was formulated to explain its origin and associations, and in this process the god received a name. Whether all of this happened simultaneously or at intervals is uncertain, and it may be difficult to come to a satisfactory conclusion.[20] Investigation of the meaning of the names of

20. Morenz, *Egyptian Religion*, pp. 23–24, and Hornung, *Conceptions of God*, pp. 66–74, opt for simultaneity.

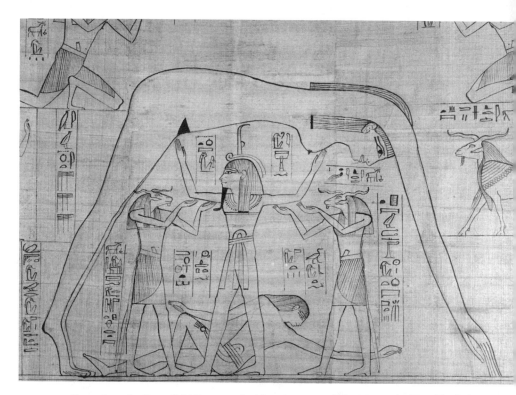

13. Scene from the Greenfield Papyrus, the hieratic papyrus belonging to the First Chief of the Concubines of Amun, Nesitanebtasheru (Twenty-first Dynasty). Shu, associated with air, separates Nut, a solar goddess, and Geb, a chthonic god. British Museum, London, 10554. Photo courtesy of the Trustees of the British Museum.

the deities often does not help to clarify the order of progression. Hathor (Ḥwt-Ḥr) is the name of the goddess pictured as a woman, often with bovine ears, and it is traditionally translated "Mansion of Horus." Thus the last part of her name (Ḥr) refers to the god Horus, and so might perhaps suggest that he, rather than she, came into being first. However, we have very early representations of bovine-associated goddesses who are clearly celestially related, and these images may be depictions of Hathor. Still, we cannot determine with certainty that in very early times they were understood in fact to be Hathor.[21] They may have

21. The goddesses Bat, Mehetweret, and Ihet are associated with similar representations. See François Daumas, "Hathor," *LÄ* 2:1024–33; and Hornung, *Conceptions of God*, p. 103.

14. The god Hapy (both left and right) uniting Upper and Lower Egypt (symbolized by the lotus and papyrus plants), carved in sunk relief on the throneside of a statue of King Ramesses II (Nineteenth Dynasty). Luxor Temple, Thebes. Photo © 1991 by Byron E. Shafer.

represented an entirely different deity or some aspect of a goddess only later identified as Hathor. Despite such problems, divine names can sometimes be useful in identification since they are usually descriptive. For example, Horus, who was pictured as a falcon (fig. 16), had a name that was perhaps derived from the word *ḥry*—"the one who is above/far from." Such a designation clearly reflected his association with the sky,

15. Stela of Iuny, Chief King's Scribe (Nineteenth Dynasty), with Renut, his wife, adoring the gods Osiris and Isis. Ashmolean Museum, Oxford, 1883.14. Photo courtesy of the Visitors of the Ashmolean Museum.

16. Ptolemaic or Roman statue of the god Horus in the form of a falcon. The forecourt of the Temple of Horus, Edfu. Photo © 1991 by Byron E. Shafer.

and Hathor's name, which included the name of Horus, connoted her celestial identification as well as her relationship with Horus.

It is not possible to determine the significance of the names of all the gods, but the naming process itself was an important step in the development of the concept of divinity. In ancient Egyptian beliefs, the name was an integral part of the personality.[22] It had to be preserved, even into the afterlife. Some inscriptions on monuments consisted of severe warnings to anyone who would destroy or obliterate the name of the owner; other texts listed rewards for anyone who would repeat the name, thereby helping to maintain the individual's eternal existence. To know the name of an individual was to have some control over him or her. The Egyptians believed they could harm enemies by inscribing their names on pottery bowls and then smashing the bowls.

The same dynamics surrounded the names of deities. Once the force/power was identified and given a name, prayers and offerings could be made to it; it could be worshiped by name; it could be invoked, implored, even feared and adored. To know the name of a god was to gain some advantage or control over the deity and over the powers it represented. It was important even for the gods themselves to know a name. In a text from the New Kingdom, the sun god Re, who abounds in names, is bitten by a snake fashioned by the goddess Isis. She had conjured the demon from Re's own being in order to learn the secret name that was the source of Re's supremacy.[23] The reader of the text never learns the name. As Egyptians believed that some mystery was necessary to preserve the dimensions of divine power, their visual images and written descriptions of the gods pointed only to some aspects of the deities and were not intended to detail every aspect. Deities were understood to retain some of their original conceptual abstraction. Not every element of their essence was fully concretized.

The gods were conceived of mainly in human terms, but not every quality attributed to them was totally human. Like mortal creatures, the gods were created, but the deities ultimately derived from a primordial being who had been responsible for his own creation. When the gods came into being, their births were described as extraordinary or mirac-

22. For a brief discussion of these elements of the personality, see Stuart Fleming, Bernard Fishman, David O'Connor, and David P. Silverman, *The Egyptian Mummy: Secrets and Science*, University Museum Handbook Series 1 (Philadelphia: University Museum, 1980), pp. 2–3.
23. The God and His Unknown Name of Power, trans. John A. Wilson, *ANET* 12–14.

ulous. The gods had birthdays, and those of certain deities were cele-brated on the five epagomenal days that were added to the Egyptian calendar of twelve thirty-day months to make a 365 day year.[24] During their existence, all gods required sustenance in the form of both offer-ings and worship. As implied in The Destruction of Mankind, it was mortals that provided these services. According to this text, Re became angry at mortals' evil plotting and took action to have them destroyed. He later relented, however, and prevented their total annihilation.[25]

Information found in texts suggests that the gods were not thought to die in the usual mortal sense, but the references to their death are not always consistent. Some texts note that deities lived for only a fixed length of time, and the story The Blinding of Truth by Falsehood refers to "the god's tomb."[26] Various texts and representations allude to the death of Osiris, but the actual event was not related during pharaonic times, for it was believed that an event narrated in detail would be rendered eternal. Osiris could be slain but not killed. No death of Osiris is mentioned in the collection of religious spells called the Coffin Texts, but his resurrection is constantly referred to.[27] It was only later, during the Greco-Roman Period, when beliefs had changed, that an account of Osiris's death was written down. In the religious literature Re, the king of the gods, was said to die symbolically every sunset and to be reborn at the dawn of each new day. Other texts, however, describe him as aging and aged.[28]

As the legends, myths, and stories surrounding the forces/powers/beings developed, so did the anthropomorphic associations. Some de-ities became identified with the environment, some with the cosmos, some with creation, some with kingship, and some even with human-kind. In order to deal with the rapidly increasing number of higher beings, the Egyptians formulated a hierarchy for their gods. The gods

24. See the references in Peter Kaplony, "Geburtstage (Götter)," *LÄ* 2:477–79.

25. For the translation, see *AEL* 2:197–99.

26. Morenz, *Egyptian Religion*, pp. 24–25, and Hornung, *Conceptions of God*, pp. 151–65; The Blinding of Truth by Falsehood, trans. Edward F. Wente, *LAE* 127, 131.

27. Hornung, *Conceptions of God*, pp. 152–53. See, e.g., Coffin Text spells 16, 17, and 148, in Adriaan de Buck, *The Egyptian Coffin Texts*, 7 vols. (Chicago: University of Chicago Press, 1935–1961), 1:47–53 and 2:209–26; translated in R. O. Faulkner, *The Ancient Egyptian Coffin Texts*, 3 vols. (Warminster: Aris & Phillips, 1973–1978), 1:10, 125–27.

28. For a discussion of the death of Re, see David P. Silverman, "Textual Criticism in the Coffin Texts," in *Religion and Philosophy in Ancient Egypt*, ed. William Kelly Simpson, Yale Egyptological Studies 3 (New Haven: Yale Egyptological Seminar, Department of Near Eastern Languages and Civilizations, Yale University, 1989), pp. 39–40.

were described, like mortals on earth, as living in a complex society, and as having separate family groupings. The Egyptians were making their gods more human. The gods' complex relationships often led to arguments and rivalries, and their passions and emotions developed. The ancient Egyptians depicted this complicated world of divine beings very well both in their religious and literary texts and in their statuary, reliefs, and paintings.

These portrayals represent a highly developed system that had long before been concretized and anthropomorphized. The depictions shed little light on the origins of such ideas, being so far removed from them in time. The Egyptians, however, had no problem relating their beliefs on the subject, nor were they reluctant to record their versions of the creation of the world, the gods, and their environment (fig. 17). Although these theologies provide valuable information about certain aspects of religion, they are late enough in time to evidence little concern with divinity before it was anthropomorphized.

The Egyptians had several cosmogonies, some of which conflicted with others. Each major center of religion had its own version of the creation, characterized by a main creator deity who generated associated gods and goddesses. These treatises dealt with the form that original concepts of divinity eventually took, and they were complemented by other texts and by depictions in art.

Each cosmogony had some consistency within its own framework. Despite the fact that religion is basically conservative, however, one must recognize that the Egyptian gods were constantly evolving and that their interrelationships were constantly changing. Erik Hornung has noted: "In their constantly changing nature and manifestations, the Egyptian gods resemble the country's temples, which were never finished and complete, but always 'under construction.'"[29] Amidst the changes, however, certain constants enable one to perceive some underlying structure to the system of the gods.

THE GODS

Some scholars think it futile to try to organize the gods of Egypt into groups. First, it can be argued that any such effort results in a

29. Hornung, *Conceptions of God*, p. 256.

17. Figure of Tutankhamun as the god Nefertem upon the lotus, illustrating a creation myth, from the tomb of the king (Eighteenth Dynasty). Egyptian Museum, Cairo, 60723. Photo © 1991 by David P. Silverman.

structure that is the product of a modern mind, not an ancient one. Second, proposed groupings result in so much overlapping that the boundaries of the categories dissolve. The multiple roles of certain divinities allow some of them to function in more than one grouping at a time, and some deities appear in a particular classification during one

18. Painted figure of the goddess Ma'at, in the tomb of Queen Nefertari (Nineteenth Dynasty). Valley of the Queens, Thebes. Photo © 1991 by David P. Silverman.

period but not during another. In response to these arguments, one may ask: Since the Egyptians were an extremely logical people who even deified the concepts of order, balance, and harmony in the form of the goddess Ma'at (fig. 18), would it not seem possible that consciously or unconsciously they organized an underlying structure to the system of their gods? It is clear that the Egyptians understood that the deities formed an obvious hierarchy. Evidence for this belief is found in the way the gods are portrayed in myths and stories, in the roles they take in religious literature, in their titles and epithets, in the prominence and actions accorded to them in tomb and temple decoration, and even in the number and sizes of temples dedicated to the various gods and the number of priests who served them.

Nevertheless, the following presentation makes no effort to discover and document that system, whatever the possibility that it existed. Rather, it attempts to arrange the deities into categories that seem today to be logical. Perhaps the results may facilitate the modern reader's comprehension of the vast array of gods and goddesses that made up the ancient pantheon. A modern grouping of the deities undoubtedly involves some simplification, for the Egyptians worshiped numerous gods for thousands of years. Several divinities, such as Isis and Serapis, survived even the collapse of the Egyptian civilization and found devotees in newly adopted lands. Given such variety and complexity over so long a period of time, some deities would inevitably shift from one category to another or span more than one category, whatever the classification suggested. The structure proposed here is admittedly oversimplified, but it appears appropriate to the organization found in Egyptian culture. It is hoped that it does some justice to the great range of the Egyptian pantheon and to the intricacies of the interrelationships among the deities.

Gods Associated with Natural Phenomena and Abstraction

Many Egyptian deities were associated with elements of the ancient Egyptian environment, both perceived and imagined, and some of them were also associated with cosmic functions. Each of the various myths of the creation of the universe incorporates those gods and goddesses related to the geographic areas where it originated, such as Memphis, Heliopolis, or Hermopolis. The Egyptians envisioned a different creator god as the preeminent figure in each version of the myth—Atum, Amun, Ptah, Khnum, the Aten.[30] Before creation could take place, however, three powers had to be present, all of which together represented the energy necessary for the creation: Ḥu (divine utterance), Ḥeka (magic or divine energy), and Sia (divine knowledge). Some of the divinities that appear in the myths of creation, such as Amun and Ptah, transcend their identification with natural phenomena and become important gods with national significance. Others, such as Amaunet and Kauket, are relatively unknown outside this grouping and remain relatively minor.

---

30. The various theologies of creation were rather late both in development and in date and may reflect a contemporaneous systemization of thought rather than an attempt to preserve an older system.

For the element air, one finds individual deities as well as paired counterparts, such as Amun and Amaunet, the first of whom was also of significance on the national/state level.[31] The god Shu was also related to air (fig. 13) and was paired with Tefnut, who was associated with moisture.[32] Before creation could begin, there had to be primordial water; it was represented by Nun. His consort Naunet symbolized the sky.[33] The heavens could also be embodied in the goddess Nut, who was paired with the chthonic god Geb (fig. 13).

The phenomena of heaven and earth were so basic to Egyptian life that they were associated with many other deities as well. Hathor, Bat, and Horus were only a few of the others identified with the sky; and Osiris, Aker, and Ptah-Tatenen were among the other earth gods.[34] The Nile itself was not deified, but the yearly inundation that brought the fertile alluvial soil essential to Egypt's agricultural economy took the form of the god Hapy (fig. 14).[35] Certain areas of the river, however, appear to have had patron deities.[36] Storms were the provenance of the god Seth, who also represented chaos, evil, and confusion, among other negative qualities.[37] The goddess Ma'at, in many ways his positive counterpart, represented the deified concept of world order, balance, harmony, justice, and truth.[38] Darkness fell under the aegis of Kuk and Kauket, who, along with Ḥuḥ and Ḥauḥet, endlessness and boundlessness, were two of the four pairs called the Ogdoad of Hermopolis, the eight primary deities in the Hermopolitan theology (fig. 19).[39]

Just as there were many divinities in ancient Egyptian religion who

31. See the comments and references in Eberhard Otto, "Amun," *LÄ* 1:237–48. For Amaunet and remarks on doublets, see Otto, "Amaunet," *LÄ* 1:183, and Hornung, *Conceptions of God*, pp. 83–85.

32. For references, see Herman te Velde, "Schu," *LÄ* 5:735–37, and Ursula Verhoeven, "Tefnut," *LÄ* 6:296–304.

33. For these deities, see Reinhard Grieshammer, "Nun," *LÄ* 4:534–35.

34. For comments on these deities and for references to other sources treating them, see the entries corresponding to their names in *LÄ*.

35. Baines, *Fecundity Figures* [n. 18], pp. 115–16; and Hornung, *Conceptions of God*, pp. 77–79.

36. Khnum, for example, was sacred to the area around the First Cataract.

37. See Herman te Velde, *Seth, God of Confusion*, 2d ed., PÄ 6 (1977), pp. 99–108. Te Velde discusses in depth all the aspects of this complex deity, including the positive side of his nature.

38. Ma'at is a deified concept of the ideal that allows the world to function properly. See Wolfgang Helck, "Maat," *LÄ* 3:1110–19.

39. See Reinhard Grieshammer, "Kek, Keket," *LÄ* 3:380, and Hartwig Altenmüller, "Heh," *LÄ* 2:1082–84. The other couples are (1) Amun and Amaunet and (2) Nun and Naunet.

19. Late Period bronze grouping of the Hermopolitan Ogdoad ("Eight Gods") with Thoth. Staatliche Kunstsammlungen Kassel, Federal Republic of Germany. Photo (neg. #A 6508) courtesy of Staatliche Kunstsammlungen Kassel.

had celestial associations, there were many who were related to the primary bodies in the heavens. The sun, perhaps the most obvious environmental element, was in many ways the most vital to life. It was the source of light, heat, and regeneration. Re was apparently the most common solar deity, especially in the earlier periods. He was amalgamated, or syncretized, with other deities to form such new gods as Re-

20. Statuette of Amun-Re, in silver overlaid with gold foil, about 900 B.C.E. British Museum, London. Photo © 1991 by Byron E. Shafer.

Horakhty (Re-Horus of the Two Horizons) (figs. 8, 31), Re-Atum, and Amun-Re (also known as king of the gods) (fig. 20). The sun had many visible manifestations. Khepri (fig. 21) was the form of the solar orb as it came into being in the morning and traveled across the sky during the day. Generally Re referred to the midday sun and Atum to the setting sun. During his daily and evening journeys through the heavens and the underworld, the solar deity had to battle his eternal enemy Apophis, the serpent.[40] Also conceived of as a distinct entity was the disk of the

40. Morenz, *Egyptian Religion*, pp. 145, 316nn31–32, 168, and 323n45; Hornung, *Conceptions of God*, pp. 158–59; te Velde, *Seth*, pp. 99–108.

21. Painted figure of the god Khepri, in the tomb of Queen Nefertari (Nineteenth Dynasty). Valley of the Queens, Thebes. Photo © 1991 by David P. Silverman.

sun, called the *aten,* and it was referred to from the early periods onward. Later it received special attention and devotion, and for a brief time in the fourteenth century B.C.E. it was worshiped as a god. The pharaoh Akhenaten raised the Aten to the rank of a supreme and essentially unique deity in his newly formed religion.

The moon was also associated with a variety of deities, the most prominent being Thoth, who also was sacred to Hermopolis, a city in Middle Egypt (fig. 19).[41] Thoth was the scribe of the gods and was the patron god of the scribal profession. Another important lunar deity was Khonsu, who also was one of the sacred family members in the triad of Thebes (fig. 11).[42] Among other divinities sometimes linked to the moon were Osiris, Min, Shu, and Khnum.[43]

41. See Bleeker, *Hathor and Thoth* [n. 4], pp. 114–15.
42. See Hellmut Brunner, "Chons," *LÄ* 1:1960–63.
43. See Bleeker, *Hathor and Thoth,* pp. 114–17.

Of the other heavenly bodies, only the star Sirius, called Sopdet, and the constellation Orion, called Saḥ, received enough prominence to be worshiped. These deities were eventually subsumed under Isis and Osiris, respectively.

While the desert clearly was a visible constant in the world of the ancient Egyptians, it was never elevated to cult status. The deities Ash and Onuris, however, had associations with it, and Seth, who was related to some aspects of the environment, was sometimes identified with it. The mountain in the landscape of the Theban necropolis could be venerated in the form of the serpent goddess Meretseger. Specific trees of the valley could be connected to a divinity as important as Hathor.[44] Each of these environmental elements was in some way a reference point for the concept embodied by the deity and was intended to reflect a characteristic or trait of the god.

Local and National Deities

Ancient Egypt was a composite of many local areas, each having its own particular traditions and customs. During the early pharaonic period these districts were organized into administrative units called nomes. Twenty-two nomes were established for Upper (southern) Egypt by the middle of the Old Kingdom. The nomes of Lower (northern) Egypt were not finally fixed until a much later period, when they eventually numbered twenty. Each of these precincts had associated deities and its own standard, often topped with a personification of the particular area.[45] Many of the nomes (fig. 22) reflected more ancient local divisions, and it is clear that the earliest Egyptians worshiped divinities whose areas of influence were originally limited to fairly small provinces. It is also apparent, however, that these Egyptians may have recognized gods whose powers transcended local limitations.[46] In any event, each nome had associated with it certain local deities, and the Egyptian language even had a term for the concept. *Njwty,* "local god," derives from *niwt,* "city." The deities were worshiped in local cult temples.

From time to time one of these local deities transcended its original

44. Ibid., pp. 34–37; and Hornung, *Conceptions of God,* p. 41.
45. See Wolfgang Helck, "Gaue," *LÄ* 2:385–408.
46. Hornung, *Conceptions of God,* pp. 73–74, states: "One must distinguish clearly between the old local deities with their often indefinite, descriptive names, and the local manifestations of the 'great gods,' such as Amun of Karnak, Re of Sakhebu, or the various provincial Horuses." See his discussion, pp. 70–74.

22. Statue of King Menkaure (Fourth Dynasty) flanked by Hathor (left) and the personification of the Seventh Upper Egyptian Nome (right), from the valley temple of the king's pyramid. Egyptian Museum, Cairo, JE 46499. Photo © 1991 by David P. Silverman.

provincialism and gained national prominence. Montu, worshiped in the Theban nome by the end of the Old Kingdom, became preeminent throughout Egypt during the Eleventh Dynasty.[47] As national god, he was eventually eclipsed by Amun. Like his predecessor, Amun already had a cult in the Theban nome, but, unlike Montu, Amun was also recognized as a primeval deity, one of the Ogdoad (eight gods) of Hermopolis. Amun was not eclipsed totally as the supreme deity, but he was eventually syncretized with Re, whose cult center from the early periods was Heliopolis. The divinity Amun-Re then emerged as king of

47. See J. F. Borghouts, "Month," *LÄ* 4:200–204.

the gods, a position he would retain for most of the rest of Egyptian history (fig. 20).

It is important to note, however, that when a geographic area is associated with a deity of national repute, it does not necessarily follow that that particular god was the original cult figure of the location. Osiris, for example, was generally referred to as "the Lord of Abydos," but he was a relative latecomer to Abydos. From an early date that city had been sacred to Khenty-Imentyw (Foremost of the Westerners), a local god, whom Osiris absorbed.

The presence of local gods in Egyptian religion from an early period and the tradition of strong local customs seems to imply that the smaller geographic districts significantly influenced the development of the deities who would eventually gain national importance. Sometimes, as with Montu and Amun, that was the case. Certain gods and goddesses, however, appear to have been influential only in particular localities through most of Egyptian history, but they seem to have had much wider recognition only during the developmental stages of the civilization. Thus there was a certain fluidity to the range of the deities, which could expand or contract.

Examples of the more usual case, in which the range expanded, were two local goddesses associated with the important cities of Nekheb in Upper Egypt and Buto in Lower Egypt. They were respectively the vulture Nekhbet and the cobra Wadjit. In time Nekhbet and Wadjit became the prominent protector deities of Upper and Lower Egypt, and representations of them can be found decorating a variety of objects, including crowns, jewelry (fig. 23), architectural elements, and weapons.

An example of the less usual case, in which the range contracted, was Neith, whose recognition was limited to Sais in the Delta for much of later Egyptian history. Before that she had been known throughout Egypt, primarily for her protective responsibilities with regard to canopic equipment. Even earlier, however, during the Early Dynastic Period and slightly later, Neith had had much more influence and range.

Undoubtedly many of these changes had political implications. Seth, a god who had national significance in the Early Dynastic Period, was later identified as the one who brought disorder and confusion and was associated with some of the negative elements of the environment. These elements, enhanced over time, became incorporated in a very complex nature. In the earliest periods, however, Seth could be held in high esteem, and later, in the Ramesside Period, his name appeared as

23. The goddesses Nekhbet (vulture) and Wadjit (cobra) on a pendant from the tomb of King Tutankhamun (Eighteenth Dynasty). Egyptian Museum, Cairo. Photo © 1991 by Leonard H. Lesko.

an element in the names of several rulers. His nature underwent many changes, so he could appear in several categories. This variety can be seen in his depiction as the evil murderer of his brother Osiris; as an effective aid to the sun god in repelling the latter's archenemy, the serpent Apophis, during the hours of the night; and as a complex figure with traits almost opposite to the qualities of order, balance, and harmony incorporated in the goddess Ma'at. At one point Seth is the enemy and hostile uncle of Horus; at another the two contenders are reconciled (fig. 24).

A local god often was not the only deity worshiped in a particular area. Egyptians frequently envisioned their divinities in small groups. They could be paired, as they were in some of the regional cosmogonies. More often they belonged to family groupings, which usually consisted of father, mother, and child. At Thebes the sacred triad was Amun, Mut, and Khonsu (fig. 11); at Memphis it was Ptah, Sekhmet, and Nefertem (fig. 10); and at Abydos it was Osiris, Isis, and Horus. Such family groupings, which were extremely common throughout Egypt, often linked gods and goddesses from different precincts and with varying significance. Hathor of Dendereh, for example, was linked to Horus of Edfu. The temple at Edfu was dedicated to Horus (fig. 16), and only he was in residence. He was often portrayed with his consort, Hathor of Dendereh. She, however, together with her sons Ihy and Horus-Sematawy, was in residence at the temple dedicated to her at Dendereh.[48]

48. See Bleeker, *Hathor and Thoth*, pp. 62–70, 75–79.

24. Horus (left) and Seth (right) crowning King Ramesses III (Twentieth Dynasty). Restored granite statue group. Egyptian Museum, Cairo. Photo © 1991 by Leonard H. Lesko.

A few gods had strong cultic associations with a particular area but also played a role in the national religion. Thoth, a deity associated with writing, had, at least in the historical period, a very strong cult following in Hermopolis. He and his consort, Seshat, known mainly as a goddess associated with writing, were represented on temple walls throughout the land (fig. 9). Their portrayal was particularly common in scenes of coronation. The goddess Bast(et), depicted in feline form, was related to the eastern Delta city of Bubastis, but there were references to her in the area of Memphis as early as the Old Kingdom.[49] She seems often to have been identified with Sekhmet (one of the Memphite triad), whose ag-

49. See Eberhard Otto, "Bastet," *LÄ* 1:628–30. Bernard V. Bothmer has pointed out to me that the first large-scale hieroglyphs in sunk relief are found on the facade of the Valley Temple of Khafre. They contain the epithet "beloved of Bastet." On a smaller scale, sunk hieroglyphs are found at Giza in the Fourth Dynasty tombs of Queen Mersyankh III and Min-khaf.

25. Ptolemaic relief of the god Sobek in a scene of coronation. The Great Temple, Kom Ombo. Photo © 1991 by David P. Silverman.

gressive nature was indicated both by her name, which means "the powerful one," and by her portrayal as a lioness (fig. 10). The god Khnum had a strong cultic relationship with the Upper Egyptian city of Esna, and Neith could appear there as consort. Khnum was often portrayed on the walls of temples as a creator god fashioning the ruler from clay on his potter's wheel. In such a role he was frequently associated with the goddess Heqat as consort. From the early periods, Khnum was also worshiped in the area of Aswan, and from the New Kingdom onward, the goddesses Satis and Anukis joined him there in a triad.

The crocodile was a ubiquitous creature in ancient Egypt, and it was often identified with the god Sobek (fig. 25), who had cult followings in the Faiyum, far to the south in Kom Ombo, and elsewhere. Although many of the associations between a god and a region were established during early periods and might reflect original local customs, it is also possible that some of these relationships developed or were arranged in later, even much later, periods.[50]

50. For comments on these deities and for references to other sources treating them, see the entries corresponding to their names in *LÄ*.

Funerary Deities

One of the most recognizable groupings of deities today is that of the gods of the mortuary religion, for so much of the Egyptian culture that survives reflects this aspect of civilization. The category consists of numerous powers. Some of them function in other areas as well, but others are limited to funerary activities alone.

In view of the preparations made for burial as early as predynastic times, funerary beliefs must have existed from a very early period. Some of the deities in this grouping retained their positions and their relationships throughout Egyptian history. Others, however, experienced change. According to the earliest beliefs, Anubis was clearly the ruler of the underworld, but Osiris, a deity associated with the Delta and with the earth and vegetation, eventually supplanted him.[51] Anubis was left with the responsibilities and rituals of embalming, while the new god became the ruler of the realm of the dead (fig. 26). Osiris's exalted position was in evidence through his royal regalia and his titles. Once established in this role, Osiris maintained his preeminence throughout Egyptian history. His family group included his wife (and sister) Isis (fig. 27), his brother Seth (fig. 24), his sister Nephthys (fig. 28), and his son Horus (fig. 29).

Many of the myths surrounding Osiris and his family are reflected in sources from the earliest periods, but the most complete versions date from the New Kingdom through the Roman Period. The myth in its most basic form was perhaps based on actual events. It reports the murder of Osiris by his brother Seth. Isis and Nephthys, their sisters, manage to collect the parts of the dismembered body, and Isis then revives her husband/brother long enough to be impregnated by him. She later gives birth to Horus. While still a youth, Horus vies with Seth for the right to succeed his father on the throne. Seth's role as the evil brother takes on greater dimensions when one realizes his power over the forces of chaos and confusion and the need to bring him (and ultimately them) under control so that the land could function again. This myth was obviously related to the passing of kingship in Egypt: the dying pharaoh was identified with Osiris, and the ruler-to-be was identified with Horus.

---

51. Osiris was originally the embalmed god, while Anubis was the one who performed the act of embalming. Later Osiris, who was identified with the deceased king, became the ruler of the underworld. See J. Gwyn Griffiths, "Osiris," *LÄ* 4:623–33.

26. Painted figure of the god Osiris, in the tomb of Queen Nefertari (Nineteenth Dynasty). Valley of the Queens, Thebes. Photo © 1991 by David P. Silverman.

27. Painted scene of King Ramesses III (Twentieth Dynasty) introducing his son Amenherkhopeshef to the goddess Isis, in the prince's tomb. Valley of the Queens, Thebes. Photo © 1991 by Byron E. Shafer.

The chthonic realm of Osiris, together with his association with fertility and rejuvenation, represents only one aspect of the afterlife. There was also a solar sphere, presided over by the sun god Re or his syncretized form, Amun-Re. In the myth associated with that sphere, the sun, with whom the dead king is identified, passes away each sunset, fights with and triumphs over the forces of evil during the twelve hours of night, and is reborn at each new sunrise.

In the two gods Osiris and Re is manifest the Egyptians' understanding of a dual eternal existence, one related to Osiris and reflecting his infinite everlasting existence, and one related to Re and reflecting his cyclical rejuvenation.[52]

The concept of the afterlife was originally limited to royalty. In time, however, the nobility and privileged classes came to have hope of attaining the same type of eternal existence. By the New Kingdom such access was within reach of even more of the population. To qualify for entry

52. Edward F. Wente, "Funerary Beliefs of the Ancient Egyptians," *Expedition* 24 (Winter 1982): 22–24.

28. Figure of the goddess Nephthys, the New Kingdom or Third Intermediate Period. British Museum, London. Photo © 1991 by Byron E. Shafer.

into an eternal existence, one had to have lived an exemplary life on earth and to know the correct responses to make and actions to take when confronted by the gods and demigods of the underworld. There were also guidelines for behavior and directions for appropriate routes that would prove useful, and certain recitations had to be used for the expected transformations. Such funerary spells were first collected for royalty and are now called the Pyramid Texts, because they appear on the walls of the interior chambers of the pyramids (fig. 1). In time the collection was edited and incorporated into a body of spells used by the upper classes. These spells are now called the Coffin Texts, since the greatest number of them were recorded on the interior walls of coffins

29. On a barque, a variant Ennead ("Nine Gods") of Heliopolis, six generations of gods: Re the Creator (right), Atum, Shu and Tefnut, Geb and Nut, Osiris and Isis, and Horus the King (left); painted scene in the tomb of King Ay (Eighteenth Dynasty). Valley of the Kings, Thebes. Photo © 1991 by Leonard H. Lesko.

(fig. 30). Around the advent of the New Kingdom an even larger share of the population gained the means of access to an eternal existence when the funerary spells were again edited and supplemented. Now called the Book of the Dead, these texts were recorded mainly on papyri (figs. 31, 32), but certain spells are found on coffins, amulets, tomb walls, and statuary. Other collections of funerary and mythological texts were meant to explicate the afterlife further, thereby ensuring entry.

Even with all of these aids, the ancient Egyptians still had to prove worthiness before a tribunal over which Osiris sat as judge. The heart of the deceased, representing the individual's entire earthly existence, was weighed against the measure of that which embodied harmony, justice, order, and truth—the goddess Maʿat, or her symbol, the feather. Thoth, the scribe of the gods, recorded the verdict, and a fantastic creature stood nearby, ready to devour those not deemed justified (fig. 32). Those who were judged worthy were rewarded with immortality.

Often the four sons of Horus—Imseti, Hapy, Duamutef (fig. 33), and Kebehsenuef—were also present at the judgment. They functioned mainly as the protectors of the lungs, the liver, the stomach, and the intestines. The Egyptians considered those internal organs essential for an afterlife, so they had to be mummified and protected. Four goddesses—Isis, Nephthys, Selket (fig. 34), and Neith—guarded those organs as well.

Many other divine forces had roles in the funerary religion. Some, such as Hathor (fig. 6) and Ptah (fig. 35), played more significant roles in

30. Spells carved in columns on the inner wall of a coffin of the Middle Kingdom. Egyptian Museum, Cairo. Photo © 1991 by David P. Silverman.

31. Hieroglyphic funerary papyrus (Book of the Dead) belonging to Neferrenpet (Nineteenth Dynasty). A baboon offers the Sacred Eye to Re-Horakhty while Neferrenpet and three gods look on. University Museum, University of Pennsylvania, Philadelphia, E2775. Photo (neg. #23173) courtesy of the University Museum, University of Pennsylvania.

32. Spell 125 and the judgment scene from the hieroglyphic funerary papyrus (Book of the Dead) belonging to the Royal Scribe Ani (Nineteenth Dynasty). Represented are (left to right) Ani's wife, Tutu; Ani; Renenet and Meskhenet; Ani's *ba*; Ani's heart being weighed by the god Anubis against a feather symbolizing Ma'at, "truth" or "order"; the god Thoth; and Ammut, "the Devourer." Above, twelve gods witness the judgment. British Museum, London, 10470. Photo © 1991 by Byron E. Shafer.

other categories, and their funerary functions were less significant.[53] The god Sokar could function much like Ptah in other realms, but in funerary religion he was eventually syncretized with Osiris (fig. 6).

The underworld itself was personified by the divinity Aker, and one of the mythological texts is devoted to him.[54] Many minor deities inhabited the underworld. Some took the form of animals, some humans, and some hybrids. Some of these creatures were present to wreak havoc on the deceased and to make the passage through the underworld difficult;

53. See Herman te Velde, "Ptah," *LÄ* 4:1177–80.

54. For the Book of Aker and other mythological texts relating to the underworld, see Alexandre Piankoff, *Egyptian Religious Texts and Representations*, vol. 3, *Mythological Papyri*, Bollingen Series 40/3 (New York: Pantheon, 1957), pp. 3–28.

33. Painted scene of King Ramesses III (Twentieth Dynasty) introducing his son Amenherkhopeshef to the god Duamutef, in the prince's tomb. Valley of the Queens, Thebes. Photo © 1991 by Byron E. Shafer.

others were there to aid and comfort the deceased. The knowledge of what was in the underworld and how it could successfully be dealt with was contained both in the texts and in the illustrations dealing with funerary religion. Possession of Pyramid Texts, Coffin Texts, the Book of the Dead, or any other funerary or mythological text helped to ensure a successful transition to the next world and, if one survived the trials, an eternal life like that of the gods.

Household and Personal Gods

Most ancient Egyptians had only limited access to the state gods in the temple. During the festivals, however, the people could see and approach them. At such times priests would bring out the boat-shaped receptacles in which the divine images were housed and carry them on

34. Figure of Selket, one of four goddesses protecting the canopic equipment in the tomb of King Tutankhamun (Eighteenth Dynasty).
Egyptian Museum, Cairo, 60686.
Photo © 1991 by David P. Silverman.

their shoulders, parading these barques in and around the public areas
of the temple (fig. 36).

The populace could always express personal devotion to a divinity by
acquiring and possessing small amulets, stelae, and votive images of the
god. Still, they apparently desired even closer relationships with their
gods, to whom they looked for aid. It was believed that certain high-
ranking gods such as Amun, who was a supreme power, and Ptah, who
was a force in creation, could hear the prayers of individual persons.
Special sections of the temple were reserved for persons making appeal
to Amun;[55] and we find ears carved on the surfaces of stelae dedicated to

55. See Lynn H. Holden, "The People's Religion," in *Egypt's Golden Age: The Art of
Living in the New Kingdom, 1558–1085 B.C.* (Boston: Museum of Fine Arts, 1982), pp. 296–
307.

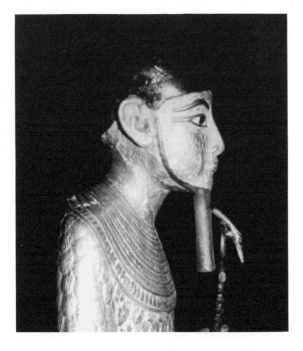

35. Figure of the god Ptah, from the tomb of King Tutankhamun (Eighteenth Dynasty). Egyptian Museum, Cairo, 60739. Photo © 1991 by David P. Silverman.

Ptah, who in this role was often amalgamated with the god Sedjem, the personification of hearing.

Some professions had particular deities as patrons: Thoth, of scribes; Ptah (fig. 35), of craftsmen; and Imhotep, of physicians. Among the many other deities related to medicine were Sekhmet, Selket, and Hor-pa-khered (in Greek, Harpocrates). The relatively large number of gods related to medicine is a measure of the Egyptians' concern about disease. They recorded much on the subject, and the medical papyri indicate that many causes of illnesses and many prescriptions for cures were associated with particular divinities. The goddess Sekhmet could both bring illness and dissipate it. Selket could protect a person from the sting of a scorpion, the creature most usually associated with her (fig. 34). Hor-pa-khered, a form of the god Horus (literally, Horus the Child), was often invoked for healing. Water was poured over a stela with his image carved on it (fig. 37), and the proper spell was recited. The ritual liquid then acquired special powers to cure poisonous bites and stings. The goddesses Taweret (fig. 6) and Meskhenet (fig. 32) and the god Bes were called upon to protect women in childbirth and their infants. Bes was frequently associated with other protective situations as well, and for

36. Painted scene of the barque of the god Amun. Temple of King Sety I (Nineteenth Dynasty), Abydos. Photo © 1991 by David P. Silverman.

that reason he appeared as a decorative element on household items and furnishings.

The ancient Egyptians produced votive statuettes of many deities for personal worship and devotion. Included among these figures were objects in the form of a snake, representing the image of either Renenutet or Meretseger, a goddess associated with farming and the harvest. Mummies of animals associated with particular deities also served a votive purpose (fig. 38), and they were placed in niches inside catacombs sacred to the god represented by the mummy.

Another type of divinity belonging to the category of household and personal gods was the deified individual. The pharaoh fitted this type well, especially pharaohs who reigned during the New Kingdom, when the practice of worshiping the still-living ruler, both in person and through his cult, had become well recognized.[56] Of course all kings

56. For studies of this practice, see Dietrich Wildung, *Egyptian Saints: Deification in Pharaonic Egypt*, Hagop Kevorkian Series on Near Eastern Art and Civilization (New York: New York University Press, 1977); and Lanny Bell, "Aspects of the Cult of the Deified Tutankhamun," in *Mélanges Gamal Eddin Mokhtar* 1, BdÉ 97/1 (1985), pp. 33–59, noting the references therein. See also David P. Silverman, "Royalty in Literature," in *Ancient Egyptian Kingship: New Investigations*, ed. David O'Connor and David P. Silverman (Cambridge: Harvard University Press, forthcoming).

37. Late Period healing stela (the Metternich Stela) with the figure of Hor-pa-khered (Harpocrates) in the center. The Metropolitan Museum of Art, New York, Fletcher Fund, 1950 (50.85). Photo © 1991 by David P. Silverman.

were identified at death with both Re and Osiris and therefore were considered divinities. Mortuary cults continued their worship and maintained their funerary establishments. A few pharaohs, however, were so popular that they also were worshiped separately and functioned as intercessors between the populace and other deities. One of the most popular of these kings was Amenhotep I, who continued to be wor-

38. Mummified falcon, associated with the god Horus. Egyptian Museum, Cairo. Photo © 1991 by David P. Silverman.

shiped for centuries after his death. Throughout the New Kingdom many votive stelae were inscribed to him with prayers, and during the Ramesside Period his oracle was often consulted in legal decisions.

Such special treatment was not limited to royal figures. Throughout the ages, personages who had attained great stature and a high level of recognition in their profession were deified, and cult followings developed thereafter. Some of these individuals were honored by votive statues and reliefs carved in their image or dedicated to them, and some were even worshiped in shrines. In the Old Kingdom, Imhotep, the architect of King Djoser's funerary complex at Saqqara, was first considered a great sage, then the son of Ptah, and eventually a god associated with medicine. During the Middle Kingdom a chapel was built on Elephantine Island for the worship and honor of the nomarch Heqaib both during his life and after his death. Amenhotep son of Hapu, an extremely competent high official under Amenhotep III in the fourteenth century B.C.E., gained a cult in Thebes within a few generations of his death. It was especially important with regard to medicine.[57]

Foreign Gods

The Egyptian pantheon included some deities that were clearly of foreign origin, gods who had non-Egyptian names, primary cults outside the boundaries of Egypt, and a historical presence in a foreign land. They were frequently identified with indigenous Egyptian gods, but

57. See Dietrich Wildung, "Imhotep," *LÄ* 3:145–48; and his *Imhotep und Amenhotep: Gottwerdung im alten Ägypten*, MÄS 36 (Munich and Berlin: Deutscher Kunstverlag, 1977), pp. 5–250. For additional remarks on Amenhotep son of Hapu, see Wildung, *Imhotep und Amenhotep*, pp. 201–97; and Wolfgang Helck, "Amenophis," *LÄ* 1:219–21. For remarks on Heqaib, see Labib Habachi, "Heqaib," *LÄ* 2:1120–22.

they continued to maintain their non-Egyptian origin. The best examples are attested in the period of the New Kingdom and include the gods Baal and Resheph and the goddesses Anath and Astarte, all from Ugarit and Canaan. Baal was often related to Seth. A title or other attribute may point to the origins of other deities outside of Egypt. Dedwen, whose name first occurs in the Pyramid Texts, was mentioned occasionally throughout Egyptian history, but his roots may have been to the south, in Nubia. The god Ash, attested with some regularity in Egypt, may also have originated in the south, as he was frequently called "Lord of Nubia."[58] Once these deities had been introduced, however, they remained within the Egyptian pantheon. A title containing the name of a foreign location is not definitive evidence of a foreign origin. Quite a few Egyptian gods and goddesses acquired epithets referring to areas beyond the borders of their own country. Hathor, for instance, clearly an Egyptian goddess, could be referred to as the "Lady of Byblos." Titles indicating foreign sovereignty for deities seem to demonstrate nothing more than the Egyptians' chauvinism and imperialism, and the portability of their gods.

The ancient Egyptians were well aware of the distinctions among these classes of deities, and it was appropriate for them to devote attention to a variety of gods, as the occasion demanded. In addition, they worshiped the state gods, attended festivals, and took part in lay service in the temples.

KINGSHIP AND DIVINITY

In modern times the ancient pharaohs have often been characterized as gods on earth. Such a description implies a clear distinction between the ruler and his subjects. It does not, however, deal with the issue of the monarch's inherent mortality, nor does it indicate the limits or extent of the perceived divine nature of the king. The ancient Egyptians' perception of the king, implied in various textual and artifactual references, was not static. It underwent changes during the more than three thousand years of Egyptian history.[59]

58. For references to and discussions of these foreign gods, see the following entries in *LÄ*: Rainer Stadelmann, "Baal," 1:590–91; William Kelly Simpson, "Reschef," 5:244–46; Jean Leclant, "Astarte," 1:499–509; Leclant, "Anat," 1:253–58; Eberhard Otto, "Asch," 1:459–60; Wolfgang Helck, "Götter, fremde in Ägypten," 2:643.

59. References to several studies on kingship and its nature together with comments on the subject can be found in Jürgen von Beckerath, "König," *LÄ* 3:461; and Hellmut

From early times the epithet *netjer* (*nt̲r*) referred directly to the king as a god. Sometimes the term occurred alone; at other times it appeared with modifying or descriptive words. Another epithet from early times referred to the king as a descendant of a god—*s³R'*, "son of Re." Later the Egyptians developed other terms, such as *tjt*, "image" of a god, and *pr '³*. The latter, an expression meaning "great house" and referring to the palace,[60] was an abstraction that attributed a corporate nature to the king, much as "White House" can denote the president of the United States. Sometimes the king was also referred to as "like" (*mj*) a deity. Ordinarily all these royal epithets were used in specific types of documents.

In all written materials the names of kings were treated differently from the names of both their subjects and the gods. The personal and throne designations of royalty were ordinarily the only names encircled within a cartouche. Despite isolated exceptions, this rule was generally followed throughout Egyptian history except during the reign of Akhenaten, when the name of the divine Aten regularly appeared within a cartouche. Interestingly enough, one of Akhenaten's designations, Waenre, could be written without a cartouche during this time.

Unlike the traditional deities, the earthly ruler needed to observe jubilees of revivification in order to ensure the fertility of the land.[61] Like a private person, the king needed a tomb to ensure his afterlife. Ordinarily gods did not have tombs.[62] Gods could age, but their actual death was rarely recorded.[63]

Adding to the complexity of the concept of divine kingship was the development of the cult of the living king, which essentially treated the king like a god while he was still alive.

Before a monarch ascended the throne, his subjects undoubtedly were aware of his growth and maturation, and, therefore, they were not ignorant of his human origin. He could have been one of many sons

Brunner, "König-Gott-Verhältnis," *LÄ* 3:461–64. See also Henri Frankfort, *Kingship and the Gods: A Study of Ancient Near Eastern Religion as the Integration of Society and Nature* (Chicago: University of Chicago Press, 1948); Georges Posener, *De la divinité du pharaon*, Cahiers de la Société Asiatique 15 (Paris: Imprimerie Nationale, 1960); Ramses Moftah, *Studien zum ägyptischen Königsdogma im Neuen Reich*, SDAIK 20 (1985); and *Ancient Egyptian Kingship*, ed. O'Connor and Silverman.

60. See Ogden Goelet, "Two Aspects of the Royal Palace in the Egyptian Old Kingdom" (Ph.D. diss., Columbia University, 1982).

61. The exception to this rule during the Amarna Period is discussed below.

62. But see The Blinding of Truth by Falsehood, *LAE* 127, 131.

63. Silverman, in *Religion and Philosophy*, ed. Simpson, pp. 39–40, and note the references therein.

born to the pharaoh and his main wife. If no such heir had been born, the monarch could be the son of a minor wife, as were Thutmose IV and perhaps even Tutankhamun. Indeed, in the absence of a more direct successor a more distant relative could become pharaoh. At times the relationship between a king and his successor is not at all clear to us. Tutankhamun's successor, Ay, was a trusted adviser and mentor to the royal family but may not have been closely related to it. If the royal family had no survivors at all, a new line began with a person whose roots were not royal, such as Amenemhat I of the Twelfth Dynasty and Ramesses I of the Nineteenth Dynasty. Undoubtedly royal conspiracies were also a part of Egyptian history, with factions supporting one candidate over another and sometimes engaging in foul play. The population must have been aware of such situations.[64] The extent of the propagandistic literature extolling a pharaoh's right to the throne is implicit evidence that the populace was not totally unaware of their ruler's human origin.

Most Egyptians at the end of the Eighteenth Dynasty would not, however, have had access to the tomb of the general who became the last king of the dynasty—Horemhab. They could not have seen either the evidence of his human origins in the decorations of his Memphite tomb or the attempt to alter it so that the man interred there appeared to be a royal figure. Of course, some people, especially the artisans involved, knew that Horemhab had had royal insignia recarved on all his images after he became pharaoh, to reflect his new status. And many more individuals became aware of the situation when Horemhab eventually had a completely new tomb constructed in the royal tradition on the west bank of Thebes in the Valley of the Kings and when he began large-scale building projects on the east bank, within the precincts of the Karnak and Luxor temples.

The long-lived pharaoh Ramesses II had colossal monuments built throughout Egypt, which he furnished with numerous large-scale images of himself, seemingly attesting to his divinity. He even had a cult worshiping him while he was still alive (fig. 39). The stature of such lofty testimonials seems diminished, however, when one notes that a letter written during the reign of this king apparently alluded to him as simply "the general."[65]

64. Harem conspiracies occurred in ancient Egypt. See Manfred Weber, "Harimsver-schwörung," *LÄ* 2:987–91. Assassinations were not unknown, either. See Jürgen von Beckerath, "Königsmord," *LÄ* 3:535.

65. See Jac. J. Janssen, "Nine Letters from the Time of Ramses II," *OMRO* 41 (1960): 31–47.

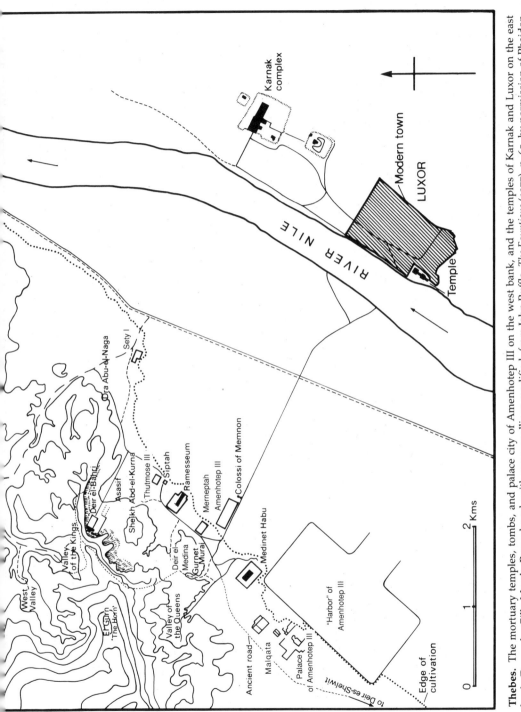

Thebes. The mortuary temples, tombs, and palace city of Amenhotep III on the west bank, and the temples of Karnak and Luxor on the east bank. Drawn by Gilly March. Reproduced, with some spellings modified, from John Ruffle, *The Egyptians* (1977). p. 65, by permission of Phaidon Press, Oxford.

39. Ramesses II, the living king (Nineteenth Dynasty), depicted as a god, and the deity Re-Horakhty portrayed on a diminutive scale in the center of the king's four colossal statues. The Great Temple, Abu Simbel, wherein the cult of the living king was practiced. Photo © 1991 by Byron E. Shafer.

The pharaoh Hatshepsut had her divine birth depicted on the walls of her mortuary temple at Deir el-Bahri (fig. 40), but on the wall of a nearby grotto political satirists took another point of view: there they sketched her in a decidedly unroyal situation, passively engaged in sexual activity.[66]

This dual divine/human perspective on kings is not quite so apparent in relation to deities. While the gods' behavior and activities tended to be humanized, they underwent no metamorphosis from one sphere to another, remaining constantly divine. The king, by contrast, seemed to possess aspects of the human at some times and of the divine at others.

66. David P. Silverman, "Wit and Humor," in *Egypt's Golden Age*, p. 278. See also Edward F. Wente, "Some Graffiti from the Reign of Hatshepsut," *JNES* 43 (1984): 52–54 and the references therein.

He clearly originated in the world of the human, but he could function in both worlds. The gods belonged to an invisible world inhabited only by the divine. They did not ordinarily appear on earth, except in their representations as two- or three-dimensional figures in reliefs or statues. The king operated on earth as an individual active among humanity.

A king had to earn his immortality, whereas a god was inherently immortal. The king's victories in battle were given to him by the deities after appropriate offerings and prayers. The monarch had to maintain *ma'at* and to indicate that he was acting appropriately. Both in art and in official texts, the monarch was portrayed as the one who presented *ma'at* to the gods so that they might live on it.

The view of the king expressed in literary texts can be quite distinct, for many of them originated in popular legends and oral traditions. In

40. View of the mortuary temple complexes of the monarchs Hatshepsut and Thutmose III (Eighteenth Dynasty) and Nebhepetre Mentuhotep (Eleventh Dynasty). Deir el-Bahri, western Thebes. Photo © 1991 by John Baines.

Khufu and the Magicians, the pharaoh is an intolerant tyrant who
stands in contrast to a benevolent sage. Supernatural powers seem to
belong to the sage rather than to the pharaoh.[67] In The Tale of the
Doomed Prince, the pharaoh is an ineffectual father who cannot protect
his son from his fate.[68] In The Tale of the Two Brothers, the ruler is a
relatively minor figure, and his influence on the action is minimal.[69]
One manuscript reports that the king's emissary (a reflection of the king)
has scarcely been treated with dignity. In The Report of Wenamun,
which many scholars believe to be factual rather than literary, references
to the monarch himself, as well as to his agent, are far from respectful.[70]
These images of the rulers surely conflicted with the depictions on temple walls, the descriptions in religious texts, and the concepts inherent
in monumental architecture and statuary, but they may well reflect the
real feelings of the people.

The unavoidable question arises: How could the ancient Egyptians
rationalize this apparent human/divine dichotomy in their rulers? Perhaps it was not a conflict to them. They may have conceived of the king
as a being who partook of both realms. Such thinking may have paralleled their understanding of the implicit duality in their world—Upper
Egypt and Lower Egypt (the Two Lands that made up Egypt), balance
and chaos, light and darkness, the solar and the chthonic, and a myriad
of other paired couplets. A modern individual might view these elements as standing in conflict, but an ancient Egyptian was capable of
viewing them as elements of a functioning composite. A ruler envisioned as both human and divine was best suited to intercede between
the human and divine worlds. The king functioned as the high priest of
every god, making offerings directly to each deity. He thus stood between the god and humankind. Because of the perceived fluidity of the
human and divine components of the king's nature, it was not difficult
for Egyptians to develop variations on and additions to their concept of
kingship. By the early New Kingdom, deification of the living king had
become an established practice, and the living king could himself be
worshiped and supplicated for aid as a god.

During different periods of time and in distinct genres of texts the
king could be referred to by a variety of terms. Some inscriptions of the

---

67. For Simpson's translation of this part of Papyrus Westcar, see *LAE* 15–30, esp. 22–
24.

68. For Wente's translation of this story, see *LAE* 85–91, esp. 86.

69. For Wente's translation of this story, see *LAE* 92–107, esp. 101–7.

70. For Wente's translation of this report, see *LAE* 142–55.

Old Kingdom already specify the king as a god. Other inscriptions call him the "good god," and in one he is said to have been given understanding by the god while still in the womb, because he was more noble than any other deity.[71] Throughout the Old Kingdom the king was said to have the powers of the gods: Ḥu (divine utterance), Sia (divine knowledge), and Ḥeka (divine energy and knowledge of magic). A king's use of the epithet "son of Re" and later of "image of Re" tended to emphasize his divinity. The importance accorded to the living king and his actions during the Old Kingdom was so great that references to him and his reign were often recorded in tombs of private persons who had been directly affected by him. Harkhuf considered the letter he received from the boy-king Pepy II so significant that he had a copy of it carved on the walls of his tomb.[72] The official Rawer recorded an event at court in which the king's baton had come into contact with him.[73] Individuals took pride in events that were related to royalty, and they regarded them as indications of their actual contact with the ruler and of their own importance.

Later Middle Kingdom representations of pharaoh, however, often did not display the imperious, detached demeanor that royal images had in the Old Kingdom. The king's expression was more human (fig. 41), perhaps more characteristic of his mortal element.[74] Yet a hymn to Senwosret III, one of the rulers of this period, identified him with numerous deities.[75] Moreover, some autobiographical texts referred to the ruler as a creator god.[76] Whether or not the motive for such inscriptions was propagandistic, their existence indicates that the concept of the king's divinity was present in this period.

The pharaoh was frequently described as acting like a particular god

71. For the hieroglyphic text, see Kurt Sethe, *Urkunden des Alten Reiches*, Urk. 1 (Leipzig: Hinrichs, 1903), 1:39, 15–16; and for a translation, see Alessandro Roccati, *La littérature historique sous l'Ancien Empire égyptien*, Littératures Anciennes du Proche-Orient (Paris: Cerf, 1982), pp. 96–98.

72. For the hieroglyphic text, see Sethe, *Urkunden des Alten Reiches*, 1:128–31, and for a translation see *AEL* 1:26–27.

73. For the hieroglyphic text, see Sethe, *Urkunden des Alten Reiches*, 1:232, 5–8; and for a translation, see Éric Doret, *The Narrative Verbal System of Old and Middle Egyptian*, Cahiers d'Orientalisme 12 (Geneva: P. Cramer, 1986), p. 61, ex. 95.

74. Dietrich Wildung, in a lecture in Denver in 1988 titled "Royalty in Art," noted that such a style may have emanated from the nonroyal sector.

75. *AEL* 1:198–201.

76. See, e.g., Khnumhotep's remark that the ruler appears as Atum himself. For the text, see Adriaan de Buck, *Egyptian Readingbook* (Leiden: Nederlands Instituut vóór het Nabije Oosten, 1963), p. 68, ll. 9–10.

41. Head of a statue of King Senwosret III (Twelfth Dynasty). Egyptian Museum, Cairo, 486. Photo ©
1991 by David P. Silverman.

or as being "in the likeness of" a specific deity. Such expressions came to
be used in association with many divinities, thereby relating the pharaoh to virtually all of the pantheon. Furthermore, during the New
Kingdom there appeared to be a conscious effort, both in texts and in
scenes, to equate the king with the powers of the divine world. Whether
the proper description of this phenomenon is "identification with the
god," "incarnation of the god," or "manifestation of the god," it is clear
that the king had a mortal aspect and that intertwined with it was an
element of the divine.[77]

Several studies on the extent of the pharaoh's divinity have come to
differing conclusions.[78] Though in many ways royal powers and abilities
may not have been equal to divine forces, the king often appeared as a
member of the divine organization and was often referred to as such.
Unlike the gods, however, he was inextricably related to his human
subjects, having been born in their ranks. He fitted in between the

77. Hornung, *Conceptions of God*, pp. 139, 141, where he suggests "incarnation."
78. See the references in n. 59 above and in Hornung, *Conceptions of God*, pp. 141–
42nn116–20.

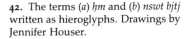

42. The terms (*a*) *ḥm* and (*b*) *nswt bjtj* written as hieroglyphs. Drawings by Jennifer Houser.

a   *b*

society of humanity's world and the society of the gods' world. He was an integral element of both. Without him neither realm could function, and the universe would end. Because the role of the king was a fixed element in the pattern of divine order, his existence was part of *maʿat*. Through his position the monarch maintained *maʿat* and offered *maʿat* to the gods. When the king ruled, a proper balance was maintained, enabling the ordered universe to persist. Therefore, the king was essential to world order.

Perhaps it is possible to comprehend better the human and divine aspects of the king if one understands that the ancient Egyptians envisioned in their ruler both a being and an office, the former originally mortal and the latter always divine. When the two were amalgamated, divine kingship began. Both of these original components remain recognizable, although the distinction between them may be clearer in some periods than in others. The dichotomy between the two is evident in texts. In Old Kingdom biographical inscriptions, when the king is referred to by others or by himself, the term used is *ḥm*, "majesty" (fig. 42a). This word refers to the living embodiment of the king, that is, to his person, and it does not occur in royal funerary inscriptions, such as the Pyramid Texts. Another expression, "King of Upper and Lower Egypt" (*nswt bjtj* [fig. 42b])—or simply "king" (*nswt*)—appears to refer to the ruler when he acted in the capacity of his office.[79] Subjects could not refer to the ruler directly as "King of Upper and Lower Egypt"; they first had to use the term *ḥm*, "majesty" or "living embodiment." Legal, administrative, and economic decrees that were issued through his official position designated him as "King of Upper and Lower Egypt." Individuals could swear an oath in the name of the "king" (*nswt*) or in the name of a god.[80] This flexibility implies that Egyptians viewed the di-

79. For a study that documents these terms and the distinctions between them, see Hans Goedicke, *Die Stellung des Königs im Alten Reich*, ÄgAbh 2 (1960).
80. On oaths, see John A. Wilson, "The Oath in Ancient Egypt," *JNES* 7 (1948): 129–56.

43. Stela of King Semerkhet (First Dynasty), on which is carved a *serekh* with the Horus-falcon perched on top. Egyptian Museum, Cairo. Photo © 1991 by David P. Silverman.

vine office of the king and the status of divinity similarly, a fact that should not be too surprising.

Henri Frankfort felt that the initiation of the new pharaoh into the rites of succession identified him with the gods.[81] Once in his new position, the king would reenact the succession of Horus after the death of his father, Osiris. The living king was identified with Horus, the falcon, while the dead king was identified with Osiris (and Re). The falcon as a symbol of kingship had appeared already in the Early Dynastic Period. Frequently it was represented perched atop the *serekh*, an architectonic design symbolizing the palace. In a rectangular space between the falcon Horus and the *serekh* was the name of the king (fig. 43). This motif,

81. Frankfort, *Kingship and the Gods*, pp. 123–39.

which continued in use throughout most of Egyptian history, combined the name of the king, the palace, and the god Horus. In royal statues, we find the same deity with its protective wings enveloping the head of the enthroned king; for example, Khafre of the Fourth Dynasty (fig. 44). Again it was Horus who perched above a seated figure of King Pepy I of the Sixth Dynasty. From the rear, one can see that Horus stands on a *serekh* that forms the back of the throne. The concept continued in the Ramesside Period, when Horus became an integral part of the headdress on a figure of the king, with its outstretched wings wrapped around the crown. All these representations stand as evidence that the king was seen as Horus in the palace. In the pharaoh's succession and coronation he recreated the myth (parts of which were recorded as early as the

44. Statue of King Khafre (Fourth Dynasty), with the wings of the Horus-falcon enfolding his head. Egyptian Museum, Cairo, 14. Photo © 1991 by David P. Silverman.

Pyramid Texts) of Horus rightfully ascending the throne of his deceased father. On that occasion, the king received the crowns of the Two Lands and became a divine king, joining his being with that of the divine Horus.

When the new pharaoh stepped into his role, he transcended mortal time; he became the king who always had been and always would be. Not only was he identified with Horus, he was also associated with the omniscient creator gods who had brought original order out of chaos during primeval times—Atum, Ptah, Re, and all other cosmogonic deities (fig. 29). It was probably for this reason that the new king was shown or described offering *ma'at* to the creator gods. He, like them, had set the world aright, a role repeatedly portrayed in temple scenes and ritual literature.

In order to establish his credentials, the pharaoh had texts of restoration composed. In these inscriptions he claimed that the land had been in disorder before he had come to the throne and that he had restored its original balance. In the case of Tutankhamun, the king who returned the land to orthodoxy after the Amarna heresy (fig. 45), the texts did accompany a genuine period of upheaval. So did the inscriptions of rulers who began dynasties after the chaotic Intermediate periods. More often, however, such texts were symbolic rather than historically descriptive. Hatshepsut sought to authenticate her claim of restoration by relating it to an actual historical occurrence and inscribing it on the architrave of a temple to the goddess Pakhet at the Speos Artemidos in Middle Egypt. There she referred to her restoration of the land after the destruction and devastation caused by the Hyksos, and she alluded to her efforts to eliminate the abomination of her god. Was her claim total hyperbole bordering on plagiarism? The Hyksos had, in reality, been conquered by the pharaoh Ahmose more than seventy years earlier. From an ancient Egyptian perspective, Hatshepsut's statement was appropriate, for once conducted through the rites of succession, she was, in symbolic terms, the only king who had ever existed. Such a concept may have underlain the not uncommon royal practice of "borrowing" predecessors' exploits, statues, and monuments, appropriating them as one's own. Recarving an earlier monarch's statuary to reflect the features and titulary of the new ruler was not considered an act of sacrilege, for the statue represented the office of the king as well as the king's person.

The king's accession and coronation and the rituals and texts involved with them ensured and corroborated his divinity, but we can also find his divinity implied in religious texts. As early as the Coffin Texts, we

45. Golden mask placed over the mummy of King Tutankhamun (Eighteenth Dynasty), with a protective uraeus (cobra) and vulture head sculpted on his headdress. Egyptian Museum, Cairo, 60672. Photo © 1991 by David P. Silverman.

find indications that the divine had intended the king for rule even before he was born. "Prophetic" texts, albeit always recorded after the fact and therefore always propagandistic in intent, stated that a divine being had implied or otherwise sanctioned the choice of the successor. The king's divine birth was illustrated on the walls of New Kingdom temples and in later times on the walls of birth houses. But the concept of an individual's divine birth had validity only after he had become "King of Upper and Lower Egypt." He could not claim divine birth until his coronation had taken place. Only then did he possess the divine nature.[82]

While the rites of coronation might alter the status of the individual

82. For the role of the divine *ka* in the divinity of the pharaoh, see Lanny Bell, "Luxor Temple and the Cult of the Royal *Ka*," *JNES* 44 (1985): 251–94; and David P. Silverman, "Royalty in Literature," in *Ancient Egyptian Kingship*, ed. O'Connor and Silverman.

who was becoming pharaoh (at least in terms of the images used in texts and art), in the eyes of the populace, the rites did not metamorphize completely the mortal into a divine being. Some scholars even question Frankfort's understanding of the extent to which the ruling king was perceived to be divine.[83] After a very careful analysis of textual references to the king, Georges Posener sees strict limits put on the king's divinity and notes clear distinctions made in references to the king and to the gods.[84]

The divinity of the dead king is a much less controversial concept than the divinity of the living king. The cult of the deceased ruler is well attested from early periods, and it continued throughout Egyptian history. The earliest religious texts provide many references to the deceased king's identification with a variety of gods. In the utterances of the Pyramid Texts the king is related mainly to Osiris and to Re, but other gods are also mentioned. Osiris and Re occur again and again in royal mortuary literature and iconography. These two deities symbolize the two distinct aspects of the funerary religion, the chthonic (Osiris) and the solar (Re); and they reflect the two measures of eternity, resurrection leading to the linear infinite (Osiris) and the daily cyclical rebirth (Re). In death the king became one with these deities.[85]

Royal figures were not the only ones who could receive the benefit of divine association after death. Once Coffin Texts had been compiled, probably as early as the end of the Old Kingdom, their funerary spells became available to the high nobility.[86] The collection included many recitations that dealt with divine transformations and identifications; some of them were edited versions of earlier spells; and others were

83. See the discussion and references in Silverman, "Royalty in Literature."

84. Posener, in *De la divinité du pharaon*, pp. 1–14, examines the references to the nature of the ruler in a variety of sources. He notes the extent of the dependence of royalty on deities, pp. 23–35, and the limited number of truly supernatural acts performed by the king, pp. 47–76.

85. For these concepts, see Wente, *Expedition* 24 (Winter 1982): 22–24.

86. Note the discoveries described in Michel Valloggia, *Le mastaba de Medou-nefer*, Balat 1, Fouilles de l'Institut français d'Archéologie orientale 31/1 (Cairo: Imprimerie de l'Institut français d'Archéologie orientale, 1986). The evidence suggests that Coffin Texts may have been used before the First Intermediate Period. See also Jørgen Podemann Sørensen, "Divine Access: The So-called Democratization of Egyptian Funerary Literature as a Sociocultural Process," in *The Religion of the Ancient Egyptians: Cognitive Structures and Popular Expressions*, Proceedings of Symposia in Uppsala and Bergen 1987 and 1988, ed. Gertie Englund, Acta Universitatis Upsaliensis: Boreas 20 (Uppsala, 1989), pp. 109–28, and Ragnhild Bjerre Finnestad, "The Pharaoh and the 'Democratization' of Post-mortem Life," in the same volume, pp. 89–94.

original compositions. By means of these spells nonroyal individuals could aspire to divine afterlife. A further democratization of the funerary religion took place in the New Kingdom with the appearance of the group of spells now called the Book of the Dead. These spells were inscribed and illustrated on papyri (figs. 31, 32), a process that required less time to produce than that for elaborate carving and painting of the coffins that held the Coffin Texts. Thus the Book of the Dead was less expensive and more widely available. Eventually mythological texts that detailed other mysteries of the underworld, originally available only to royalty, became available to a wider audience. In addition, the citizenry began to appropriate other royal prerogatives, as in an inscription from the early New Kingdom in which a private person claimed to have godlike omniscience.[87]

Although the association with divinity was exclusive to royalty less and less as time went on, the special status of the kings was maintained through extensive royal mortuary cults. Large complexes were established to perpetuate the memory of the monarch even though he had passed on to the next world, and maintaining these establishments required constant attention. Funerary temples were part of the repertoire of royal architecture from the Old Kingdom onward. Although the building plans evolved and changed over the centuries, their essential elements remained the same. Inside the temple, the statues of the deceased king received daily care. On holidays, priests brought out the royal cult statues, along with the statues of other deities, and paraded these images in the public areas of the temple for worship and adoration. The rituals and scenes associated with the funerary complexes have usually been understood as symbolizing the afterlife. In the 1980s, however, studies such as those by Zahi Hawass and William Murnane showed that much of the iconography and many of the texts and decorations in the mortuary complexes appear to emphasize the king's divinity by reaffirming his kingship. They do not center on aspects of the eternal life.[88]

87. See the autobiographical inscription in Kurt Sethe, *Urkunden der 18. Dynastie*, Urk. 4 (Leipzig: Hinrichs, 1909), 4:1071, 9. There Rekhmire's knowledge is said to cover everything on earth, in heaven, and among hidden places in the underworld. See also Norman deGaris Davies, *The Tomb of Rekh-mi-Re at Thebes*, Egyptian Expedition Publications 11 (New York: Metropolitan Museum of Art, 1943), 1:pl. XII and 2:79.

88. Zahi Hawass, "The Funerary Establishments of Khufu, Khafra, and Menkaura during the Old Kingdom" (Ph.D. diss., University of Pennsylvania, 1987); and William J. Murnane, *United with Eternity: A Concise Guide to the Monuments at Medinet Habu* (Chicago: Oriental Institute, University of Chicago, 1980), pp. 1–2, 6–74.

One king attempted to deny many of the funerary aspects of ancient Egyptian religion by introducing new beliefs and by altering or eliminating traditions that had been followed for more than two thousand years. The early years of the man who became King Amenhotep IV were lived during the relatively calm, prosperous, and productive reign of his father, Amenhotep III. Art, architecture, and literature flourished. Royal and noble women were prominent and held high status. The most notable of these women was Amenhotep III's wife, Queen Tiye, whose presence on monuments and in texts indicates her importance. The royal marriage was even recorded on the undersides of large commemorative scarabs, which were then distributed.

Amenhotep III had been relatively successful in military affairs, and by diplomacy he managed to maintain many gains made on the battlefield. Life in Egypt was therefore quite peaceful, a circumstance that afforded the king time to involve himself in other activities. In Thebes he constructed a magnificent palace city, known today as Malqata. It included several royal domiciles and also, to accommodate the royal barges, a manmade harbor that was more than one and a half miles long.[89]

The available records from the reign of Amenhotep III reveal no clear development of conflict between the monarch and the priests of the god Amun, who were becoming increasingly powerful. Perhaps a clash was avoidable in part because the king himself was powerful and popular and in part because Anen, a high official in the priesthood of Amun, was a brother of Queen Tiye.

During this apparent calm, Amenhotep III instituted new directions in religion, the most consequential of which proved to be the prominence given to the disk of the sun, called the Aten. The Aten had appeared in religious literature since a much earlier time, and it had even been described as a universal deity. In the New Kingdom, the Aten's prominence as a god expanded to some degree, but its significance did not increase very noticeably until the reign of Amenhotep III. Then the name of the Aten came to be used in the names of the palace, royal barge, and part of the army; and the Aten may well have had its own shrine in Thebes.[90] At the same time, the king apparently empha-

89. See David O'Connor, "Malqata," *LÄ* 3:1173–77.

90. See Sir Alan Gardiner, *Egypt of the Pharaohs: An Introduction* (Oxford: Clarendon, 1961), p. 217; and Donald B. Redford, *Akhenaten: The Heretic King* (Princeton: Princeton University Press, 1984), pp. 170–72. Redford discusses Amenhotep III on pp. 34–54.

46. Sandstone statue of Amenhotep IV (Eighteenth Dynasty) from Karnak. Egyptian Museum, Cairo. Photo © 1991 by David P. Silverman.

sized and extended his own divine kingship while he was still alive.[91]

Amenhotep IV (fig. 46), the son and successor of Amenhotep III, brought the Aten to its zenith, so that it superseded all other deities. This pharaoh was a man of distinctive nature, character, and personality, and one should not minimize the role he personally played in determining and directing the religious changes that occurred while he was king (fig. 47).[92] Perhaps it was partly political astuteness that motivated him. Aware of considerable potential for conflict between the monarch and the ever more powerful priesthood of Amun, he may have hastened the advent of a newly developing religion devoted exclusively

91. See the references cited in n. 82 above.
92. For comments on the characteristics of this individual, see Redford, *Akhenaten*, pp. 57–203, and the references therein.

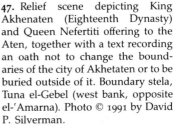

47. Relief scene depicting King Akhenaten (Eighteenth Dynasty) and Queen Nefertiti offering to the Aten, together with a text recording an oath not to change the boundaries of the city of Akhetaten or to be buried outside of it. Boundary stela, Tuna el-Gebel (west bank, opposite el-'Amarna). Photo © 1991 by David P. Silverman.

to the Aten in order to supplant the power of the priests and cult of Amun. Royal fears about "church-state" relations probably would not have been unfounded, since later pharaohs did vie for power with the high priests of Amun at the end of the Twentieth Dynasty. One such high priest of Amun, Herihor, was depicted in royal regalia on the walls of the Khonsu Temple at Karnak. Aside from such possible political/religious motivation, one should not underestimate Amenhotep IV's contemplative, perhaps philosophical leanings as factors that helped shape his doctrines. Neither should one underestimate the role of Amenhotep IV's feelings about himself and about his status in relation to both humanity and divinity. His ideas concerning his own position had undoubtedly been shaped by his life as son and heir of one of Egypt's most popular and powerful rulers, a monarch whose beliefs in his own divinity had been expressed in a variety of texts and reliefs. He even had an entire room of the Luxor Temple devoted to depictions of his divine birth.[93]

93. See Bell, *JNES* 44 (1985): 251–94, and Silverman, "Royalty in Literature," in *Ancient Egyptian Kingship*, ed. O'Connor and Silverman.

Though the impetuses for Amenhotep IV's religious program may be unclear, the results are apparent.[94] Only a few years after ascending the throne, he had effected major changes in Egyptian religion and kingship. Because the king's extensive accomplishments took place within the short span of about twenty years, a modern viewer might suppose that the modifications he introduced had occurred abruptly. The king moved in well-orchestrated and progressive steps, and his innovations were, for the most part, rooted in precedent. The changes he initiated clearly involved structure, planning, and methodology. Had the king not possessed good administrative skills, a peaceful transition would not have been possible. The image of this ruler as a philosopher-king who appeared to be concerned more with otherworldly issues than with his own kingdom may have been current in ancient times; it has persisted in modern times.[95] Yet the records show that he did use diplomatic skills learned in his father's court, more successfully at some times than at others, and that he employed military force when necessary.

During the first few years of his reign, Amenhotep IV made some subtle but decisive moves. The king began the construction of several temples to the Aten. Simultaneously he increased the significance of the Aten to the extent that the god Amun, whose name formed part of the king's own names, first was reduced to a shadow of his former importance and then ultimately was omitted from the developing doctrines. Such a dramatic increase in the prestige of a divinity certainly had precedent. In earlier periods, Re, Montu, and Amun had each come to prominence through support and promotion by pharaohs who constructed and decorated monuments on behalf of their chosen god.

The art of the first years of Amenhotep IV's reign was characterized by an exaggerated style that seems bizarre and almost surreal in comparison with that of earlier reigns (fig. 46).[96] The distinctive physical characteristics of the king appeared not only in his own images but also in those of his family and subjects (fig. 48). These traits clearly identified these figures with that of the king, and such an effect was obviously

94. For further discussion of Akhenaten, see Donald B. Redford, "The Concept of Kingship during the Eighteenth Dynasty," in *Ancient Egyptian Kingship*, ed. O'Connor and Silverman. For other suggestions see Silverman, "Royalty in Literature," in the same volume.

95. However, see Redford, *Akhenaten*, pp. 164–68 and 185–203, where he notes some of Akhenaten's shortcomings.

96. Cyril Aldred, *Akhenaten and Nefertiti* (New York: Brooklyn Museum and Viking Press, 1973), pp. 48–57. Cf. also Wildung, "Royalty in Art" [n. 74].

48. Relief fragment of Queen Nefertiti, who is modeled to reflect the features of her husband, King Akhenaten (Eighteenth Dynasty), offering a bouquet to the Aten, one of whose rays, ending in a hand, touches the uraeus on her crown. Ashmolean Museum, Oxford, 1893.1–41(71). Photo © 1991 by Byron E. Shafer.

intended. Modified within a few years, this early style soon resulted in a freshness and naturalness that had rarely been expressed by Egyptian artists of the past (figs. 49 and 50). The later phases, however, continued to reflect the eccentricities of the royal physique and physiognomy, but much of its manner of representation survived the king and his revolution. Its effects can be observed well into the Ramesside Period.

The king also introduced new styles of expression in the texts. During previous reigns, formal inscriptions had been composed primarily in the

49. Relief depicting King Akhenaten (Eighteenth Dynasty) and Queen Nefertiti on a small shrine in the form of a temple facade, from Tell el-'Amarna. Egyptian Museum, Cairo. Photo © 1991 by David P. Silverman.

classical style, with elements of the less formal spoken language rarely employed. Now such features regularly occurred in all texts, in some ways presaging their use in the nonliterary texts of the later New Kingdom. Occasionally a "Late Egyptianism" had appeared in classically written inscriptions of the past,[97] but during the Amarna Period texts consciously and consistently included some of these elements that derived ultimately from the spoken language. Their frequent appearance has led some scholars to assume that the king was attempting to extend the understanding of the written language to more of the population. Close examination, however, reveals the contrary to have been the case: he was making the language more exclusive. The grammar is less a reflection of Late Egyptian vernacular and more a hybrid composed of both the classical and spoken idioms.[98] It appears to have been quite

97. B. Kroeber, "Die Neuägyptizismen vor der Amarnazeit" (doctoral diss., Eberhard-Karls-Universität, Tübingen, 1970), has noted the use of such elements of the vernacular in earlier texts. See also David P. Silverman, "Plural Demonstrative Constructions in Ancient Egypt," *RdÉ* 33 (1982): 64–65. See also Silverman, "Royalty in Literature," in *Ancient Egyptian Kingship*, ed. O'Connor and Silverman.

98. For a grammatical analysis of some of the texts in the tombs at Akhetaten, see Shlomit Israeli, "A Grammatical Analysis of the First 23 Pages of the El Amarna Texts: Bibliotheca Aegyptiaca VIII," in *Papers for Discussion*, ed. Sarah Israelit-Groll (Jerusalem: Hebrew University, 1982), pp. 278–302.

50. Sculpture of the head of a princess (Eighteenth Dynasty), found at Tell el-'Amarna. Egyptian Museum, Cairo. Photo © 1991 by David P. Silverman.

artificial, and many of the patterns and usages were unique. Much like the new art, the new language was meant to relate directly to the king, and the new royal style was to be one more instance of the pervasive influence of this all-powerful individual.

After the first few years of his reign, Amenhotep IV began thinking about moving Egypt's capital to a city other than Thebes. Changing the location of the capital city was not without precedent. Memphis had been the capital before Thebes. At some point after the king's fifth year, the site for his new capital was chosen, and its occupation was begun. Called Akhetaten ("Horizon of the Aten"), the city lay far down river (north) from Thebes and had been sacred to no other god. Most of the move to Akhetaten and most of the process of occupying it took place during the following year. Like the language and art of the same period,

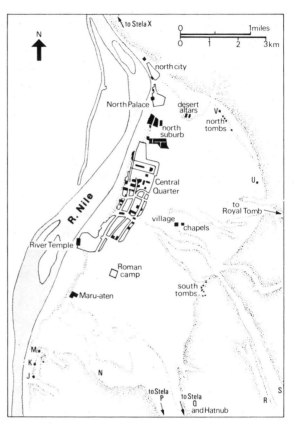

Akhetaten (el-'Amarna). The site of the capital city built by King Akhenaten (Eighteenth Dynasty) and abandoned shortly after his death. Drawn by Brian and Connie Dear. Reproduced from John Ruffle, *The Egyptians* (1977), p. 78, by permission of Phaidon Press, Oxford.

Akhetaten's city plan and architecture followed the new directions the king was taking in relating society to himself.[99] While planning the city and mobilizing the emigration, Amenhotep IV changed his name to Akhenaten. Earlier monarchs had altered parts of their names, but none had changed his name so drastically. "Akhenaten" reinforced the king's denial of Amun and his emphasis of the Aten. Clearly the king not only was elevating the new deity but also was raising his own status by close association with this new god.

Within a few years Akhenaten must have developed his doctrines further, for not only was the Aten emphasized but all other gods were

99. See David O'Connor, "Palace and City in New Kingdom Egypt," in a forthcoming volume of the series Sociétés urbaines en Égypte et au Soudan, Cahier de Recherches de l'Institut de Papyrologie et d'Égyptologie de Lille.

avoided. Eventually he attempted to obliterate the name and image of Amun so that no visual or written stimuli would call Amun to mind. Akhenaten wanted his subjects to worship only the Aten, and he sought to erase all memory of Amun from the minds of his people. Those individuals charged with expunging the names and images of Amun from the monuments were zealous, and they began to remove as well the names and images of other gods and even occurrences of the plural noun "gods." At first solar deities were tolerated, but soon even their titles, epithets, and images were among the traditional religious elements discarded by Akhenaten. Ma'at, however, was tolerated throughout the period.

Through these actions, the king purposely removed any rivals to the Aten. Whether strong political or economic factors motivated this program remains uncertain. Undoubtedly such factors played some role in it. However, the directness, speed, and perseverance of the movement suggest a very strong ideological motivation.

Monotheistic tendencies were clearly evident in the new religion. They are reflected in its texts, terminology, iconography, and underlying concepts. Some of these elements had precedents in earlier periods, but Akhenaten's religion went further toward monotheism than any of the world's religions had previously attempted. In fact, some scholars state that Akhenaten's beliefs introduced monotheism to the world.[100] Perhaps Akhenaten did pioneer a concept that was to have a profound effect on the development of the world's religions. In any event, within a relatively short period of time this individual strongly affected Egyptian religious traditions that were over two thousand years old.

Akhenaten's program touched all aspects of Egyptian culture. The art and architecture of the period were unmistakable. The content and language of the texts were unique. Even the concepts associated with kingship were altered. The focus shifted not only to the Aten, but also to the living divine king, who was proclaimed the son of the Aten. The religion stressed the solar aspects, while chthonic deities, notably Osiris, became less and less important, as did eschatological doctrines and the cult of the deceased king. The funerary divinities who for so long had been an essential element of Egyptian religion became insignificant in Akhenaten's doctrines. Emphasis on the divinity of pharaoh reached new heights as Akhenaten closed the gap between the living king and the

100. Hornung, *Conceptions of God*, p. 246, states: "Now, for the first time in history, the divine has become one. . . ."

supreme power. Perhaps he sought to recapture or even to surpass the status of kingship enjoyed by the Fourth Dynasty monarchs who built the great pyramids.

Through these actions Akhenaten managed simultaneously to raise the level of kingship and to lower the level of divinity, putting them almost on a par. Akhenaten and the Aten came to share prerogatives that formerly had been distinctive either to monarchs or to gods. In earlier reigns, the names of royalty were written within the oval band called a cartouche. Now the cartouche, however, enclosed not only the names of the royal family but the Aten as well. In former times kings had celebrated jubilees and worn the uraeus. Now the Aten also celebrated these festivals, and bore the uraeus. Usually only royalty had received the epithet "Given life for ever and ever," but now both the Aten and Akhenaten received it. Official texts of the past had been dated to the reign of a king, but those composed during Akhenaten's rule could be dated also in terms of the Aten. Earlier typical funerary-offering formulas had mentioned the king and the deity separately. Now these formulas referred to the king and the Aten as if they were a single being.[101] Before, the disk of the sun had not been rendered anthropomorphically. Now it was depicted with rays terminating in human hands, sometimes offering items to the king (fig. 51). In the past, the king had been the high priest, or first prophet, of the god, and Akhenaten followed this tradition, serving as the first prophet of the Aten. Akhenaten's personal status was so high, however, that he rated his own first prophet, as if he were a great god. He followed earlier models in presenting *ma'at* to his god, the Aten, but now Akhenaten was said himself to live on *ma'at*. In earlier periods the statues of the gods had been paraded in barques during festivals (fig. 36). But the Aten had no statue. Now the royal family was displayed in these barques to the adoring population. The Aten could be worshiped only through the king.

Like other Egyptian gods, the Aten was celebrated in hymns. During the Amarna Period, however, the content of the hymns was related less to traditional struggles than to overall positive expressions, and the hymns' literary merits were emphasized. Unlike other Egyptian gods, the Aten was not the subject of myths. No elaborate stories or documentations of divine activity explained the Aten's existence or relation to

101. See Winfried Barta, *Aufbau und Bedeutung der altägyptischen Opferformel*, Ägyptologische Forschungen 24 (Glückstadt: Augustin, 1968), p. 109.

51. Relief from a shrine showing the rays of the Aten offering life (*ankh*) to King Akhenaten (Eighteenth Dynasty) and Queen Nefertiti, from Tell el-ʿAmarna. Egyptian Museum, Cairo. Photo © 1991 by David P. Silverman.

humankind. Akhenaten's doctrines did not include legends mentioning gods or descriptions of divine interrelationships that could bring the Aten closer to the individual. The Aten had no consort, nor was it united with other traditional deities in a divine triad. Rather Akhenaten had a consort, his wife Nefertiti (fig. 49); and the Aten, Akhenaten, and Nefertiti constituted the divine triad (fig. 51). The hymns that were sung and the liturgies that were performed focused on the Aten and Akhenaten.

Akhenaten and the Aten were also the focus of the decorative art in the private tombs at Akhetaten. The tomb owner was himself portrayed only briefly and then mainly in the service of the king. The traditional activities of daily life and glimpses of the underworld were not depicted. Instead the tombs contained large-scale representations of Akhenaten, often accompanied by Nefertiti, and of Akhenaten's activities.[102] Sometimes the daughters of Akhenaten and Nefertiti were portrayed with them. Invariably the Aten was overhead at the apex of the scene, its life-giving rays fanning downward, some ending in human hands offering immortal life to the royal/divine couple (fig. 51).

Such intimate depiction of the royal family was unprecedented. Yet in Akhetaten it occurred not only in tombs but also on the walls of temples and on the exteriors of public buildings and household shrines. The iconography on such surfaces had previously focused only on the deities or on the king or on their relationship with each other. In the religion of Akhenaten, scenes depicting the intensely personal activity of the royal family and showing their closeness to the deity seem to have replaced the myths and stories of the gods found in the religion of Egypt's past. Such scenes served to anthropomorphize the supreme power, the abstract deity—the Aten. They afforded the populace access to the Aten and understanding of it. Only through the medium of the king could one's relationship with the deity be established.

The familial scenes reinforced the relationship of the king with the god. The concept of closeness between the royal and the divine was not, of course, an innovation. It had been presented in funerary texts and scenes throughout Egypt's history. Akhenaten, however, extended the concept to all types of texts and iconography. Akhenaten's teachings and hymns, together with his concept of the "divine family," represented and explained the interrelationship between the living king, the Aten,

102. The importance of Nefertiti, the wife of Akhenaten, should not be underestimated, and she also could be invoked. See Redford, *Akhenaten*, pp. 78–82; and Emma Brunner-Traut, "Nofretete," *LÄ* 4:519–21.

and the cosmos.[103] Akhenaten's writings portrayed the Aten as a creator god and identified the king with it. Like the Aten, Akhenaten was a creator god. Like the Aten, Akhenaten was reborn every day, thereby becoming part of the cosmos. But Akhenaten alone was accessible both to the individual on earth and to the god in the heavens; and this system, which must have seemed logical to the king, was the correct order of the universe. It was *ma'at*.

In many ways the concepts and iconography promoted during Akhenaten's reign were variations on traditional ideas, and their development may even have had a certain logic. Yet despite the apparent care with which the program of transition was planned and despite the meticulous and coherent manner in which it was enacted, Akhenaten's concepts and iconography did not take root.

Many reasons can be suggested for the failure of the new doctrines, but primary among them were the inability of individuals to have direct access to the god(s) of their choice and the necessity to worship the new deity through the king. Undoubtedly the people reacted negatively to an official religion that deprived them of both the chthonic deities and the means for acquiring a personal/individual afterlife and immortality. People apparently found it difficult to adapt to new dogmas that did not deal with them directly and that focused so much on the divinity of the king. Moreover, traditional religion had stressed strong contrasts and had clearly delineated light and darkness, good and evil, life and death, the positive and the negative. Akhenaten's theology practically denied darkness, evil, death, and the negative; it emphasized the positive aspects of life. Since only one god, the Aten, existed, it could have no comparisons, and it had necessarily to be positive. So Akhenaten's religion emphasized life, daily cyclical rebirth, goodness, order, and the sun. The underworld with its dangers, demons, and twelve hours of darkness had no place in the concepts of the new religion. Neither did illness and corruption. In traditional religion these negative aspects symbolized realities of this life and fears about the next. Only by recognizing them could one defeat them. The complex myths, symbols, and texts of tradition dealt with these problems and dangers. In place of such myths and symbols, Akhenaten's monotheistic religion offered an almost simplistic faith in the positive. In his view, neither the new religion nor its godhead had a rival that could create conflict.

103. Jan Assmann, "Die 'loyalistische Lehre' Echnatons," *SAK* 8 (1980): 1–32. Note also therein the references to other important works.

Apparently even people who followed Akhenaten to Akhetaten did not follow his teachings completely. Excavations of private households in the city have unearthed amulets and other images of the traditional pantheon.[104] Such finds indicate that the people, at least in private, retained traditional beliefs. Indeed, a few people may even have poked fun at the "divine family," for archaeologists have found group statuettes of monkeys that apparently satirize the depictions of the personal activities of Akhenaten and his family which dominated the official iconography.[105]

People must have felt the loss of their traditional gods and doctrines deeply. Moreover, now they were also deprived of the traditional monarchy and clerical organization that had run the country for thousands of years. What was offered to them in their place was a divine living king who was reborn daily with the sun, who was at one with the Aten and the cosmos, who was the center and mediator of all, and who was order and life. This replacement, however, was not acceptable to them. Death was all too apparent and real, and people saw that the divine living king was himself mortal. Yet death was a reality that played no part in the new theology. When Akhenaten, the living link to the supreme power, ceased to exist, the new religion could not survive.

104. For references to the works on this subject, see Redford, *Akhenaten*, pp. 242–43.
105. Silverman, "Wit and Humor," in *Egypt's Golden Age*, pp. 280–81 (figs. 385, 386).

2 ANCIENT EGYPTIAN COSMOGONIES AND COSMOLOGY

Leonard H. Lesko

Many modern observers have the impression that the ancient Egyptians were quite primitive in their beliefs and ritual practices. Classical sources indicate that Egyptian religion seemed rather different and exotic even to ancient visitors from abroad. The great temples and tombs reinforce these impressions by providing visual images of a people dominated by an apparently overwhelming pantheon. On the other hand, the better the ancient Egyptian language is understood and the more the problems of the transmission of texts are studied, the greater our appreciation of the sophistication of the Egyptians' reasoning and abstraction becomes.

It has taken years to produce preliminary translations of the huge corpus of Egyptian religious literature, and these translations often defy logical interpretation and encourage wild speculation. It is often discouraging to find that translations of the edited texts of the pyramid's inner chambers (Pyramid Texts [fig. 1]), coffin interiors (Coffin Texts [figs. 30, 52]), and the papyri called the Book of the Dead (figs. 31, 32) contain some grammatically and lexicographically lucid passages interspersed with what can be described only as gibberish. The ancient Egyptians themselves had considerable difficulty understanding their texts, as is demonstrated by, for example, the widely differing interpretations preserved in the glosses appended regularly to chapter 17 of the Book of the Dead. If some of the ancients were so sure of their individual interpretations and others were unsure enough to include the

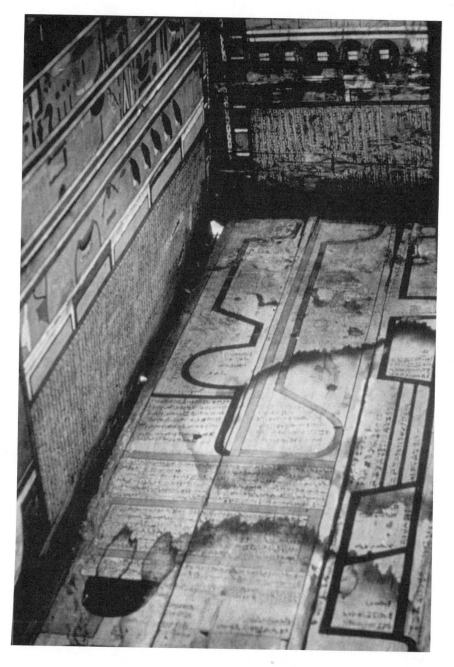

52. A Middle Kingdom coffin with the Book of Two Ways. British Museum, London, 30841. Photo © 1991 by Leonard H. Lesko.

many possibilities, modern interpreters cannot expect some single, yet-to-be-discovered document to provide the key to unlock all mysteries. Rather, we must painstakingly examine everything that survives, objects and texts, together with their context, suspending contemporary biases insofar as we can.

Let us examine several differing ancient Egyptian interpretations of the nature of the cosmos (cosmology) and of its divine creation (cosmogony).[1] The ancient Egyptians generally would have been aware of these concepts and may well have had personal preferences among them, but no particular speculations appear to have been required dogmatically, since many conflicting descriptions often occur together. From time to time many of the cosmological and cosmogonical materials in the possession of the various Egyptian cults or religions were assimilated, integrated, and interwoven by skilled persons who knew what they were doing. Their task was philosophical and theological. Their mode of expression was mythological.

COSMOGONIES

According to Egyptian tradition, at the beginning of Egypt's history (about 2950 B.C.E., or perhaps about 3110 B.C.E.) a king of Upper Egypt named Menes (possibly to be identified with either the Narmer [fig. 3] or the Aha known from surviving monuments) conquered Lower Egypt, and, after uniting (or reuniting) Egypt, he established a new capital city at Memphis and founded a temple to Ptah, the creator god of Memphis. Almost all of Egyptian mythology can be related in one way or another to these events. Existing mythology was recast and re-employed to explain them, and new mythology was produced for the same purpose. Gradually, or perhaps quickly, local myths from throughout the country were brought together into a system, and local gods from many sites were arranged in a hierarchy. Lacking textual evidence and also any reasonably complete formulation of the mythology from an early date, one cannot be sure how long it took to create this national mythology, which sought to include almost every god and thereby to

1. John A. Wilson, "Egypt: The Nature of the Universe," in Henri Frankfort et al., *The Intellectual Adventure of Ancient Man* (Chicago: University of Chicago Press, 1946), pp. 31–61, is still the best standard treatment of these topics. My account differs in dealing with more texts and in dealing with them more directly.

satisfy almost every person. It was a product of genius, however, and laid the foundation for one of the longest-lived civilizations in history.

In the form in which the major Egyptian myths survive, all are basically cosmological or cosmogonical, but they were probably only secondarily formulated for the purpose of explaining the origin of the universe. Getting back to the beginning, to the origin of the world, is essential for anyone wishing to establish the priority of a particular religious system, and in this case the religious system was practically synonymous with the governmental structure.

Until recently the divine kingship of the pharaoh was taken for granted as a cornerstone of Egyptian society and as one explanation for many of the Egyptians' outstanding achievements. The concept of divine kingship has now been challenged by several eminent scholars, who point to differences in the degree of respect and devotion shown on the one hand to the living king and on the other hand (even by the king) to deceased kings and the great gods.[2] Demonstrations of differences in respect and devotion would not of themselves validate this overall challenge. Against it stands the solid witness of almost all of the Egyptian myths, which at least in the forms that have come down to us were intended primarily to bolster the greatest myth of all: divine kingship.[3] These myths show the king to be related in one way or another to the many gods, temples, and religions of ancient Egypt. In some cases the king may have imposed himself upon a particular religious system and its mythology, but in other cases the priest-scribes who authored the religious texts voluntarily affirmed the king's divinity for one reason or another and incorporated him into their religions by formulating and propagating the myths as they did.

The best-known and perhaps most important of the early Egyptian myths is the Heliopolitan Cosmogony. Its modern name comes from the chief center of Egyptian sun worship, called Heliopolis in Greek, but originally Iwnw in Egyptian. The latter is reflected in On (Hebrew 'n or

2. For the traditional view, see Henri Frankfort, *Kingship and the Gods: A Study of Ancient Near Eastern Religion as the Integration of Society and Nature* (Chicago: University of Chicago Press, 1948). And for the dissent, see Georges Posener, *De la divinité du pharaon*, Cahiers de la Société Asiatique 15 (Paris: Imprimerie Nationale, 1960), and Dietrich Wildung, *Egyptian Saints: Deification in Pharaonic Egypt*, Hagop Kevorkian Series on Near Eastern Art and Civilization (New York: New York University Press, 1977).

3. Most of the deities and much of the myths' detail could have existed much earlier, even in prehistoric times, but they come to us in written forms dating from 2500 B.C.E. and later.

'wn), the Bible's name for the city. An early reference to the Ennead, or group of nine gods, upon whom this cosmogony focuses is Pyramid Text utterance 600:

> Atum Kheprer, you have come to be high on the hill, you have arisen on the Benben stone[4] in the mansion of the Benben in Heliopolis, you spat out Shu, you expectorated Tefnut, and you put your two arms around them as the arms of a *ka* symbol (⎣ ⎤), so that your *ka* (personality) might be in them. O Atum, place your arms around the king, around this edifice, around this pyramid as the arms of a *ka*, so that the King's *ka* may be in it, firm forever and ever. O Atum, place your protection over this king, over this pyramid of his, over this edifice of the king, so that you may guard against anything happening evilly against him forever and ever, just as your protection was placed over Shu and Tefnut.
>
> O great Ennead which is in Heliopolis—Atum, Shu, Tefnut, Geb, Nut, Osiris, Isis, Seth, Nephthys—children of Atum, extend his heart (good-will) to his child (the king) in your name of Nine Bows. Let his back be turned from you toward Atum, so that he may protect this king, so that he may protect this pyramid of the king, so that he may protect this edifice of his from all the gods [and] from all the dead, and so that he may guard against anything happening evilly against him forever and ever.[5]

Several versions of the Heliopolitan creation story can be reconstructed from the allusions found in texts from various periods. All of them begin with Atum ("the All" or "the complete one") ejaculating out of himself Shu ("air"—male) and Tefnut ("moisture"—female). Shu and Tefnut in turn give birth to Geb ("earth"—male) and Nut ("sky"—female) (fig. 13). In the next generation Geb and Nut give birth to two sons and two daughters, and the increased number of siblings leads inevitably to conflict, while the simple chthonic equivalences become more complex.

The conflict focuses on the two brothers Osiris (fig. 26) and Seth. Seth slays Osiris and dismembers his body, scattering the parts throughout Egypt (a narrative feature that provides an etiological explanation for old scattered cult centers and perhaps an imperative for the construction of

---

4. A representation at Heliopolis of the primeval hillock of creation. There is obvious wordplay here involving *wbn* ("to arise"), but the interdependence of the two words is not necessarily required. A related term is later used for "pyramidion," which probably indicated its shape.

5. See Kurt Sethe, *Die altägyptischen Pyramidentexte*, 2 vols. (Leipzig: Hinrichs, 1908, 1910), secs. 1652–59, 2:372–77. The text is translated in R. O. Faulkner, *The Ancient Egyptian Pyramid Texts* (Oxford: Clarendon, 1969). This translation, like those elsewhere in this chapter, is my own.

new shrines). Isis, the devoted sister-wife of Osiris (fig. 15), collects and reassembles the parts of Osiris's body, and he is revived long enough to engender a son and avenger, Horus. In a variety of episodes, Horus contends with his uncle Seth, losing an eye but eventually triumphing.

On one level of meaning, the struggle between Osiris and Seth represents a conflict in nature—between the fertile Nile Valley (Kemet, the black land) and the infertile desert (Deshret, the red land) or between the consistent, beneficial inundation of the Nile (Osiris) and the unpredictable, generally undesirable storm (Seth). On another level, reflected in later texts,[6] the struggle represents a conflict between two anthropomorphic heirs contending for the rule of their father, the earth, clearly symbolizing the struggle between kings of the north and south for control of the country. Originally the myth may even have been intended to resolve the question of succession by legitimizing the claim of the son against the competing claim of the dead king's brother.

Horus represents the living, reigning king, and the king of Egypt is called Horus early and often. Typical of the complexity of myth, the anthropomorphic Horus, the son, the avenger, thus achieves a much higher standing by being identified with an originally separate falcon god who represents the sky. The sound eye of Horus comes to symbolize the bright sun, and his injured eye symbolizes the sky's weaker luminary, the moon. With this amalgamation the falcon becomes a principal symbol of kingship.

As Rudolph Anthes pointed out, the Heliopolitan Ennead (or family of the nine gods preceding Horus) is certainly to be viewed as a genealogy of the king, and this genealogy was constructed from the bottom up rather than from the top down.[7] Since Atum was the chief god of Heliopolis, a city a few miles north of the new capital at Memphis, it seems curious that the conquering king from the south should be portrayed as a descendant of this major northern god. The integration and harmonization of myths was doubtless part of the effort to unify the land. The kings also bore a so-called Two Ladies title for Nekhbet and

6. Principally, The Contendings of Horus and Seth, but also The Blinding of Truth by Falsehood and The Tale of the Two Brothers. See the translations of Edward F. Wente in *LAE* 108–26, 127–32, 92–107, and of Miriam Lichtheim, *AEL* 2:214–23, 211–14, 203–11.

7. Rudolf Anthes, "Egyptian Theology in the Third Millennium B.C.," *JNES* 18 (1959): 169–212. One would think that the members of this genealogy should have been well known and consistently listed, but as a matter of fact sources contain a number of substitutions in the listing and depiction of the Great Ennead. See Winfried Barta, *Untersuchungen zum Götterkreis der Neunheit*, MÄS 28 (Munich: Deutscher Kunstverlag, 1973).

Wadjit, the goddesses of the early predynastic capitals of Hierakonpolis (Nekhen) in the south and Buto (Pe/Dep) in the north (fig. 23). Additionally, the kings of the First and Second dynasties seem to have prepared cenotaphs (that is, rather complete false burials) for themselves in the north at Saqqara, near their new capital, whereas their actual burials were most probably in the south at Abydos, a necropolis near their former family seat at This and a site sacred to Osiris.

A second major creation myth originated in Middle Egypt at Hermopolis (Ḫmnw), the city of Thoth, god of wisdom and of the moon. The myth's story begins with an ogdoad (group of eight), four couples of male and female gods who seem to represent elements of precreation chaos (fig. 19). The names of the gods of the Ogdoad are listed inconsistently in various texts. Pyramid Text 301 mentions two of the pairs:

> Your offering-cake belongs to you, Niu and Nenet,
>   who protect the gods,
>   who guard the gods with your shadows.
> Your offering-cake belongs to you, Amun and Amaunet,
>   who protect the gods,
>   who guard the gods with your shadows.[8]

Coffin Text spell 76 names the four pairs (substituting Tenem for Amun of the standard list), and this text also connects the Ogdoad with some of the Ennead as well:

> Going forth to the sky, going down to the barque of Re, becoming a living god.
> O you eight Ḥeḥ (chaos) gods, keepers of the chambers of the sky, whom Shu made from the efflux of his limbs, who bound together the ladder of Atum, come in front of your father with me, give me your arms. Bind together the ladder for me; I am the one who created you and made you, as I was created by your father, Atum.
> I am weary of the supports of Shu since I raised up my daughter, Nut, from upon me, so that I might give her to my father Atum in his precinct. I have placed Geb under my feet. This god binds together the two lands for my father, Atum; he assembles for himself the Great Flood (heavenly cow). I have placed myself between them, so the Ennead cannot see me. I am Shu, whom Atum created, from whom Re came to be. I was not fashioned in the womb, I was not bound together in the egg, I was not

---

8. For the text of utterance 301, see Sethe, *Die altägyptischen Pyramidentexte*, secs. 446–57, 1:231–35. The text is translated in Faulkner, *Ancient Egyptian Pyramid Texts*, pp. 90–91.

conceived, but my father, Atum, spat me out in the spittle of his mouth, together with my sister, Tefnut. She went forth after me. I was covered with the breath of the throat.

The phoenix (Benben) of Re was that from which Atum came to be as Heh (chaos), Nun (the watery abyss), Kek (darkness), Tenem (gloom). I am Shu, father of the gods; Atum used to send his Sole Eye seeking me and my sister, Tefnut. I made illumination for her because of the darkness, and she found me as man of millions (Heh). I am the one who begot the Heh gods again as Heh, Nun, Tenem, Kek. I am Shu who begot the gods.

O you eight Heh gods, whom I made from the efflux of my flesh, whose names Atum made, when the *mdw*[?] of Nun was created, on that day when Atum spoke in Nun, Heh, Tenem, Kek.[9]

The gods of the Ogdoad, with their names as they generally occur in later texts, show the following equivalences. Amun and Amaunet were hiddenness, Huh and Hauhet were formlessness, Kuk and Kauket were darkness, and Nun and Naunet were the watery abyss. From these eight deities came an egg bearing the god responsible for creating all other gods, humans, animals, plants, and so on. Originally Thoth may have been this creator god (fig. 19), but in texts generally coming from Heliopolis, Atum was easily inserted in his place. Coffin Text spell 76 is unusual in having Shu create the Ogdoad so that Atum has priority in time as well as in the act of creation. The contemporaneous spell 335 (the earlier version of chapter 17 of the Book of the Dead) more clearly shows the priority of Nun, which is seen in most of the later texts cited below.

For a modern reader, the most interesting of the creation myths, both because of its methods and because of its relation to the other cosmogonies, is the Memphite Theology. Unfortunately, it survives only on a very late and badly damaged stone inscription, itself supposedly copied in the time of King Shabaka (about 710 B.C.E.) from a worm-eaten original. A portion of the text reads:

Then His Majesty copied this writing anew in the House of his father Ptah, He who is south of his wall. His Majesty had found it as that which the ancestors had made but which was worm-eaten. It was unknown from beginning to end. Then His Majesty copied it anew, so that it is better than its state formerly. . . .

9. See Adriaan de Buck, *The Egyptian Coffin Texts*, 7 vols. (Chicago: University of Chicago Press, 1935–1961), 2:1–8. The text is translated in R. O. Faulkner, *The Ancient Egyptian Coffin Texts*, 3 vols. (Warminster: Aris & Phillips, 1973–1978), 1:77–80.

> The gods who came into being as Ptah:
>   Ptah upon the Great Throne . . .
>   Ptah-Nun, the father who begot Atum . . .
>   Ptah-Naunet, the mother who bore Atum . . .
>   Ptah, the Great, that is the heart and tongue of the Ennead . . .

> There came into being from the heart and there came into being from the tongue [something] in the form of Atum. The mighty Great One is Ptah, who caused all gods [to live], as well as their *ka*s, through this heart, by which Horus became Ptah, and through this tongue by which Thoth became Ptah. . . .

> His Ennead is before him as teeth and lips, that is, the semen and hands of Atum. The Ennead of Atum came into being by his semen and fingers; the Ennead [of Ptah], however, is the teeth and lips in this mouth, which pronounced the name of everything, and from which Shu and Tefnut came forth, the fashioner of the Ennead.

> The sight of the eyes, the hearing of the ears, and the smelling of the air by the nose, they present to the heart. This is what causes every "completed [concept]" to come forth, and it is the tongue that repeats what the heart thinks.

> Thus all the gods were born and his Ennead was completed. Every word of the god ("hieroglyph"? "idea"?) came into being through what the heart thought and the tongue commanded.[10]

In this text the Memphite god Ptah (fig. 35) is the one who conceives in his heart and creates with his tongue, an interesting example of creation ex nihilo and a possible antecedent both of ancient Israel's concept that God created by speaking and of Christianity's doctrine of the Logos. Ptah creates Atum and the rest of the Ennead by pronouncing their names, and because Ptah is equated with Nun and Naunet, the last of the chaotic pairs of the Ogdoad, the cosmogonies of the Ogdoad and Ennead are linked by the figure of a rather abstract, intellectual creator who stands between chaos and the physical progenitors of the cosmos. If either the original version of this document or the ideas expressed in it are genuinely old, the text represents the creation of a national mythology that linked the king to Ptah, the god of the Old Kingdom capital of Memphis, and showed the king to be the descendant and chief supporter of all the principal gods. Rival institutions based on a differing mythology could thus be circumvented, overshadowed, or even supplanted.

---

10. For the text of this inscription, see James H. Breasted, "The Philosophy of a Memphite Priest," *ZÄS* 39 (1901): 39–54; trans. John A. Wilson, *ANET* 4–6.

Although the course of Egyptian history was not made completely smooth by the constructive employment of religious propaganda, most political and social crises were understood in terms of mythology and were resolved with the use of mythology. An early instance of this phenomenon occurred toward the end of the Second Dynasty (about 2700 B.C.E.) when a claimant to the throne took the title Seth rather than Horus. This claimant, Peribsen, was apparently deposed by a Horus king of the South, who in victory assumed a Two Lords title to indicate his renewed control of the Two Lands.

The Fourth Dynasty was remarkable both for the construction of the great pyramids at Giza and for the religious, political, and economic reality to which they testify—the god-king's complete centralized control of the nation's natural, material, and human resources. The central place of these kings was symbolized in the ground plan of the necropolis of Khufu, the builder of the Great Pyramid. Elder relatives who held important posts in his reign were buried to the west of his pyramid, while his wives and his children were buried to the east in their small pyramids and large mastabas (flat-topped rectangular structures). This orderly arrangement in proximity to the king's burial has led some scholars to hypothesize that the king's divinity was unrivaled at this time, that he was the only one who had great expectations for the afterlife, and that all others who wished to enter the realm of the gods had to cling to his shirttails. Khufu may have thought so, but surely many of his subjects would have had as much confidence, or perhaps more, in the individual efforts that they described in their autobiographical inscriptions or in the boons that they sought from gods other than the king.

The official doctrine that equated the king with Horus is very well illustrated in Khafre's famous statue, where a falcon is incorporated into his headgear (fig. 44). Religious developments at the same time in nearby Heliopolis, however, gave increased impetus to the cult of the sun god, Re, which could perhaps have posed a serious challenge to the religion of the divine Horus king had not the mythology been reconstructed so that the king also became the child of that unequaled natural force, the sun (fig. 29). Beginning in the Fourth Dynasty and continuing in the Fifth, the kings styled themselves "son of Re" and many, such as Khafre, included "Re" in their own names. Fifth Dynasty kings erected solar temples at Abu Ghurab (fig. 53), and perhaps elsewhere, which were as large as their comparatively small pyramid tombs at Saqqara and

53. Altar of the solar temple of King Niuserre (Fifth Dynasty). Abu Ghurab. Photo © 1991 by Leonard H. Lesko.

Abu Sir. And to enable the king to accompany Re on his voyage through the sky and the underworld, pyramids from the end of the Fifth Dynasty and throughout the Sixth were inscribed with spells or utterances known collectively as the Pyramid Texts (fig. 1). Utterance 264 is one of the numerous texts in this collection that speak of the king's "ascension" to the sun's celestial realm:

The reed floats of the sky are set down for Horus,
    that he may cross on them to the horizon, to Horakhty,[11]
The reed floats of the sky are set down for the king,
    that he may cross on them to the horizon, to Horakhty.
The reed floats of the sky are set down for Shesemty,[12]
    that he may cross on them to the horizon, to Horakhty.
The reed floats of the sky are set down for the king,
    that he may cross on them to the horizon, to Horakhty.
The Nurse Canal is opened, the Winding Waterway is flooded,
    the Fields of Reeds are filled with water,
So that the king is ferried over thereon
    to that eastern side of the sky
    to the place where the gods fashion him,
    where he is born again, new and young.[13]

Note also this description in Pyramid Text 510:

The doors of the sky are opened,
    the doors of the cool place are ajar.
For Horus of the East at dawn,
    that he may go down and bathe in the Field of Reeds.[14]

The cool place (*ḳbḥ*) mentioned here may reinforce the idea of purification, since *ḳbḥ* also means "to purify," but the term could also be used to refer to the northern sky, the place of the imperishable stars. Pyramid Text 509 provides additional interesting details:

The sky thunders, the earth quakes, Geb quivers,
    the two districts of God roar, the earth is hacked up.
The offering is presented before this king, alive and enduring,
    so that he may go forth to the sky,
    so that he may traverse the firmament,
    so that he may cross the Ḥesaw water
    and demolish the ramparts of Shu,
    so that he may go forth to the sky.

11. "Horus of the Horizon" was a sky god in the form of a falcon. This aspect of Horus was combined with Re as Re-Horakhty to become the chief god of the Egyptian pantheon until he was challenged by Amun-Re.

12. An epithet of Horus, "He of Shesmet" (a location in the east).

13. For the text of utterance 264, see Sethe, *Die altägyptischen Pyramidentexte*, secs. 342–50, 1:183–85; trans. Faulkner, *Ancient Egyptian Pyramid Texts*, pp. 73–74.

14. For the text of utterance 510, see Sethe, *Die altägyptischen Pyramidentexte*, secs. 1128–48, 2:131–42; trans. Faulkner, *Ancient Egyptian Pyramid Texts*, pp. 185–87.

The tips of his wings are those of a great bird.
    His entrails have been washed by Anubis.
The encircling of Horus was in Abydos, and Osiris was embalmed,
    so that he might go forth to the sky among the imperishable
        stars.
His companion is Sothis,[15] his guide is the morning star,
    and they grasp his hand at the Field of Ḥetep.[16]
He sits on this iron throne,
    the faces of which are those of lions,
    the feet of which are the horns of the Great Wild Bull.[17]

Many aspects of these texts, which integrate the three major gods Horus, Osiris, and Re, help to explain the various developments of Egyptian religion in the third millennium B.C.E. Following the lead of James Henry Breasted, scholars have generally assumed a developmental progression from Horus kingship to Re supremacy to increased Osirinization, which was supposed to have led in the Middle or New Kingdom to a democratization of the hereafter and a religion that involved the common people.[18] However, the Pyramid Texts do not appear to reflect conflict between Horus kingship and the solar religion. Quite the contrary, the association of the king with Re seems clearly intended to enhance the older doctrine rather than to diminish it (fig. 29).

In the Pyramid Texts the king is also represented as the son of the goddess Hathor (fig. 5), who in this case must be seen as the spouse of Re. Hathor was a great mother goddess who probably had her own cult, but her name means "House of Horus," and on the basis of various references in the Pyramid Texts, it is clear that she was believed to be the personification of the entire Ennead and, in that sense, the mother of Horus.[19]

The Osirian religion with its themes of fertility, vindication, and resurrection later had great appeal to the common folk of Egypt, as Breasted

15. The star Sirius as a goddess was thought responsible for the annual flood. Her reemergence from behind the sun in the middle of summer marked New Year's Day.

16. Field of the god Ḥetep (or Field of Offerings) was a location in the western sky where originally the deceased in the afterlife seems to have labored on behalf of the god Osiris, but which later came to be regarded as a paradise.

17. For the text of utterance 509, see Sethe, *Die altägyptischen Pyramidentexte*, secs. 1120–27, 2:127–31; trans. Faulkner, *Ancient Egyptian Pyramid Texts*, pp. 184–85.

18. See James Henry Breasted, *The Development of Religion and Thought in Ancient Egypt* (New York: Scribner's, 1912; rpt. Harper & Row, 1959).

19. See Anthes, *JNES* 18 (1959): 169–212; his "Note Concerning the Great Corporation of Heliopolis," *JNES* 13 (1954): 191–92; and his "Mythology in Ancient Egypt," in *Mythologies of the Ancient World*, ed. Samuel Noah Kramer (Garden City, N.Y.: Doubleday Anchor, 1961), pp. 15–92.

pointed out, but in the Old Kingdom Pyramid Texts, generally intended for royalty, the devotion of the Horus king to his dead father was surely the association being stressed. A few Pyramid Texts were originally nonroyal and some so-called Coffin Texts were probably copied for wealthy common folk as early as the Old Kingdom, so there is no reason to believe that all religion before the First Intermediate Period centered on the king, as many scholars have claimed and as the king probably wanted people to believe. Nor is there reason to believe that the cult of Osiris became prominent because it was the only religion that appealed to commoners. In the Old Kingdom, for example, hundreds of men and women served as clergy in the cult of Hathor.

That several religions made real efforts to appeal to commoners can clearly be seen in the ancient Egyptian Book of Two Ways (fig. 52). This guidebook to the beyond, drawn on the inside bottoms of wooden coffins, was apparently intended originally for followers of Osiris. Later, however, it was cleverly turned into a proselytizing tract for the Re religion, with promises that anyone who knew all its spells, including a brief theology of the Re religion, could attain the same goal as the king and could travel in the sun god's barque.[20] The final spell in this rather long book is Coffin Text 1130, which begins "Words spoken by him-whose-names-are-secret," and continues:

Proceed in peace, that I may repeat to you the good deeds that my heart
    has done in the midst of the coiled one[21] in order to silence evil.
I have done four good deeds in the midst of the portal of the horizon.
I made the four winds, that every man might breathe in his time.
    This is a deed thereof.
I made the great flood, that the poor man might have power like the great.
    This is a deed thereof.
I made every man like his fellow.
I did not command that they do evil.
It is their hearts that disobey what I have said.
    This is a deed thereof.
I made their hearts to cease forgetting the West, in order to make divine
    offerings to the gods of the nomes.
    This is a deed thereof.

20. See Leonard H. Lesko, *The Ancient Egyptian Book of Two Ways*, Near Eastern Studies 17 (Berkeley: University of California Press, 1972); and Lesko, "Some Observations on the Composition of the *Book of Two Ways*," *Journal of the American Oriental Society* 91 (1971): 30–43.
21. The sun god on his barque stands within a shrine that is protected by a coiled serpent.

It is with my sweat that I created the gods,
    while humankind is from the weeping of my eye. . . .
It is for the One-who-is-weary-of-heart (Osiris) that I made night. . . .

Authoritative-utterance and Magic overthrow for me that One-of-evil-
character, so that [the deceased] may see the horizon and sit in front of it,
that he may judge the poor together with the rich, and that he may do
likewise against the evil ones. . . .

My scepter has not been taken from my hand. After [the deceased] has
spent millions of years between me and that One-who-is-weary-of-heart,
the son of Geb, then we shall sit in one place. Mounds will be cities and
vice versa; house will desolate house.

As for any person who knows this spell, he will be like Re in the east of
the sky, like Osiris in the midst of the Duat.[22] He will go down to the
entourage of flame. There is no flame against him forever.[23]

The two versions of the Book of Two Ways, both apparently composed
at Middle Egyptian Hermopolis, also included sections referring to an
afterlife in which deceased commoners become stars in the sky, alongside the moon god Thoth. Interestingly, these sections do not mention
the sky goddess Nut, whose role is well attested in the Pyramid Texts
and most other coffins and burial chambers.

The First Intermediate Period saw decentralization, rival claimants to
the throne, and upheaval, but through it all the myth of divine kingship
was maintained, though the distance between the king and the god Re
in particular became much greater. Dating to this period, sometime
around 2000 B.C.E., is one of the most profound religious documents
surviving from ancient Egypt, the Instruction for Merikare. It is set in
Tenth Dynasty Herakleopolis and contains a humble confession by King
Akhtoy, acknowledging responsibility for the sack of the Thinite cemetery, an act of sacrilege against the gods buried there. Akhtoy instructs
his son, Merikare, to revere the god Re, "for none can withstand him."
The conclusion of the text contains the most succinct and elegant descriptions extant of both the philosophy and the theology of the Re
religion. Providing an overview of the cosmology, ontology, ethics, and
eschatology of this developed religious system, it also summarizes the

---

22. On the cosmological plan or map accompanying these texts, Duat is located in the
sky nearer the eastern horizon.

23. The text of Coffin Text 1130 is found in de Buck, *Egyptian Coffin Texts*, 7:461–71. It is
translated in Faulkner, *Ancient Egyptian Coffin Texts*, 3:167–69; Lesko, *Ancient Egyptian Book
of Two Ways*, pp. 130–33; and Wilson, *ANET* 7–8.

nature and attributes of Re, the creator—hidden, omniscient, provident, responsive, and just:

> One generation of people passes to another, and God, who knows characters, has hidden himself. . . .
> The soul goes to the place it knows; it does not stray on its road of yesterday.
> Decorate your mansion of the West. Establish your place of the necropolis with straightforwardness and just dealing, for it is on that that their hearts rely.
> More acceptable is the character of the straightforward one than the ox of the evildoer.
> Act for God, that he may do the like for you, with offerings for replenishing the altars and with carving. It is that which will show forth your name, and God is aware of the one who acts for him.
> Provide for people, the cattle of God, for he made heaven and earth for their liking. He repelled the greed of the waters; he made the winds in order that their nostrils might breathe; [for] they are likenesses of him that came forth from his flesh. He shines in the sky for their liking; he has made vegetation, small cattle, and fish for them to nourish them. He has killed his enemies and destroyed his own children, because they planned to make rebellion. He makes daylight for their liking, and he sails around in order to see them. He has raised up a shrine behind them, and when they weep, he hears. He has made them rulers even from the egg, a lifter to lift [the load] from the back of the weak man. He has made for them magic to be weapons to oppose what may happen.[24]

Here the Herakleopolitan king who is supposed to have written this instruction to his son and successor certainly had a diminished view of his own position in relation to that of his god. His political situation, which seems to have been one of impending disaster, probably increased his piety. The text argues for religious observances as a means of appeasing the creator, who has the power to respond to people's needs during life in this world and to reward them after death. Like Atum and Ptah, the sun god Re here parts the waters (Nun?) and creates the winds (Shu?), but the anthropomorphism, and for that matter the polytheism, of the other creation stories is totally absent.

This Tenth Dynasty of Herakleopolitan kings eventually lost its bid to rule over all Egypt. An Eleventh Theban Dynasty, professing devotion

24. The text of the Instruction for Merikare is found in Aksel Volten, *Zwei altägyptische politische Schriften*, Analecta Aegyptiaca 4 (Copenhagen: Munksgaard, 1945), pp. 3–82 and pls. 1–4. It is translated by Faulkner, *LAE* 180–92; Lichtheim, *AEL* 1:97–109; and Wilson, *ANET* 414–18.

to its local war god, Montu, defeated the Herakleopolitans, reunited the land, and founded the Middle Kingdom. Evidence suggests that the victorious Thebans were not nearly so sophisticated as the Herakleopolitans, but, probably with support from some northern scribes as well as various priesthoods, they were able to continue in the old tradition, while at the same time satisfying their own priests, constituents, and supporters.

The Twelfth Dynasty, also Theban in origin, moved its capital and tombs from Thebes to the north, where the high artistic traditions had been maintained. The god Montu was displaced in prominence, and his attributes were generally assimilated into a new national god, Amun. As one of the Ogdoad of Hermopolis, Amun had represented the abstract concept of hiddenness, but he now became quite personalized. Surely one reason these Thebans adopted Amun was that by claiming as their own the very first of the chaotic elements, they sought to establish the priority of Thebes over both Memphis and Heliopolis. Later mythology would also claim that the burial place of the Ogdoad had been Thebes.

In typical Egyptian fashion, other gods were incorporated into Amun and his religion. Perhaps because Thebes had been supported by the nearby nomarchs of Coptos, the ithyphallic fertility god of Coptos, Min, was one of the gods incorporated. And for the sake of continuity in tradition, the previous national god, Re of Heliopolis, was amalgamated with Amun. Amun-Re became "King of the Gods" and remained so for almost all of pharaonic history (fig. 20).

Interestingly, it was a Middle Kingdom priest of the god Ptah, named Senusretankh, who seems to have been the first person outside the Heliopolitan tradition to study the Pyramid Texts. He sought the earliest and best versions of the texts and had them inscribed on the walls of his own tomb. The kings of the Twelfth Dynasty were apparently much more interested in propaganda literature. At first their purpose was to justify their claim to the throne. Later, discontented with being portrayed merely as the greatest god's companion in the afterlife, they had themselves equated with the greatest god.

The decline at the end of the Middle Kingdom was marked by the Thebans' loss of control over Lower Egypt, even though they were ruling from near Memphis. Foreigners called the Hyksos invaded the Delta from the northeast and ruled over the north from the city of Avaris. In later texts they were accused of many acts against the Egyptian gods, which they may not in fact have committed, but theoretically, because they were regarded as followers of Seth, the slayer of Osiris, they had to be expelled.

Another Theban family rose to the task and with the help of Amun-Re succeeded in expelling the Hyksos and reuniting the Two Lands. The early Eighteenth Dynasty, devoted to Amun-Re, had clear connections with a moon god as well. Though he may have been the same Hermopolitan Thoth who appears in the names of the Thutmoside kings, this moon god was described and worshiped at Thebes as Khonsu, the son of Amun-Re and of Mut, "the Mother" (fig. 11).

The Theban version of the creation story is probably best preserved in the Khonsu Cosmogony, which survives in a Ptolemaic text that attempts through elaborate punning and fanciful new descriptions to explain the connection of Thebes with the Hermopolitan Ogdoad and with Ptah, the Memphite creator (fig. 54):[25]

> Words spoken by Amun-Re, King of the Gods, august being, chief of all the gods, the Great God, lord of the sky, earth, the other world, water, and mountains, the august soul of the Kem-atef serpent, father of the semen, mother of the egg, who engendered everything living, the hidden soul who made the gods, who formed the land with his semen, father of the fathers of the Ogdoad in the tomb chamber in the necropolis in the place Djeme, who created this place in Nun, overflowing seed the first time. The first snake made heaven because of his desire. . . . Earth came into existence, the sky spat forth an egg, like the egg of a falcon. It was as the face . . . earth. That is how the second snake came into being with the face of a beetle likewise, while the cow before this predecessor went forth. . . .
>
> Amun in that name of his called Ptah created the egg that came forth from Nun . . . as Ptah of the Ḥeḥ gods and the Nenu goddesses who created heaven and earth. He ejaculated and made [it] at this place in the lake, which was created in Tjenene,[26] it flowed out under him, like that which happens, in its name of "grain of seed." He fertilized the egg and the eight came into existence from it in the district around the Ogdoad. He languished there in Nun, in the Great Flood. He knew them; his neck received them. He traveled (ḫns) to Thebes in his form of Khonsu. He cleared his throat from the water in the flood. Thus came into existence his name of Khonsu the Great in Thebes, the august being in the seed. He turned his face to this seed. It was his Maʿat, that great one who raised herself as a power from the ground, a necklace on his breast fashioned to the likeness thereof, brought from the . . . high land in Nun. Thus came into existence

25. See Richard A. Parker and Leonard H. Lesko, "The Khonsu Cosmogony," in *Pyramid Studies and Other Essays Presented to I. E. S. Edwards*, ed. John Baines et al., Occasional Publications 7 (London: Egypt Exploration Society, 1988), pp. 168–75 and pls. 34–37.
26. A Memphite sanctuary of Ptah.

Thebes in her name of Valley. Thus came into existence Hathor the Great, in
the midst of the "grain of seed" in that name of hers of Nunet. Then he put
his body upon her, and he opened (*pth*) her as Ptah, the father of the gods.
Thus came into existence the Ogdoad . . . consisting of its four males, and a
wife for each one. It is this that Thebes made, together with the four drops
that were in her. They are the men and ladies of Tanen.[27] The land of Thebes
rejoiced at Tanen, inasmuch as Tanen had created the Ogdoad in Thebes.
They were water-borne to the Island of Flames, and thus came into existence his form, the first primeval one of the Great Flood.

Here Amun-Re is described as father of the fathers of the Ogdoad,
which should be contradictory, but since both *Khonsu* and *Ptah* are considered emanations of Amun, this god can travel (*ḫns*) to Hermopolis to
produce the egg to bring forth the Ogdoad and also open (*pth*) Hathor to
produce the Ogdoad. The Khonsu Cosmogony actually portrays the
Ogdoad's connection with Thebes as twofold, since Amun-Re came
from Thebes to produce the Ogdoad at Hermopolis, and the Ogdoad at
some point is supposed to have returned south to be buried at Djeme, in
the Theban necropolis.

It was the warlike Amun-Re who sanctioned the Thutmoside kings'
military expeditions into Asia, and as a result this god's temple (Karnak)
and priests became prosperous and powerful. A unique episode, however, interrupted that process when Egypt was near the zenith of its
power. No one fully understands the episode, but all regard it as one of
the major events in history.

In the fourteenth century B.C.E., after nearly two centuries of rule by
the Eighteenth Dynasty, a pharaoh changed his name, devoted himself
almost exclusively to a comparatively new god, transferred his residence
to an entirely new site in Middle Egypt (fig. 47), neglected his allies in
Asia, and apparently began to spend more time with his wife and
daughters than with traditional administrative and ritual functions. It
may never be known whether Akhenaten (fig. 46) acted as he did out of
religious commitment or out of mental derangement; in response to
urging by his wife, Nefertiti (fig. 48), or by the priests of Heliopolis; or
solely out of contempt for the powerful priesthood of Amun-Re. It is
known that his exclusive devotion (monolatry) toward a single, generally nonanthropomorphic aspect of the solar cult, the sun disk itself,
approached very near monotheism.

27. Generally called Tatenen, an earth god frequently associated with Ptah in the New
Kingdom and later.

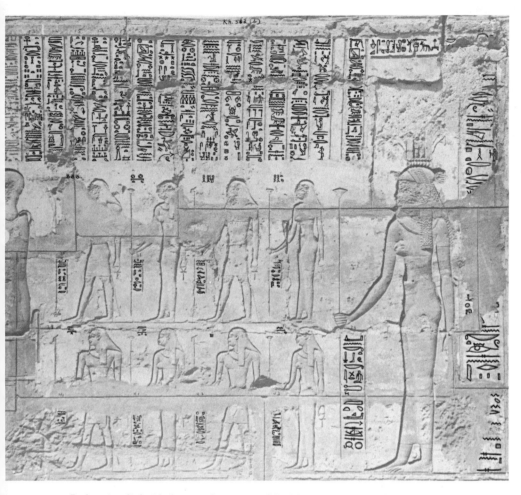

54. Ptolemaic relief with the text of a portion of the Khonsu Cosmogony and a depiction of the pairs of the Ogdoad standing in front of the goddess Hathor. Room 5 of the Khonsu Temple, Karnak. Enhanced photograph courtesy of Richard A. Parker and Leonard H. Lesko.

Akhenaten's hymn to Aten, the sun disk, attained literary and contemplative heights seldom reached in other Egyptian texts:

How plentiful it is, what you have made,
  although they are hidden from sight.
O unique god, beside whom there is no other,

you created the earth for your own sake, while you were alone,
humankind, all large and small cattle,
everything on land, that goes on foot,
and those in the air, that fly with their wings.
The hill countries of Khor and Kush and the land of Egypt,
you set every person in his place, you provided for their needs,
each one having his food, and his lifetime is counted out.
Tongues are distinct in speech, and their characters likewise.
Their skin colors are different, for you differentiated the foreign peoples.
In the Duat (underworld) you made a Nile
that you may bring it forth as you wish to nourish the commoners,
according as you made them for yourself, their total master,
who became weary for them, lord of every land,
who shines for them, the Aten of daytime, great in majesty.
All distant foreign lands, you made them live, for you placed a Nile in the
sky
that it might descend for them and make waves upon the mountains
like the sea to irrigate their fields in their towns.
How efficient are your plans, Lord of Eternity, a Nile in the sky for
foreigners
and for the small cattle of every foreign land that go on foot,
a Nile that comes back from the underworld for Egypt.[28]

This Hymn to the Aten, which perhaps influenced the later biblical
literature of Israel (for example, Psalm 104), had antecedents in earlier
Eighteenth Dynasty hymns to Amun-Re. Even the important phrase
"unique god, beside whom there is no other" (italicized in the translation above) has an earlier parallel in Amun-Re's description as the "soli-
tary unique one, without his peer."

Late in Akhenaten's reign his agents began to erase the name and title
"Amun-Re, King of the Gods." It is the eradication of the Egyptian word
for "gods," *ntrw*, that is largely responsible for scholars' suggestion that
this period witnessed a "monotheistic revolution." However, archaeological evidence from the capital city of Akhetaten, modern Tell
el-'Amarna, shows that even here many people continued their devo-
tions to other gods, and it seems that Amun-Re of Thebes was the chief
object of the attacks. The new developments of the Amarna interlude

28. For the text of The Hymn to the Aten, see Norman de Garis Davies, *The Rock Tombs of
El Amarna*, vol. 6, Archaeological Survey of Egypt 18 (London: Egypt Exploration Fund,
1908), pl. 27. The text is translated by William Kelly Simpson, *LAE* 289–95; Lichtheim, *AEL*
2:96–100; and Wilson, *ANET* 369–71.

were short-lived, moreover, and Akhenaten's two immediate successors, Semenkhkare and Tutankhamun (fig. 45), attempted reconcilia-
tion with the priesthood of Amun, though without renouncing the
Aten. The real historical significance of these theological events is seen
in the later devastating reaction against this "heresy" and against all
who had participated in it. The monuments of the Amarna Period were
destroyed, and whenever the names of the Amarna pharaohs were
found, they were obliterated.

The succeeding Ramesside Period (Nineteenth and Twentieth dynasties), about 1300–1100 B.C.E., is apparently filled with contradictions,
and because of the wealth of materials available from various sources it
is one of the periods most deserving of synchronic analysis. The royal
names of kings of this period indicate that they either were "born of Re"
(Ramesses or Ramses) or were "Sethian" (Sety, Sethnakht), that is, associated with Seth, the traditional enemy of Osiris and Horus (fig. 24). The
kings erected many monuments to Amun-Re at Thebes and made lavish
burial preparations for themselves in the south, but they lived and ruled
near the site of the old capital in the northeast Delta used by the hated,
foreign Hyksos. They had divisions of their army named for Seth, but
the kings paid great homage to Osiris at Abydos, and their sons served
as priests of Ptah.

The Ramesside tombs at Thebes are replete with guidebooks for the
afterlife voyage with Re through the hours of night, past the portals and
their demon keepers.[29] The tombs of nobles from this period omit most
of the autobiographical texts and scenes of daily life which had been so
popular earlier in favor of scenes depicting temple cults, funerary rites,
and deities.

The rich literature from this period consists mainly of stories that are
largely mythic and frequently are related to the Osiris-Seth-Horus episodes. What is remarkable is that despite all the outward appearances of
a very conservative religious reaction (for example, a return to polytheism), most of these literary texts seem to make a mockery of all the
gods.[30] The myth of The Destruction of Mankind is essentially one of
these literary stories that happened to be copied on the walls of several

29. See Erik Hornung, *Ägyptische Unterweltsbücher*, 2d ed., Bibliothek der Alten Welt:
Der Alte Orient (Zurich and Munich: Artemis, 1984).
30. See Leonard H. Lesko, "Three Late Egyptian Stories Reconsidered," in *Egyptological
Studies in Honor of Richard A. Parker*, ed. Leonard H. Lesko (Hanover, N.H.: University
Press of New England, 1986), pp. 98–103.

Ramesside royal tombs.[31] It is interesting for its anthropomorphism as well as for its etiologies.

Re, the god who came into being by himself, when he was king of humans and gods together. Then humankind plotted something in the presence of Re. Now, His Majesty (life, prosperity, health) was old. His bones were of silver, his flesh of gold, and his hair of real lapis lazuli.

Then His Majesty perceived the things that were being plotted against him by humankind. Then His Majesty (l.p.h.) said to those who were in his following: "Summon for me my Eye, also Shu, Tefnut, Geb, and Nut, as well as the fathers and mothers who were with me when I was in Nun, as well as my god Nun also, who brings his entourage with him. You are to bring them secretly. Let humankind not see. Let their hearts not flee. . . ."

Then these gods were brought in. . . .

Then Re said to Nun: "O eldest god, from whom I came into being, O ancestor gods, humankind, which came into being from my Eye, has plotted things against me. Tell me what you would do about it. I am seeking. I cannot slaughter them until I hear what you say about it."

Then the majesty of Nun said: "My son, Re, the god greater than he who made him and mightier than they who created him, sitting on your throne, the fear of you is great when your Eye is against those who scheme against you. . . ." . . .

Then they said . . . "Cause your Eye to go that it may catch for you those who scheme evilly. The Eye is not foremost in it in order to smite them for you. Let it go down as Hathor."

Then this goddess came and slaughtered humankind in the desert. Then the majesty of this god said: "Welcome in peace, Hathor, who did for me the deed for which I came."

Then this goddess said: "As you live for me, I have prevailed over humankind, and it is pleasant in my heart."

Then the majesty of Re said: "I shall prevail over them as a king in diminishing them." That is how Sekhmet came into being, the [beer] mash of the night, to wade in their blood beginning from Herakleopolis. . . .

Then the majesty of this god said: "Go to Elephantine and bring me hematite abundantly." . . . Moreover, maidservants crushed barley to make beer, then this hematite was added to this mash. It was like the blood of humankind. Then seven thousand jars of the beer were made and the majesty of the King of Upper and Lower Egypt, Re, came together with these gods to see this beer. . . .

Then the majesty of Re said: "How good it is! I shall protect humankind

31. For the text of The Destruction of Mankind, see Charles Maystre, "Le livre de la vache du ciel dans les tombeaux de la Vallée des Rois," *BIFAO* 40 (1941): 58–75; trans. Wilson, *ANET* 10–11; and Lichtheim, *AEL* 2:197–99. See also the text, translation into German, and commentary by Erik Hornung et al., *Der ägyptische Mythos von der Him-melskuh: Eine Ätiologie des Unvollkommenen,* OBO 46 (1982).

with it." . . . "Please carry it to the place in which she expected to slay humankind." Then the majesty of the King of Upper and Lower Egypt, Re, went to work in the end of the night to have this sleepmaker poured out. Then the fields were filled with liquid for three palms [depth]. . . .

When this goddess went at dawn she found this place full of water. Her face was beautiful therein. She drank, and it was good in her heart; and she returned drunk, without having perceived humankind.

This mythic story, unlike the typical mortuary literature, has a traditional palace setting. It may have been an attempt to rationalize plague as a divine punishment that had miscarried, in part because of the human foibles attributed to the gods. The text also provides an explanation for the origin of beer and for the drinking of beer, perhaps to excess, at the Festival of Hathor.

Ramesses (or Ramses) II had four statues carved at the back of the shrine of his famous rock-cut temple at Abu Simbel. The gods so commemorated were Ptah, Pre-Harakhti,[32] Amun-Re, and Ramesses II himself (fig. 55). After recognizing the three previous national gods of Egypt, Ramesses had himself placed on their level.[33] Perhaps there is some consistency in his megalomania, his erection of monuments as much to himself as to any other gods, and also in the literary texts of the period which make the other gods look foolish, thereby enhancing Ramesses' own status as god-king (fig. 39).[34]

After the long, sixty-seven-year reign of Ramesses II, his son, Merneptah, had to deal with Libyans and Sea Peoples as well as "the people of Israel," who may have undertaken their "exodus" from Egypt slightly earlier.

Ramesses (or Ramses) III, of the Twentieth Dynasty, the last great pharaoh of the New Kingdom, was apparently slain in an attempted coup that originated in his harem. His assassination and the eventual takeover of the throne by the priests of Amun-Re (Twenty-first Dynasty) brought the myth of divine kingship and the history of pharaonic Egypt to a low ebb. Afterward, in the Third Intermediate Period, foreign rulers and rulers supported by foreigners tried to resurrect the myths, mainly for their personal advantage. One foreign ruler of the Twenty-fifth Dy-

32. The Late Egyptian form of Re-Horakhty with a definite article, "The Re, Horus of the Horizon," with reference to the Heliopolitan sun god.

33. Herman te Velde, "Some Remarks on the Structure of Egyptian Divine Triads," *JEA* 57 (1971): 81, goes a step further in his interpretation of this group by stating that "the pharaoh seems to represent the unity of this triad."

34. See Lesko, in *Egyptological Studies*, ed. Lesko, pp. 98–103.

55. Four gods—(left to right) Ptah, Amun-Re, King Ramesses II (Nineteenth Dynasty), and Pre-Harakhti—seated along the rear wall of the sanctuary. The Great Temple, Abu Simbel. Photo © 1991 by Byron E. Shafer.

nasty, a Nubian named Piye (formerly read Piankhy), was quite extraordinary both in his deep personal devotion to Amun and in his vigorous attempts to reestablish the old order in Egypt, the formerly great country to his north which was rapidly declining before his eyes.[35]

Throughout the Late Period, the religion of the common people continued to center on Osiris and Re, though they also venerated local and household gods. The cultic worship of animals became very popular as well. In earlier periods the animal representations of the gods had apparently symbolized attributes of power and had enabled a largely illit-

35. See James H. Breasted, *Ancient Records of Egypt*, vol. 4, *The Twentieth to the Twenty-sixth Dynasties* (Chicago: University of Chicago Press, 1906), secs. 816–83, for a translation of the Piankhy Stela. He discusses the text in secs. 796–815. See also Sir Alan Gardiner, *Egypt of the Pharaohs: An Introduction* (Oxford: Clarendon, 1961), pp. 335–40.

erate population to identify the cast of gods in the ritual scenes depicted on art objects and the walls of temples and tombs.

The papyrus copies of the Book of the Dead, which were also popular in this period, provided spells for overcoming obstacles in the afterlife, and the book permitted anyone who could afford to have a personalized copy to be found innocent in a judgment before Osiris and to join Re in the sky. Interestingly, the most important vignettes of the so-called Theban recension of the Book of the Dead generally illustrated Osiris, whereas the text (including passages that accompanied these vignettes) clearly reflected the book's old association with the Re religion of Heliopolis. Some uncertainty, confusion, and/or dissension concerning the book's mythology is evident in glosses attached to chapter 17:

I am Atum when I was alone in Nun. I am Re in his appearances in glory,
     when he began to rule that which he had made.
    Who is he?
    "Re when he began to rule that which he had made" means: when
     Re began to appear in the kingship which he exercised as one
     who existed before the liftings of Shu had occurred, while he
     was on the hill which is in Hermopolis. . . .
I am the great god who came into being by himself.
    Who is he?
    "The great god who came into being by himself" is water; he is Nun,
     the father of the gods.
    Another version: He is Re.
He who created his names, the Lord of the Ennead.
    Who is he?
    He is Re, who created the names of the parts of his body. That is how
     these gods who are in his following came into being.
He among the gods who cannot be repulsed.
    Who is he?
    He is Atum, who is in his sun disk.
    Another version: He is Re, when he arises on the eastern horizon of
     the sky.
Mine is yesterday, I know tomorrow.
    Who is he?
    As for "yesterday," it is Osiris. As for "tomorrow," it is Re on that
     day when the enemies of the All-lord are destroyed and his son
     Horus is made to rule. . . .[36]

36. See Edouard Naville, *Das aegyptische Todtenbuch der XVIII. bis XX. Dynastie*, 3 vols. (Berlin: Asher, 1886). The text and glosses of chap. 17 are found in 1:23–30 and 2:29–74. For translations, see Thomas George Allen, *The Book of the Dead, or Going Forth by Day.* Studies in Ancient Oriental Civilization 37 (Chicago: University of Chicago Press, 1974), pp. 26–32, and Wilson, *ANET* 3–4.

Some very important eschatological questions are answered in chapter 175 of the Book of the Dead, and this could well be a religious
response to the live-for-today attitude expressed in such literary texts as
the Song of the Harper. A portion of chapter 175 reads:

Words spoken by Osiris (Name of deceased):
    "O Atum, what does it mean? I am departing to the desert, the silent
land."
    "It has no water, it has no air, deep, deep, dark, dark, boundless,
boundless, in which you live in the peace of heart of the silent land. Sexual
pleasures are not enjoyed in it; but a blessed state is given to you in
exchange for water, air, and sexual pleasure, and peace of heart in exchange for bread and beer." So said Atum.
    "In the sight of your face? I will not suffer being deprived of you. Every
god has assumed his place in the forefront of the barque, Millions of
Years."
    "Your place belongs to your son, Horus." . . .
    "O Atum, what is my span of life?"
    "You will exist for millions of millions of years, a lifetime of millions. I
have caused that he send the great ones. Further I shall destroy all that I
have made, and this land will come back into Nun, into the floodwaters, as
in its beginning. I am a survivor, together with Osiris. I have made my
form in another state, serpents, which people will not know and gods will
not see. How good is what I have done for Osiris, more distinguished than
all other gods. I have given him the desert, the silent land, with his son
Horus as heir upon his throne which is in the Island of Flame. Further, I
have made his place in the barque of Millions of Years. Horus remains on
his palace facade, for the purpose of founding his monuments. The soul of
Seth has been more distinguished than all other gods, because I have
caused the restraint of his soul, which is in the barque, because he wishes
to fear the divine body."
    "O my father, Osiris, may you do for me what your father, Re, did for
you. I remain on earth, so that I may establish my place." "My heir is
healthy, my tomb is strong. They are my supporters on earth. My enemies
have been given into woes, for Selket is piercing them. I am your son, my
father, Re. You do these things for me for the sake of life, prosperity, and
health, while Horus remains on his palace facade. May you cause that this
my time of passing to the revered state come."[37]

For a person concerned about the negative aspects of death, this text
promises a blessed state, peace of mind, a "beatific vision," a lifetime of
millions of years, a place of repose in the desert, a son as successor,
punishment of one's enemies, and the eventual destruction of the created world.

37. For the text of chap. 175, see Naville, *Das aegyptische Todtenbuch,* 1:198–99; trans.
Allen, *Book of the Dead,* pp. 183–85, and Wilson, *ANET* 9–10.

During the reign of the Ptolemies (305–30 B.C.E.) truly great temples were constructed at some ancient cult sites, and countless smaller temples, temple additions, gates, and inscriptions were erected or added at other places. All of the main structures at the temple of Horus at Edfu are Ptolemaic (fig. 16). The vast main temple and its surrounding wall are covered from top to bottom with scenes and texts dealing with Horus, his myths and rituals. Separate huge temples for the great goddesses Hathor, at Dendereh, and Isis, at Philae (fig. 56), are evidence not only of their usefulness in furthering the myth of divine kingship but also of their growing importance in the minds and hearts of the people, quite apart from their connection to the old Ennead. Small birth houses, *mammisi*, commemorate the birth of Horus many times at each of these sites.

A papyrus text from the early Ptolemaic period, probably from Thebes, illustrates both the continuity of the long-lived Re religion and the religion's successful assimilation of the earlier Heliopolitan and Hermopolitan cosmologies.

> The All-Lord said, after he had come into being:
> I am he who came into being (*ḫpr*) as Khepri. When I had come into being, being came into being, and all beings came into being, after I came into being. Numerous were the beings coming forth from my mouth, before heaven came into being, before earth came into being, before the ground and snakes had been created in this place. . . .
> I planned in my own heart, and a multitude of forms of beings came into being in the forms of children and in the forms of their children. I was the one who copulated with my fist. I masturbated with my hand. I spewed from my own mouth. I spat out Shu, and I sputtered out Tefnut. It was my father, Nun, who brought them up, with my Eye following after them since eternity, when they were far from me.
> After I had come into being as the sole god, there were three gods beside me. When I came into being in this land, Shu and Tefnut rejoiced in Nun, where they were. They brought me my Eye with them. After I had joined together my members, I wept over them. That is how humankind came into being from the tears which came forth from my Eye. . . .
> I created all serpents and whatever came to be from them. Then Shu and Tefnut bore Geb and Nut. Then Geb and Nut bore bodily Osiris, Horus Khenti-en-irti,[38] Seth, Isis, and Nephthys, a female one after a male one of them, and they brought forth their multitudes on this land.[39]

38. "He who is in front of the two eyes (sun and moon)."
39. For the text in transcription, see R. O. Faulkner, *The Papyrus Bremner-Rhind*, BiAe 3 (1933), pp. 59–69; trans. Wilson, *ANET* 6–7.

56. Ptolemaic sunk relief figure of Isis. The Temple of Isis, Philae. Photo © 1991 by Leonard H. Lesko.

COSMOLOGY

The ancient Egyptians were reasonably interested both in the world around them and in what was beyond their boundaries and their reach. Their own world was neatly delineated and organized by the Nile River, which provided irrigation, transportation, communication, drinking water, water for washing, a disposal system, and plentiful fish, fowl, and game. The Egyptians' geographical orientation was toward the south—the source of the Nile. Accordingly, Upper Egypt was in the south and Lower Egypt in the north, while one word meant both "west" and "right" and another both "east" and "left." The Two Lands were Upper and Lower Egypt, symbolized respectively by the sedge plant and either the papyrus or the bee. Another designation for the entire country was Two Banks, referring to both sides of the river, but probably the most important distinction was between the Black Land and the Red Land, the cultivable land and the desert.

The Egyptians used the word *ta* (⟐) for "land," but distinguished between the plural *tau*, "plains," and *khasut* (⟐), "hill country," the latter generally referring to foreign lands. For the Mediterranean Sea they regularly used *wadj-wer*, "the great green," but they could use *shen-wer*, "the great encircler," which seems to have been a prototype for the Greek *okeanos*. Their universe was "all that the sun encircles," but if this phrase implies that the sun was thought to have gone around the world on a single circular course, then apparently the phrase reflected a cosmology different from that in the religious texts discussed here.

Obviously the ancient Egyptians viewed and described the world around them in a variety of ways. The personifications and metaphors of the myths and stories were imaginative, poetic, very complex, and often humorous, but they certainly did not represent the sum total of the Egyptians' cosmological or scientific thinking on the subject. In religious texts, for example, the earth could be described and depicted as the god Geb lying flat on his back, while the sky goddess, Nut, arched her body over his. The Egyptian hieroglyphs for "earth" and "sky," by contrast, had nothing to do with these personifications. The earth was depicted as a flat stretch of land, rather long but not too deep, consisting partially at least of stone and sand: ⟐. The sky was drawn as a thin canopy with supports on its ends: ⟐. Note also that an Egyptian word for "firmament," *bia*, is clearly related to the words for "marvels" or "wonders," *biau*, and "iron," *biat*. Apparently the Egyptians made a connection between the marvelous meteoric iron that they used for ritual purposes and the material of which the sky's canopy was thought to be made. This idea would be consistent with the reflection of the sun's glory as it passed from east to west beneath the polished metal canopy, and perhaps also with its passage from west to east *above* this canopy. In the latter case, the sun's glory would be glimpsed through the stars, the holes left in the canopy when meteorites fell. Clearly the earth was not thought to revolve around the sun, but neither was the sun thought to revolve around the earth.

The rather objective description of the cosmos reflected in Egyptian lexicography was in some ways consistent with the mythological descriptions of the heavenly cow and of the sky goddess Nut. The great Cow of Heaven, who might also be identified with the goddess Hathor, stood supported by gods who held each of her legs. She gave birth to the sun as Ihy every day, and the sun disk traversed her belly to be swallowed by the goddess at night. In another mythological tradition, Nut gave birth to the sun god Re, who passed below her arched body during the daylight hours, was swallowed by her at sunset, and passed through her body at night.

The artwork illustrating these myths shows the stars as gods sailing on crescent-shaped barques along the bellies of the goddesses rather than as openings in their bodies. This representation gives greater prominence to the stars, for they travel independently, like the sun. On the one hand, this idea may reflect the greater influence of an astral cult, which could not be omitted in a cosmological scheme. In the Old Kingdom Pyramid Texts, the king himself is said to become a star, ideally in the northern sky, among the "imperishable stars" that never disappear from view.[40] On the other hand, the notion of the stars' independent movements may also reflect the improved astronomical observation and knowledge that led to considerable advances in timekeeping and calendar making.

The Egyptian sun, which modern scholars describe as a disk, was actually conceived of as a sphere, as seems clear from ancient relief carvings. For the mythmakers the "disk" might require wings or a beetle for propulsion and could either be a barque or contain a barque. This vessel carried Re, who was depicted in anthropomorphic form inside his shrine, and a number of attendant protective deities—the group called "entourage of flame" in the Coffin Texts.[41] Early religious literature described the journey of the sun barque as it sailed across the sky to the

---

40. For example, Pyramid Text 302: "The sky is clear, Sothis lives, because the king is a living one, the son of Sothis, and the Two Enneads have cleansed themselves for the king in Ursa Major, the imperishable." For the text of utterance 302, see Sethe, *Die altägyptischen Pyramidentexte*, secs. 458–63, 1:235–39; Faulkner, *Ancient Egyptian Pyramid Texts*, pp. 91–92.

41. Coffin Text 1032, found in de Buck, *Egyptian Coffin Texts*, 7:262. Differing translations of the phrase have been made by Lesko, *Ancient Egyptian Book of Two Ways*, p. 15, and Faulkner, *Ancient Egyptian Coffin Texts*, 3:129. The evidence of Coffin Text 1128 seems to confirm "entourage" or "company" over a "circle" to be passed.

horizon and *descended* to the purifying Field of Reeds in the eastern sky to be born anew.[42] There is little doubt that the sky in the description was Nut, and the place names, such as the Winding Waterway, Nurse Canal, Field of Reeds, and Doors Thrown Open, may even have related to her female anatomy. Nut also frequently personified the coffin, the womb containing the one to be reborn, and this personification was extended to the tombs' burial chambers.

The ancient Egyptian Book of the Ways of Rosetau, known today as the Book of Two Ways, is preserved on the interiors of Middle Kingdom coffins from el-Bersheh. It provides the earliest real map of the heavens, designed specifically for the purpose of guiding the "equipped spirit" (*akh-aper*) of the deceased on its journey in the afterlife (fig. 52). For the benefit of those followers of a lunar cult who desired to become stars in the night sky, the map included the location of Thoth's mansion in the place of *ma'at* (truth). The map also located the mansion of Osiris and the Field of Ḥetep ("peace" or "offerings") (fig. 57), where the deceased might continue to serve Osiris, the god of "those who are there." The largest part of the plan indicated the path followed by the sun god, with his attendants and followers, on his voyage first from east to west along a blue waterway through the inner sky and then back again from west to east on a black-land way through the outer sky. The paths described in this book and in later guidebooks from New Kingdom royal tombs (Amduat, Book of Gates, Book of Caves) were beset by demons whose names and features had to be known if one was to pass the obstacles/gateways they guarded. One who did not pass them successfully could not continue forever on this cyclical journey. The major obstacle to be encountered was the demon Apophis, the giant serpent who threatened to devour the sun, a personification clearly reflecting the Egyptian's familiarity with solar eclipses.

The Egyptian place names Rosetau, Imḥet, and Duat are all regularly translated as Underworld or Netherworld, but such consistent translations are often inaccurate and misleading since all these places were located in the sky above, at least originally. Rosetau is particularly interesting because the term, translated literally, means "passage of dragging," a reference to the sloping entranceway of a tomb. At a rather early date the term was extended to the entire necropolis, originally of Memphis and later of Abydos. Subsequently, the word was regularly

42. See Pyramid Texts 264 and 510 above, pp. 98–99.

57. Painted scene depicting the Field of Ḥetep, in the tomb of Sennedjem (Nineteenth Dynasty). Deir el-Medina, western Thebes. Photo © 1991 by Leonard H. Lesko.

used as a general term for the beyond or afterworld, including the heavens. Duat and Imḥet were separate locations in the sky. Duat, probably related to the words for "morning" and "morning worship," referred to the eastern horizon of the sky, and Imḥet referred to the west, essentially the heaven that Imentet ("the west") later became. The two fields—the Field of Reeds and the Field of Ḥetep—are likewise associated respectively with the eastern and western horizons, the former as a place of purification and the latter as the nearest thing to an Egyptian Elysian Fields or paradise (fig. 57). Coffin Text spells 464–68 and chapter 110 of the Book of the Dead describe this well-watered place with abundant grain and all kinds of fruit trees as a place where the dead could indulge any desire, doing what they had enjoyed on earth.[43]

Early sources indicate that the Egyptians had the concepts of an undersky (Nenet) and of an underworld where they would have to contend with such unpleasantnesses as living upside down and eating ex-

43. See Leonard H. Lesko, "The Field of Ḥetep in Egyptian Coffin Texts," *JARCE* 9 (1971–72): 89–101.

crement. Interestingly, the spells provided to protect against such indignities were directed to solving specific problems rather than to avoid the place altogether, so the place should probably not be seen as a direct antecedent for the notion of hell.

Conceptualizing both an ascent to the sky to join the gods and how to accomplish it required the Egyptians to engage in considerable speculation. Such an ascension, of course, presumed that the judges in Osiris's tribunal would find one innocent of the most obvious sins, those listed in chapter 125 of the Book of the Dead (fig. 32). To ascend, one probably also needed both faith and good works. One needed at least to have paid attention to ritual matters, as the Instruction for Merikare makes clear. As for means of ascent, numerous possibilities, presumably alternatives, are described: one might be borne aloft on the back of a falcon, goose, or other bird; be wafted upward with burning incense; carried by the clouds; one might climb on ladders formed by the outstretched arms of gods or travel on a reed float or barque that was sailed, rowed, or towed.

Two other mythological descriptions of the sky relate to bird imagery and were probàbly put forth before the promulgation of the nationally accepted cosmogonies or in spite of them, perhaps to enhance local cults. In one, the whole sky is represented by the falcon, Horus, with wings outstretched. His one good eye is the bright sun, and his other eye, injured in the conflict with his uncle Seth, is the pale moon. Certainly this "Great Horus," grander than either Re or Thoth, would not have been a concept of Heliopolitan or Hermopolitan origin. The other mythological description represents the sky as a vulture. Perhaps this image goes back to the iconography of Nekhbet, the Predynastic goddess of Upper Egypt (fig. 23), or perhaps it is linked with Theban Mut (written with the vulture hieroglyph) "the Mother," consort of Amun-Re (fig. 11). Such apparently incompatible cosmological concepts can represent either originally separate traditions or later attempts at rationalization.

One final Egyptian cosmological concept deserves mention here. In Ptolemaic hieroglyphs, the name of the god Ptah is written $\overline{\underline{\text{T}}}$. This writing, based on acrophonics, is composed of the *p* of *pt* ("heaven"), the *t* of *ta* ("earth"), and the *ḥ* of *ḥeḥ* ("support of heaven"). The image is not unlike the artistic representation in which the sky goddess Nut is separated from the earth god Geb by the air god Shu (fig. 13). In this Ptolemaic writing of his name, Ptah, the "fashioner" god, incorporates both the male aspect of Geb and the female aspect of Nut, and the writing carries further the concept of Ptah's androgyny found earlier in the Memphite Theology, which identified Ptah-Nun and Ptah-Naunet. Thus this Ptah provides a further symbolic link between the Ennead (*p*, heaven and Nut; *t*, earth and Geb) and the Ogdoad (*ḥ*, *ḥeḥ* and Nun/Naunet).

EPILOGUE

Because it is impossible to know when each of the cosmogonical myths and cosmological concepts originated and how long each of them was prevalent, there is a definite tendency to ignore the problem and to present the phenomena as if all were applicable during the entire span of Egyptian history. To maximize benefits, future studies should avoid the pitfalls of a phenomenological approach as much as possible. Where sufficient quantities of data have survived, a synchronic approach focusing on all the relevant material from a single time period and perhaps from even a single location would enable a more accurate reconstruction of the world view held by at least some ancient Egyptians. Sufficient quantities of resources to pursue synchronic studies seem to exist for the First Intermediate Period, the Eighteenth Dynasty, the Nineteenth Dynasty, and the Ptolemaic Period, and if one were to pursue the data, one would unquestionably find significant differences between the phenomena of any two of those periods.

I have tried to treat at least the cosmogonical material in approximate chronological order, and, through a diachronic approach, to indicate the beliefs that seem to have been fairly consistent, along with the various additions or modifications effected by changing historical circumstances. The Memphite Theology and the Khonsu Cosmogony were treated as late copies of old texts, but how old? On the basis of language and content, both seem to date back to at least the early Eighteenth Dynasty.

The cosmological notions that have been presented were just that—notions. Taken together they do not constitute a definitive cosmology or a carefully reasoned or argued system. They are suggestions or speculations, sometimes clever, often contradictory, always whetting our appetites for more.

3 SOCIETY, MORALITY, AND RELIGIOUS PRACTICE

John Baines

INTRODUCTION: RELIGION, ORDER, AND MISFORTUNE

Egyptian religion consisted of a vast range of beliefs and practices and is difficult to comprehend as a whole. It must be subdivided greatly for study, while on a theoretical level it may be best not to think of religion as a unity. The Egyptians lived with and participated in this diversity. It would hardly have occurred to them to question the basis of religious beliefs and practices or to ask whether all of them belonged together. They had no single term for "religion" that would have facilitated any discussion of such issues. "Religious" beliefs were essential and largely unquestioned presuppositions underlying the conduct of life. These beliefs related additionally to the character and the organiza-

This chapter is closely related to my article "Practical Religion and Piety," *JEA* 73 (1987): 79–98. Here I concentrate on problems of society and morality which are assumed or only alluded to there; but some duplication and self-citation is inevitable. I have taken advantage of the space available to give fuller examples. The topics are vast and can only be sketched; omission does not imply unimportance or irrelevance.

The three principal chapters in this book sometimes approach similar questions from different angles, occasionally drawing on the same textual evidence. This diversity of views is valuable and has not been harmonized artificially.

I am very grateful to J. C. A. Baines, Richard Parkinson, and David Silverman for commenting on drafts and suggesting references, and to Anthony Leahy, Andrea McDowell, Jaromir Malek, and Harco Willems for help with bibliography. The final version was prepared during a Humboldt-Stiftung fellowship at the University of Münster.

tion of society. Society interacted with religious beliefs, but these beliefs cannot be interpreted in exclusively social terms. The connection between the two was, however, closer in Egypt than it usually is in lands where world religions hold sway, because Egyptian religion belonged to a single society.

There are various possible approaches to the study of religious practice. One is to examine beliefs about creation and about the nature of the gods, and to move from there to relations between the gods and humanity. Another is to start from society, and to see religious practice from that perspective. The previous chapters used the first approach; I attempt the second. The basic difficulty in the study of social life lies in the nature of the ancient evidence. Most of what is known about ancient Egypt relates to the small elite; there is little direct evidence for the lives and attitudes of the rest of the people. The beliefs of the elite existed in relation to the wider society, even though they often ignored that society. Where the elite did present the wider society, it would be unwise to take their picture at face value.

Connections between central beliefs, society, and the wider natural world are not straightforward,[1] but there was a continuity between the elite's presentations of the created order of the cosmos and its social hierarchies and the role humanity played in that cosmos. In the cosmogony, the world, including the gods, the king, and humanity, was created at a definite but remote past time, and would ultimately come to an end. In the present, the king took on for humanity the task of dealing both with the gods and with the negative forces that surrounded the ordered world. Disorder lurked at the edges of Egypt—in the desert and in the underworld—and the ordered cosmos was shot through with "uncreated" elements that threatened to engulf it and had to be countered. Whereas order was determinate, disorder was indeterminate and could never be vanquished completely. Constant vigilance was needed. In contrast with largely negative "uncreated" disorder, the god Seth embodied the positive aspects of the brute force and destructiveness that exist within creation.[2] The Egyptians came to reject Seth and persecute him as an enemy only in the first millennium B.C.E.

---

1. Compare the title of Henri Frankfort's classic work, *Kingship and the Gods: A Study of Ancient Near Eastern Religion as the Integration of Society and Nature* (Chicago: University of Chicago Press, 1948).

2. For positive aspects of disorder, see Erik Hornung, *Conceptions of God in Ancient Egypt: The One and the Many*, trans. John Baines (Ithaca: Cornell University Press, 1982; London: Routledge & Kegan Paul, 1983), pp. 178–84. On Seth, see also Hornung, "Seth: Geschichte und Bedeutung eines ägyptischen Gottes," *Symbolon* n.s. 2 (1974): 49–63.

Ordered creation had constantly to be affirmed against the forces of disorder.[3] Not only the king and humanity but also the gods were involved in this enterprise. All beings, except perhaps the creator, were mortal. Among the gods, Osiris, who once lived and ruled on earth, was distinctive for being dead and ruling in the underworld (fig. 26).

This problematic and ultimately pessimistic view of order and disorder[4] is the opposite of what a monument like the Great Pyramid may symbolize. The pyramid affirms overpowering human, or rather royal, achievement. As a medieval Arabic poem proclaims, it is "feared by time, yet everything else in our present world fears time." Documents of that period, which show that people had a conception of a perfect "antiquity," may confirm that it was built in the hope of instilling such fear, but in the awareness that the triumph over time which it promised could not ultimately be achieved.[5]

In evaluating this instability of the Egyptian cosmos, one should recall that many societies consider the present world to be short-lived. Many Christians have thought that the Second Coming of Christ and the end of the world could occur at any time. Contemporary society could be consumed in a nuclear holocaust. In comparison, the Egyptians had a very long perspective both on the beginning of time and on its end, but they conceived of order as being insecurely founded. One could see their view as a cosmic analogy for the fragility of any social order, or as tempering the apparently unchanging character of Egyptian order. Whichever of these perspectives may be nearer the truth, the Egyptians' local and cosmic visions were connected. The insecurity of the foundations of order did not need to be a constant concern in everyday life. Nonetheless, the problems of order in society and of how and why events affect the individual could gain urgency from their cosmic background. Yet that background could be a source of reassurance, because it showed that all, from the highest to the lowest, might be affected by the untoward, which could be seen as a manifestation of chaos or disorder. Everyone, including the gods, was in it together.

Thus the Egyptians' general conceptions of order were relevant to mundane events throughout society. On public monuments of the state

3. Compare Hornung, *Conceptions of God*, pp. 157–59, 172–84.
4. See Hellmut Brunner, "Gefährdungsbewusstsein," *LÄ* 2:479–83. For psychological extensions, see Jan Assmann, "Furcht," *LÄ* 2:359–67. See also n. 83 below. The Arabic poem is cited in al-Maqrīzī, *Khiṭaṭ* (Bulaq ed. of A.H. 1294 [1877]), 1:121.
5. See John Baines, "Ancient Egyptian Concepts and Uses of the Past: 3rd to 2nd Millennium B.C. Evidence," in *Who Needs the Past? Indigenous Values and Archaeology*, ed. Robert Layton (London: Unwin Hyman, 1989), esp. pp. 134–35.

and of the elite, these conceptions are embodied in a system of decorum which presents a restricted view of society within the context of celebrating the gods and the king. Temples and other major structures on which this system was displayed related chiefly to the official cults. In discussing religious practice, I am not primarily concerned with those cults, whose relevance for most people was rather limited. Instead, I focus on religious actions of any kind that responded to the problems of people's lives, particularly problems that threatened ordinary existence or social relations, or that threatened continued life. If Egyptian beliefs and practices are to be comprehended, it is necessary to review a vast range of phenomena, to study how they relate to one another, and to view them without prejudice. Distinctions between religion and magic or superstition do not help understanding. It is difficult to define what counts as religion, and it may not be relevant to try to do so.[6]

It may seem one-sided to concentrate on misfortune in relation to religion, because Egyptian rituals focused on celebrating the gods and what the gods continually did for the world, and on the positive aspects of the cosmos. But most of these rituals formed part of the official temple cults, from which people were largely excluded. The king and his priestly deputies were the main beneficiaries of the sweetness and light they presented as pervading the cosmos. In practice, the elite as a whole received these benefits through their privileged position and, for many of them, through their participation in the cults. King and elite presented the cosmos in positive terms because rules and conventions required it to be so, and because the function of the divine cult was to honor the deity and induce in him or her the good disposition that would continue to confer benefits on the king and humanity.[7] Cult consisted of regular daily service for the deity, which was performed on a cult statue. In daily rites the deity was purified, fed, clothed, and praised. Periodic festivals took the deity out of the temple in procession, sometimes to visit other deities in other temples. These festivals were the occasions when the majority who were not involved in the cult came closest to the gods, but even then the cult image was shut inside a shrine and invisible. The

6. See John Baines, "Interpretations of Religion: Logic, Discourse, Rationality," *Göttinger Miszellen* 76 (1984): 25–54. The same looseness of definition is valuable for the study of morality; see next section.

7. Hornung, *Conceptions of God*, pp. 197–216. See also Siegfried Morenz, *Ägyptische Religion*, Die Religionen der Menschheit 8 (Stuttgart: Kohlhammer, 1960), pp. 60–116 (= *Egyptian Religion*, trans. Ann E. Keep [London: Methuen; Ithaca: Cornell University Press, 1973], pp. 57–109).

outward form of rituals thus appears to be more material than spiritual. The cost of maintaining these cults was borne by endowments, but estates of the gods did not become economically significant until the New Kingdom.[8]

Since in theory the gods provided for all of humanity, and humanity responded with gratitude and praise, the cult could be seen as having universal implications. In practice, however, the gods' benefits were unequally divided. The privileged received the rewards of divine benefi- cence and returned gratitude, while the rest suffered misfortune in greater measure and had no official channel for interacting with deities. In this inequality Egypt was not and is not unique.

The condition of ordinary Egyptians was probably comparable with, or only a little worse than, that of most people in premodern societies. The small elite were the exceptions. The elite's presentation of their ideology on public monuments is so persuasive, however, that scholars often neglect or fail to comment on its omission of most of humanity and their conditions of life. Other Egyptians may not have found the elite's presentation so convincing, and they must surely have been aware that they were omitted. Here gaps in the evidence, of which very little shows participation by ordinary people in official religious practice, are almost as significant as the evidence itself.

The beneficence of the gods could not be taken for granted. They might not be so well disposed as they were said to be. They could be capricious, or vent their fury on humanity, as the creator had once done near the beginning of time.[9] If neglected, they might abandon human- ity—as they did in the time of Akhenaten (1353–1336 B.C.E.), according to his successor Tutankhamun (1332–1322 B.C.E.).[10] But gods and people were still ultimately thrown on one another for support.

The official division of the cosmos is presented in a brief text, probably of the Middle Kingdom, which describes the king's role in the cult of the

8. For the context, see Richard Holton Pierce, "Land Use, Social Organisation and Temple Economy," *Royal Anthropological Institute News*, no. 15 (August 1976), pp. 15–17.

9. This myth is narrated in a text known as The Destruction of Mankind: Erik Hornung et al., *Der ägyptische Mythos von der Himmelskuh: Eine Ätiologie des Unvollkommenen*, OBO 46 (1982); *AEL* 2:197–99. The myth is alluded to in the Instruction for Merikare, which probably dates to the Middle Kingdom: Aksel Volten, *Zwei altägyptische politische Schriften*, Analecta Aegyptiaca 4 (Copenhagen: Munksgaard, 1945); Wolfgang Helck, *Die Lehre für König Mer- ikare*, Kleine Ägyptische Texte (Wiesbaden: Harrassowitz, 1977), pp. 83–85; *AEL* 1:106, 109n. My citations of Merikare use Volten's line numbers.

10. Wolfgang Helck, *Urkunden der 18. Dynastie*, Urk. 4/22 (Berlin [East]: Akademie, 1958), p. 2027; English trans. John A. Wilson, *ANET* 251–52.

sun god. The text is worth quoting because of the place it assigns to moral concerns and to humanity. Kingship was both the central institution and the main focus of power in Egyptian society, and the text correspondingly incorporates generalized ideas of social order. Kingship also provided a metaphor for the way others were to conduct their lives, so some aspects of the king's morality were to be emulated by the elite. The text says that the king (in a sense the kingship) is on earth "for ever and ever, judging humanity and propitiating the gods, and setting order in place of disorder. He gives offerings to the gods and mortuary offerings to the spirits (the blessed dead)."[11] (Here "order" is the fundamental religious, social, and abstract concept of *ma'at*, and "disorder" is *izfet*, the opposite of *ma'at*, associated with the world outside creation.)

In this statement the role of the king is more critical for the maintenance of order than that of any single deity. He performs the cult of the gods, an assertion that refers primarily to his provision for them from the abundance of the land and its imports of exotic products. The king is said to "propitiate" the gods rather than to "worship" them; he "judges" humanity, setting them in order but also providing justly for them; and he makes mortuary offerings. The spirits to whom he offers could be either his own ancestors or the blessed dead in general. In the former case, the king may acknowledge the importance of lineage to his position, perhaps placating his ancestors as a normal mortal would. Ancestor cults were not widespread or long-lasting among the nonroyal in Egypt, but the recently dead were important to the living in various ways.[12] There is much evidence from the New Kingdom in particular for the significance of earlier kings in ideology and religion, but this does not constitute a formal royal "ancestor cult."[13] In the case of the spirits in general, the king may take on a burden of care that is vital for the

11. Jan Assmann, *Der König als Sonnenpriester: Ein kosmographischer Begleittext zur kultischen Sonnenhymnik*, ADAIK 7 (1970), pp. 17–22. The text contains a wealth of meaning and allusion, to which justice cannot be done here.

12. For limited evidence from Deir el-Medina, see Florence Friedman, "On the Meaning of Some Anthropoid Busts from Deir el-Medîna," *JEA* 71 (1985): 82–97. For a more cautious and comprehensive study of this material, see R. J. Demarée, *The 3ḫ ỉḳr n R'-Stelae: On Ancestor Worship in Ancient Egypt*, Egyptologische Uitgaven 3 (Leiden: Nederlands Institut voor het Nabije Oosten, 1983). These later practices may not be comparable with those attested from earlier times.

13. Relevant material is assembled by Donald B. Redford, *Pharaonic King-lists, Annals and Day-books: A Contribution to the Study of the Egyptian Sense of History*, Society for the Study of Egyptian Antiquities Publication 4 (Mississauga, Ont.: Benben, 1986), pp. 165–201.

cohesion of society and is common to, or aspired to, by all.[14] The cult of the gods, which is always presented as being performed by the king, was in fact carried out by relatively small numbers of priests. The rest of humanity had far better contact with the dead than with the gods.

The text presents society as consisting of four parts: the gods, the king, the blessed dead, and humanity. They are bound together by moral obligations. Evil people who are found wanting in an ethical judgment after their death are cast out of creation. The four parts of society act together to create and maintain order, while the condemned remain to be tortured eternally in the disordered realms outside the cosmos.[15] Nonhuman, nondivine living beings are absent from this model. Their omission probably relates to the text's brevity, but it also fits with a particular style of presenting the moral universe.

A more expansive style, in which all living beings owe their productive existence to the creator's benevolence, is exhibited in reliefs from an Old Kingdom solar temple and in a list incorporated into a Middle Kingdom mortuary text.[16] This style was the forerunner of important developments. Hymns from a cycle to be pronounced hourly in the cult of the sun god give an opposite picture. In these hymns the sun god's passage is threatened by hostile forces, and the officiant cajoles and commands the continuance of the "natural" order.[17] Such texts were rarely written down in contexts that have been preserved, perhaps part-

14. In commenting on a passage where the sun god is said to give "life" to the "living" (i.e., the blessed dead), Jan Assmann has suggested that "life" may derive from the next world and be mediated through the gods to the king and to humanity: *Liturgische Lieder an den Sonnengott: Untersuchungen zur altägyptischen Hymnik, I,* MÄS 19 (Berlin: Hessling, 1969), p. 88 (12). This idea is in keeping with the regenerative properties of the next world (e.g., Hornung, *Conceptions of God,* pp. 181–85), but it may restrict the notion of "life" too much.

15. Hornung, *Conceptions of God,* pp. 180–81; Erik Hornung, *Altägyptische Höllenvorstellungen,* Abhandlungen der Sächsischen Akademie der Wissenschaften, Philologisch-historische Klasse 59/3 (Berlin [East]: Akademie, 1968), and *Ägyptische Unterweltsbücher,* 2d ed., Bibliothek der Alten Welt: Der Alte Orient (Zurich and Munich: Artemis, 1984). For judgment after death, see also pp. 141, 151–53 ahead.

16. See Jan Assmann, *Ägypten: Theologie und Frömmigkeit einer frühen Hochkultur* (Stuttgart: Kohlhammer, 1984), pp. 214–15; John Baines, "An Abydos List of Gods and an Old Kingdom Use of Texts," in *Pyramid Studies and Other Essays Presented to I. E. S. Edwards,* ed. John Baines et al., Occasional Publications 7 (London: Egypt Exploration Society, 1988), pp. 124–33.

17. Assmann, *Liturgische Lieder,* pp. 113–64; Jan Assmann, *Re und Amun: Die Krise des polytheistischen Weltbilds im Ägypten der 18.–20. Dynastie,* OBO 51 (1983), pp. 22–53. See further John Baines, "Restricted Knowledge, Hierarchy and Decorum: Modern Perceptions and Ancient Institutions," *JARCE* 27 (1990): 1–23.

ly because of their central significance for the cult and partly because of the problematic nature of what they said. Their assumption that order was threatened was part of the Egyptians' basic world view, but decorum seldom allowed it to be openly presented in a this-worldly context.

The Egyptians made a clear division between normal, ostensibly optimistic religious action, which took place in the restricted context of the cult, and reactions to misfortune. This division makes it possible to concentrate on the less well-known aspect of misfortune, which is universally one of the foci of religious action. Misfortune threatens the individual's and the group's sense of life's meaning. In Egyptian terms, it may also be part of still broader threats to order that concern all of society. In other words, human misfortune may acquire more general significance as an analogy for the threatened cosmos. Misfortune poses crucial and continuing tests of a society's viability and solidarity. In earlier periods, Egyptians seem to have reacted to it on a local basis and in small groups, in keeping with a social structure that was not fully centralized. This social structure contrasted with the highly centralized political organization of the country. In some later periods, Egypt had a more integrated, urban society, which appears to have responded to adversity in rather different ways.

SOCIAL CONDITIONS

A discussion of the way in which people confronted the untoward requires presentation of the social context, so far as there is evidence for it. Where evidence is lacking, a hypothetical context must be supplied. Practical religious action needs to be related to conceptions of ethics and morality. These two terms do not refer to two different things so much as to two aspects of the same thing. Society is a "moral system" that is held together by moderated self-interest (and altruism) but is also threatened with dissolution by tensions between self-interest and the interests of wider groups.[18] Morality is integral to the normal interchanges of social life. People reflect on and systematize the problematic of social tensions and of tensions between the individual and the

18. See, e.g., T. M. S. Evens, "Two Concepts of 'Society as a Moral System': Evans-Pritchard's Heterodoxy," *Man* n.s. 17 (1982): 205–18.

group. In the process they create ethics, which is a second, more abstract level of engagement with moral issues. Official pronouncements and works of literature are often oriented toward ethics, while more indirect sources reveal a little of the workings of morality.

Hardly any Egyptian texts are so abstract as Western works on ethics. Their presentation is rooted in examples, not in general principles, but it can nonetheless be comprehensive and can approach abstraction indirectly, as in the complex ethical discourses of the story of the Eloquent Peasant.[19] In the name of ethics, the most immoral things have been done in many places and periods. Morality, which is more local and less grandiose, may bear less blame here. The contrast between the two is important, because ideology and ethics rationalize the basis for social inequality, which Egypt had in great measure, yet the king and the elite who benefit from the ideological underpinning of their position cannot ignore morality. This moral tension within the position and attitudes of the elite is a complex analogy for the general tension between interests in society.

The sources for investigating practical religion and morality are sparse and indirect. Widespread participation in religious practices that leave archaeological traces is attested from the New Kingdom, from about 1500 B.C.E.,[20] and on a much larger scale in the Late Period (from about 700 B.C.E.). In studying earlier periods, it is necessary to use analogies from these better-documented times. It is difficult, however, to say how far such analogies from later periods can be taken. If similar practices cannot be posited for earlier times, were early society and religion very different from their descendants? If they can be posited, why did the practices leave little trace? These little-studied questions are important for a rounded picture of any period. A small number of sites have yielded a wide range of evidence relating to social life during a few short, well-documented periods in dynastic history, but for most such questions only Ptolemaic and Roman times are well documented.[21] I

19. In, e.g., *AEL* 1:169–84; compare Gerhard Fecht, "Bauerngeschichte," *LÄ* 1:638–51. For the text, see Richard Parkinson, *The Tale of the Eloquent Peasant* (Oxford: Griffith Institute, 1991). I am very grateful to Richard Parkinson for discussions of this work.

20. For the archaeological record of religious practice as seen in votive offerings and an excellent discussion of the religious context, see Geraldine Pinch, *New Kingdom Votive Offerings to Hathor* (Oxford: Griffith Institute, in press).

21. See, e.g., Alan K. Bowman, *Egypt after the Pharaohs* (London: British Museum Publications; Berkeley: University of California Press, 1986); Naphtali Lewis, *Life in Egypt under Roman Rule* (Oxford: Clarendon, 1983); Dorothy J. Thompson, *Memphis under the Ptolemies* (Princeton: Princeton University Press, 1988).

focus on the third and second millennia B.C.E., for which it is necessary to reconstruct social conditions by indirect methods.

Although ancient Egypt had the largest and most stable state of its time, its world was small and uncertain—the antithesis of the size, confidence, and self-proclaimed certainty of the Great Pyramid. Despite their mass, monuments such as the pyramid leave no record, except the stones themselves, of the people who built them (as opposed to those who commissioned them). Their essential meaning and symbolism even for those who were buried in them is not understood with any assurance.[22] But something can usefully be said about the group of elite people who were involved in planning the pyramids, which, apart from their own tombs, were surely the central undertakings of their lifetimes. This is not my main concern here. Instead, I present, more hypothetically, important conditions of life among the rest of the society. Much of what follows would apply in greater or lesser measure to almost any premodern complex society.

In most periods, the elite who ran affairs of state were a close-knit group of a few hundred.[23] They were all men, and they were the fathers of the next generation of the elite. Although no rule required that positions be inherited, elite children stood an altogether better chance of reaching high office than others. The core elite with their families numbered two or three thousand people. There were perhaps five thousand more literate people, who with their families would have brought the total ruling and administrative class to fewer than 50,000, of whom perhaps one in eight were literate officeholders. They might have formed 3 to 5 percent of the population, which, in the Old Kingdom, was perhaps one to one and a half million.

The rest of society lived in relative poverty and simplicity. Their material culture was little different from that of neolithic times, and may not have been so prosperous.[24] Elite and nonelite had many children. They

22. Surprisingly, there has not been a full discussion of this question. See, e.g., I. E. S. Edwards, *The Pyramids of Egypt*, rev. ed. (Harmondsworth: Penguin; New York: Viking Penguin, 1985), pp. 271–81.

23. For computations based on the size of the Old Kingdom elite necropoleis of Giza and Saqqara, see John Baines and C. J. Eyre, "Four Notes on Literacy," *Göttinger Miszellen* 61 (1983): 65–96. These computations are problematic in detail but may be useful in suggesting an order of magnitude.

24. The argument for reduced prosperity derives mainly from the impoverished cemetery record. See John Baines, "Literacy, Social Organization and the Archaeological Record: The Case of Early Egypt," in *State and Society: The Emergence and Development of Social Hierarchy and Political Centralisation*, ed. Barbara Bender et al. (London: Unwin Hyman, 1988), pp. 192–214.

needed to if they were to increase or even reproduce themselves, because only a minority of children survived to become adults. Adults could not look forward with confidence to long careers. Evidence from Roman Egypt suggests a life expectancy at age 14 of 29.1.[25] At birth, average life expectancy must have been much less than 20. These figures may seem startling, but their plausibility for all but the elite is corroborated from a number of sources.[26]

Thus most of the elite could only hope for, rather than expect, a long career. This lack of an assured future is exemplified by statistical work on the elite of imperial Rome, whose basic conditions of health and life were probably better than but not essentially different from those of Egypt.[27] The rest of society, in their harsher circumstances of life, will have had fewer expectations. Many people throughout society will have died unexpectedly or developed sudden severe illnesses. Egyptian medicine was the best of its time, but it could do little against disease and could achieve only limited success with accidents and injuries. As in most societies, the full range of medical treatment was probably available only to the elite.[28]

Such frequent, almost routine experience of loss is something modern Westerners find hard to comprehend, and it has led to theories about periods as recent as early modern times, when it has been suggested that parents avoided emotional attachment to their children because of the exposure to grief it would bring.[29] People in many societies, includ-

25. See n. 23 above. For a neolithic parallel from Anatolia, in which the skeletal material produced the same figure of 29, see Robert and Linda Braidwood, "Çayönü—1987," *Oriental Institute News and Notes* 112 (1988): 3. For the demographic composition of an ancient elite, see Keith Hopkins, *Sociological Studies in Roman History*, vol. 2, *Death and Renewal* (Cambridge: Cambridge University Press, 1983), pp. 31–200. Egyptian monuments very commonly show large elite families with many children. These compositions are not purely idealized, but often depict specifically named individuals. The number of surviving children must have been smaller among the less fortunate.

26. For ancient Teotihuacán, a society in some ways comparable with Egypt, see Rebecca Storey, "An Estimate of Mortality in a Pre-Columbian Urban Population," *American Anthropologist* 87 (1985): 519–35. For a different context, see Fredrik Barth, *Ritual and Knowledge among the Baktaman of New Guinea* (Oslo: Universitetsforlaget; New Haven: Yale University Press, 1975), pp. 270–73.

27. See Hopkins, *Death and Renewal* [n. 25].

28. For an outstanding study of social conditions and their relation to a range of religious practices as broad as can be attested from Egypt, and far better known, see Keith Thomas, *Religion and the Decline of Magic: Studies in Popular Beliefs in Sixteenth- and Seventeenth-Century England*, rev. ed. (Harmondsworth: Penguin, 1973). On Egyptian medicine, see, e.g., P. Ghalioungui, *The House of Life, Per Ankh: Magic and Medical Science in Ancient Egypt* (Amsterdam: B. M. Israel, 1973).

29. Denied by, e.g., Sheldon J. Watts, *A Social History of Western Europe, 1450–1720: Tensions and Solidarities among Rural People* (London: Hutchinson University Library, 1984),

ing the Egyptians, dramatize their loss and involve the community, making loss bearable by making it public. Loss creates loose ends: widows of greatly varying ages, orphans, widowers who wish to marry again, aging grandparents with no source of support, and so forth. Many people suffer mutilation through disease and through accidents, which renders them unable to perform useful work because most labor is heavy and physical. These people must then depend on others for support.[30] A notable proportion become mentally unable to sustain their roles in society. In the contemporary world, such people are said to be suffering from stress or to be mentally ill; in most premodern and many modern societies, diagnoses of this common phenomenon and methods of coping with it have been different.[31] Thus, even in periods of peace and stability, the amount and range of untoward occurrences affecting most people was much greater than is the case in modern Western society.

The central context for all these occurrences, for guarding against them and providing for their consequences, was the family. As a unit, the family reaped the benefits of success, but had to care for children, for misfits, for the incapacitated, and for those who had the good fortune to become old. The basic family unit was probably large, consisting of parents, children (including married ones, often with their own children), unattached and widowed relatives, perhaps grandparents, and, among the relatively well-to-do, servants or slaves. Housing was scarce, and people lived at close quarters, accommodating remarkable numbers.[32] Visitors and unrelated people might also be present in the household, because they could not easily find somewhere to stay by themselves.

---

pp. 89–90. For a balanced discussion, see J. A. Sharpe, *Early Modern England: A Social History, 1550–1760* (London and Baltimore: Arnold, 1987), pp. 56–76.

30. See, e.g., Gy. Acsádi and J. Nemeskéri, *History of Human Life Span and Mortality* (Budapest: Akadémiai Kiadó, 1970).

31. True especially of spirit possession, which often also has a strong aspect of social leveling; see, e.g., I. M. Lewis, *Ecstatic Religion: An Anthropological Study of Spirit Possession and Shamanism* (Harmondsworth: Penguin, 1971).

32. For a large rural household, see T. G. H. James, *The Heḳanakhte Papers and Other Early Middle Kingdom Documents*, Egyptian Expedition 19 (New York: Metropolitan Museum of Art, 1962); Klaus Baer, "An Eleventh Dynasty Farmer's Letters to His Family," *Journal of the American Oriental Society* 83 (1963): 1–19. For urban housing, see Barry J. Kemp, "The City of el-Amarna as a Source for the Study of Urban Society in Ancient Egypt," *World Archaeology* 9 (1977–78): 123–39. For Greco-Roman evidence, see H. S. Smith, "Society and Settlement in Ancient Egypt," in *Man, Settlement and Urbanism*, ed. Peter J. Ucko et al. (London: Duckworth, 1972), pp. 705–19; Bowman, *Egypt after the Pharaohs* [n. 21], pp. 146–50. For a well-documented special group, see Thompson, *Memphis under the Ptolemies*, pp. 169–89.

In contrast with this diverse reality, the ideal of the elite would be relatively familiar today, except that its context was in state service: one grew up, trained for a career, got married, and set up house with one's wife and children.[33] In the grandest of circumstances, one lived on a vast, seemingly rural estate with hundreds of subordinate officials, workmen, peasants, and others.[34] Such a career, with its focus on the nuclear family, might have been possible for few, and it provided a suitably rootless ideal for those who were in theory dedicated to royal service.[35] Their estates and positions depended on the patronage of the king to whom they owed their allegiance, and their wider kinship ties were not displayed on their monuments. They appeared to owe nothing to anyone but the king. This image is the essential one projected by the great Old Kingdom tombs. In Theban New Kingdom tombs it is modified into a part-urban, part-rural presentation. For neither period should this presentation be taken at face value, because it masks realities of competition and independent ambition, but the fact that social forms were presented in these terms remains important.

The experience of most people was very different from the ideal of the elite. Most were tied to the land, which they worked for the state or for a high official. The unfortunate might be taken from their homes to work on major state works in the Nile Valley or, worse, in the desert, becoming little more than expendable units of labor. On an expedition to quarry stone in the Wadi Hammamat during the reign of Ramesses IV (c. 1155 B.C.E.), more than 10 percent of the people who set out did not return. This was not the harshest or most distant place from which minerals were extracted, and the fact that these figures were publicly recorded shows that they were not considered discreditable.[36] Some

33. The outline of such a life is presented in many of the biographies that give more than a sketch of a mature career. For marriage and setting up house, see the biography of Ahmose son of Ebana: Kurt Sethe, *Urkunden der 18. Dynastie,* Urk. 4/1, 2d ed. (Leipzig: Hinrichs, 1930), pp. 1–2; English trans. *AEL* 2:12, 14n7.

34. Examples can be found in most major tomb publications and illustrated books, but the social or career ideals implied by the compositions as a whole have not been analyzed.

35. Especially pronounced in biographies of the Amarna Period. See Jan Assmann, "Die 'loyalistische Lehre' Echnatons," *SAK* 8 (1980): 14–16; John Baines, "Literacy and Ancient Egyptian Society," *Man* n.s. 18 (1983): 585–86 with n. 34.

36. For the exploitation of people's labor in state institutions, see, e.g., William C. Hayes, *A Papyrus of the Late Middle Kingdom in the Brooklyn Museum* (Brooklyn: Brooklyn Museum, 1955). For the expedition with high mortality, see Kenneth A. Kitchen, *Ramesside Inscriptions, Historical and Biographical,* vol. 6 (Oxford: B. H. Blackwell, 1983), p. 14, l. 9; Louis A. Christophe, "La stèle de l'an III de Ramsès IV au Ouâdi Hammâmât (N° 12)," *BIFAO* 48 (1949): 20–21, 24–26n(r).

kings of the later New Kingdom made capital of their efforts to mitigate these somber conditions, setting up inscriptions vaunting their concern and provision for their workers.[37] But even in these cases, the groups addressed were professional workmen rather than the conscripted unskilled laborers who made up the majority on most expeditions. The laborers must have been taken temporarily from their normal environment and made completely dependent on state provision. As the Wadi Hammamat inscription makes clear, they had no special reason to trust the quality of the state's provision.

Such cases highlight one concomitant of life's uncertainty: life was cheap, especially that of the poor and of those who did not conform. Most ancient complex societies were brutal.[38] Egypt's bland public image should not mislead people into thinking that Egyptian society was very different in this respect. A second corollary of life's uncertainty, one that is not quite so apparent, was the importance of age. The material from Roman Egypt used for assessing life expectancy did not include any individual who was with certainty more than sixty-four years old, but some, such as King Ramesses II, who reigned sixty-six years (1279–1213 B.C.E.), lived much longer. Even if most people died young, many still survived to an advanced age, and those who did survive were resilient.[39] Because they were few, they selected themselves as leaders, frequently forming the power behind much younger kings. In the wider society, too, some men pursued active lives to remarkable ages. High mortality and gerontocracy go together. This authority of the aged may also have related to that of their elders, the dead.

Thus the king and the elite appropriated a high proportion of the

37. E.g., Sety I at Kanayis: Siegfried Schott, *Kanais: Der Tempel Sethos I. im Wâdi Mia*, Nachrichten der Akademie der Wissenschaften in Göttingen, Philologisch-historische Klasse, 1961/6 (Göttingen: Vandenhoeck & Ruprecht, 1961) = Kenneth A. Kitchen, *Ramesside Inscriptions, Historical and Biographical*, vol. 1 (Oxford: B. H. Blackwell, 1975), pp. 65–70; Ramesses II at Heliopolis: A. Hamada, "A Stela from Manshiyet eṣ-Ṣadr," *Annales du Service des Antiquités de l'Égypte* 38 (1938): 217–30 = Kitchen, *Ramesside Inscriptions*, vol. 2 (1979), pp. 360–62.

38. Compare the comments of Jean-Marie Kruchten, *Le décret d'Horemheb: Traduction, commentaire épigraphique, philologique et institutionnel*, Université Libre de Bruxelles, Faculté de Philosophie et Lettres 82 (Brussels: Université de Bruxelles [1982]), p. 206. See also n. 83.

39. For models of age at death in relation to life expectancy derived from skeletal material, see Theya Molleson, "The Archaeology and Anthropology of Death: What the Bones Tell Us," in *Mortality and Immortality: The Anthropology and Archaeology of Death*, ed. S. C. Humphreys and Helen King (London and New York: Academic Press, 1981), pp. 19–21.

resources of Egyptian society and rendered society very unequal. Inequality lessened people's capacity to be self-sufficient in facing life's problems. The means of provision for calamity were largely removed from ordinary people, most of whom either lived on the land or lived in towns but derived their livelihood from the land. They paid their rent, taxes, or dues and retained little more of what they produced than they needed for subsistence.[40] In a disastrous flood or a year when the inundation of the Nile was inadequate for a harvest, the state, or in decentralized periods the local grandee, had either to supply people's needs for subsistence or to face the threat of social dislocation. Late Old Kingdom and First Intermediate Period inscriptions contain numerous references to famine and to how their dedicatees averted or mitigated its effects for their people or for a region.[41] Social dislocation, when it came, did not lead to a new order with greater equality or individual self-reliance. Instead, another grandee took over. Although one extant text states that all were created equal, people had no conception of a social order of a different type from the one they had long known.

DECORUM, MORALITY, AND BIOGRAPHY

These harsh conditions of life, within which the often casuistic Egyptian presentation of morality must be comprehended, were almost the opposite of what is shown in reliefs in private tombs of the Old, Middle, and New kingdoms, or of what is implied by royal inscriptions. Such a contrast can be found in many societies if the display of the elite is compared with the life of the deprived. In Egypt this contrast had extra significance because the elite's display of their own circumstances and surroundings on the monuments was constrained by the global

40. On the scale of governmental granary provision, see Barry J. Kemp, "Large Middle Kingdom Granary Buildings (and the Archaeology of Administration)," *ZÄS* 113 (1986): 120–36 (some calculations problematic); compare Lin Foxhall and H. A. Forbes, "[*Sitometreia*]: The Role of Grain as a Staple Food in Classical Antiquity," *Chiron* 12 (1982): 41–90. For evidence for the form of large-scale granaries, see Charles Cornell van Siclen III, *Two Theban Monuments from the Reign of Amenhotep II* (San Antonio: author, 1982), pp. 18–46.

41. See Jacques Vandier, *La famine dans l'Égypte ancienne*, Institut français d'Archéologie orientale, Recherches d'archéologie, de philologie et d'histoire 7 (Cairo, 1936); and *Moʿalla: La tombe d'Ankhtifi et la tombe de Sébekhotep*, BdÉ 18 (1950); Waltraud Guglielmi, "Hunger," *LÄ* 3:82–84. See further Wolfgang Schenkel, *Die Bewässerungsrevolution im alten Ägypten* (Mainz: von Zabern, 1978), pp. 37–49.

system of decorum that governed the public presentation of order. By implication, to represent deprivation or the untoward would be to allow disorder to intrude into order.[42]

Decorum, which operated on all monuments of characteristic Egyptian style, affected what might be depicted in scenes or presented in texts, and how and in what context anything might be shown. Decorum evolved very slowly, allowing an increasing range of religious and other material to be shown. This development accompanied a general expansion of the uses of representation and writing. The principal expansions in decorum accompanied major historical developments in the central Old Kingdom, the Middle Kingdom, the Eighteenth Dynasty, and Ramesside times—a period of well over a millennium. Despite these expansions, the general effect of decorum was probably to slow the proliferation of religious material in public contexts. A subject would not be displayed on monuments simply because it existed in society. Most subjects must have existed for long periods before contexts were created or forms devised for presenting them within the system of decorum. This point applied especially to the omnipresent reality of suffering, which never became a normal topic within decorum.

Much of Egyptian practical religion concerned people's responses, behind the surface of decorum, to the very frequent events that disturbed order. Presentation of such disturbances is almost necessarily absent from the monuments, which were massively committed to the official order, but such texts as the story of the Eloquent Peasant make the connection between personal suffering and official order. Royal and divine texts and reliefs omitted human concerns, so that there was no place to state the reality that order was not universal. These omissions do not imply a desire to falsify reality, but rather demonstrate a lack of focus on such issues. In addition, many of the preserved sources for Egyptian religion were public and were set up with their owners' prestige in mind, so it is not surprising that they omit compromising material.

The limits to presenting "deviant" material can be seen in the finest Old Kingdom tombs of high officials, such as that of Ti.[43] These tombs

42. John Baines, *Fecundity Figures: Egyptian Personification and the Iconology of a Genre* (Warminster: Aris & Phillips; Chicago: Bolchazy-Carducci, 1985), pp. 277–305; for the system in texts, see, e.g., Baines, "The Stela of Emhab: Innovation, Tradition, Hierarchy," *JEA* 72 (1986): 41–53.

43. Much illustrated. For publications of the tomb as a whole, see Georg Steindorff, *Das Grab des Ti*, Veröffentlichungen der Ernst von Sieglin Expedition in Ägypten 2 (Leipzig:

contain numerous relief scenes in which people who fall short of the physical ideal are depicted, hapless peasants are beaten to force them to pay their rents, and boatmen fight as they bring their catch home (this seems to be a game).[44] Such scene types are among the few that show violence among Egyptians (as opposed to violence they inflict on foreigners). The general absence of public presentations of violence could correspond to a low level of violence in Egyptian society, although both indirect arguments and evidence from the more variously documented Late Period suggest that the sources may here disguise realities, while certain types of violence, such as homicide and feuding, may have been kept outside the institutional framework of the state.[45]

These Old Kingdom tomb scenes must be set in context. A figure of the tomb owner, for whom the composition was carved, dominates the wall surface and brackets as many as eight registers of scenes of "daily life." He stands or sits, often with his wife and perhaps one or two children, and impassively observes the scenes, probably taking pleasure in these colorful manifestations of life on the land under his control.[46] The picaresque details in the scenes do not alter the overall message that everything is right with the world, but rather enhance its interest for the somewhat detached observer. Yet the context in which these "manorial"

Hinrichs, 1913); Lucienne Épron, François Daumas, and Henri Wild, *Le tombeau de Ti*, 3 vols., Mémoires de l'Institut français d'Archéologie orientale 65 (Cairo, 1939–1966).

44. See Kent R. Weeks, "The Anatomical Knowledge of the Ancient Egyptians and the Representation of the Human Figure in Egyptian Art" (Ph.D. diss., Yale University, 1970) (imperfect physique); Ahmed M. Moussa and Hartwig Altenmüller, *The Tomb of Nefer and Ka-hay*, AVDAIK 5 (1971), pls. 6 (beating peasants), 10–11, 15 (boatmen); Walter Wreszinski, *Atlas zur altägyptischen Kulturgeschichte*, pt. 3: *Gräber des alten Reiches*, with Hermann Grapow, ed. Heinrich Schäfer (Leipzig: Hinrichs, 1936–), pl. 68 (beating peasants); Norman de G. Davies, *The Rock Tombs of Deir el-Gebrâwi*, vol. 1, Archaeological Survey of Egypt 11 (London: Egypt Exploration Fund, 1902), pl. 8 (beating peasants; Middle Kingdom).

45. For the general context, see Pierce, *Royal Anthropological Institute News* 15 (1976): 15–17. For the best-known community, Ramesside Deir el-Medina, the evidence for violence adduced by Dominique Valbelle, *"Les ouvriers de la Tombe": Deir el-Médineh à l'époque ramesside*, BdÉ 96 (1985), pp. 305–12, is meager and in part questionable. This comment does not apply to the elite, among whom there is ample indirect evidence for factional struggle around the kingship, as well as the violent desecration of tombs, which probably had counterparts in actions among the living. See also Harco Willems, "Crime, Cult and Capital Punishment (Mo'alla Inscription 8)," *JEA* 76 (1990): 27–54. For Late Period material, see, e.g., Thompson, *Memphis under the Ptolemies*, pp. 214–52; J. D. Ray, "The Complaint of Herieu," *RdÉ* 29 (1977): 97–116, esp. 116. The unconventional First Intermediate Period inscriptions of Ankhtify include a seeming allusion to the ending of feuds, and so may attest to their occurrence: Vandier, *Mo'alla* [n. 41], pp. 163–64; *AEL* 1:85–86.

46. Sources are very abundant. See, e.g., William Stevenson Smith, *A History of Egyptian Sculpture and Painting in the Old Kingdom*, 2d ed. (London: Geoffrey Cumberlege, Oxford University Press, for Museum of Fine Arts, Boston, 1949), pls. 34a, 55a–b, 56b, 60b.

dependents are presented probably implies a moral dimension. The owner offers them a livelihood and protection against injustice and misfortune in return for their services. There is nothing explicitly religious in what is shown.

"Autobiographical" texts found increasingly from the later third millennium B.C.E. admit that all is not right with the world. They state that the men they praise "gave bread to the hungry, clothes to the naked," and so forth. Later royal texts—both instruction texts and "historical" inscriptions—take up this idea. This magnanimous role belongs to the whole elite rather than specifically to the king, who has a more cosmic, less centrally moral purpose to fulfill. Extended versions of these formulas enumerate many ways in which the fortunate might help the unfortunate, such as looking after the widow and the divorced woman or, in a country with countless large and small watercourses, ferrying people who have no boat. A hymn to a god can use the same phrases.[47]

The superficial purpose of these "autobiographical" texts was to persuade the visitor to enter a tomb in a suitable state of purity and to recite an offering prayer on behalf of the deceased, but their meaning was broader. They were also closely associated with prestige. By praising the deceased's qualities, they sought to persuade the visitor to recite the prayer. The ideals behind the actions described are universally comprehensible and constitute a "natural morality." Should those in lower social groups read the texts—which was unlikely to happen—the great would be seen to have cared for them. The great would thus be justified in appropriating the wherewithal to satisfy people's needs (which they themselves had earlier appropriated). But because so few could read and because even access to the tombs may not have been very common, the moral justification offered in these texts was probably more significant in reinforcing the elite's own sense of status than in speaking to others. Nonetheless, it is likely to reflect some broader consensus over the moral composition of society, and it must surely relate to widespread maxims and sentiments.

Were the elite to abuse their status, their tombs might be vandalized, and they might then lack a resting place for the next life. In this context,

47. For a collection of Old Kingdom inscriptions, see Alessandro Roccati, *La littérature historique sous l'Ancien Empire égyptien*, Littératures Anciennes du Proche-Orient (Paris: Cerf, 1982). For an initial analysis, chiefly of Middle Kingdom texts, see Jozef Janssen, *De traditioneele egyptische autobiografie vóór het Nieuwe Rijk*, 2 vols. (Leiden: Brill, 1946). For a hymn to a god with similar phrases, see Alan H. Gardiner, "The Graffito from the Tomb of Pere," *JEA* 14 (1928): 10–11 with pls. 5–6.

their desire for a proper progress into and existence in the next life restrained their excesses in their treatment of people in this life, because they needed a good reputation in society, whether they had to face an ethical judgment after death or not.[48] In their biographies, tomb owners sought to forestall attacks on their tombs or their memories by asserting that they had held title to their property and had settled their obligations—but tombs were vandalized.[49] It is difficult to say what conclusion ancient observers drew from vandalism.[50]

Except in the special case of tombs, this argument might imply that morality need not be closely related to religion, if religion is narrowly defined as relating exclusively to the cult and the gods. Since the norms of natural morality are almost universal, this interpretation may be valid for an outsider to the culture, and no specific aspect of religion has necessarily to impinge on morality. Egyptian ethical texts, however, go out of their way to connect the two—in relation to judgment after death, for example. In the Egyptians' terms, morality and religion can hardly be separated, and the history of the development of both in Egypt vindicates this view. The association of the general ideals of natural morality with central Egyptian religious values carries with it the implication that loss and deprivation could disturb the proper order of things. This disturbance then is not simply a potentially disruptive lack of equity in society; it involves the gods and the cosmic order. Loss is one of many things that may threaten the fragile constitution of the cosmos.

There was therefore tension in Egypt between the inequality of society, which the elite took to be natural while claiming to have mitigated its effects in individual cases, and the equally natural feeling that everyone should have some well-being. The king conformed with this morality in many respects and on occasion proclaimed his concern for the

48. See, e.g., Roccati, *Littérature historique*, p. 236, where an official denies—unconvincingly—that he was prosecuted.

49. The motif is common. See, e.g., Roccati, *Littérature historique*, p. 152; Elmar Edel, "Inschriften des Alten Reiches V: Die Reiseberichte des Ḥrw-ḫwjf (Herchuf)," in *Ägyptologische Studien*, ed. O. Firchow [Festschrift for Hermann Grapow], Deutsche Akademie der Wissenschaften zu Berlin, Institut für Orientforschung, Veröffentlichung 29 (Berlin [East]: Akademie, 1955), p. 53, with references.

50. For a possible case in which a vandal's feelings were expressed, see Étienne Drioton, "Une mutilation d'image avec motif," *Archiv Orientální* 20 (1952): 351–55. The scene described is now published: Selim Hassan, *Mastabas of Ny-'Ankh-Pepy and Others*, ed. Zaky Iskander, Arab Republic of Egypt, Antiquities Department of Egypt, Excavations at Saqqara, 1937–1938, 2 (Cairo: General Organisation for Government Printing Offices, 1975), pp. 7–9, pl. 3.

everyday social order.[51] On another level, however, he stood outside human society as the protagonist of the cosmic order. This separate status enabled him to distance himself from normal human morality. Thus the grosser royal or state exploitations involved in building the pyramids and similar undertakings might have been justified peremptorily, by reference to the cosmic needs of the king or of society.[52]

Apart from glorifying their moral worth, the great of the Old Kingdom presented a "biography" that said they had gone to and fro between town and estate, had built houses, had dug pools in their courtyards, had planted trees, and so forth.[53] They also displayed long strings of accumulated titles, distilling their careers as officials into hierarchical listings. Taken together, these two types of inscription outline the ideal for a regularly successful, complete life. In conformity with the elite family and career ideal, these biographies relate success to the king. The moral identity and the political and personal success of the great were bound together into what may seem an unrealistic whole, but an optimistic presentation of morality was part of decorum for much of Egyptian history; only Late Period texts depart significantly from it.[54] There is no reason to believe that Egyptians were deceived by it.

Unlike the title strings, the "biography" hardly relates to the king. It is the part of elite display in which people claimed moral stature. Although members of the elite ascribed success in their careers to royal favor (and their own abilities), they presented their moral actions toward subordinates as separate from the royal sphere. This presentation suggests that they aspired to moral authority in a community that included all but the king.

51. An example is the posthumous declaration of Ramesses III that he made life safe for women in the streets: W. Erichsen, *Papyrus Harris I: Hieroglyphische Transkription*, BiAe 5 (1933), pp. 95, l. 18–96, l. 16; James Henry Breasted, *Ancient Records of Egypt*, vol. 4, *The Twentieth to the Twenty-sixth Dynasties* (Chicago: University of Chicago Press, 1906), sec. 410. See also Kruchten, *Décret d'Horemheb* [n. 38].

52. The same conceptions were crucial in royal "historical" action in general.

53. This phraseology was analyzed by Elmar Edel, "Untersuchungen zur Phraseologie der ägyptischen Inschriften des Alten Reiches," *Mitteilungen des Deutschen Instituts für Ägyptische Altertumskunde in Kairo* 13 (1944): 1–90. For an argument relating the optimistic presentation of biographies and the passage of generations in this context more generally to the preservation and transmission of *ma'at* ("order"), see Jan Assmann, "Vergeltung und Erinnerung," in *Studien zu Sprache und Religion Ägyptens zu Ehren von Wolfhart Westendorf*, vol. 2, *Religion* [ed. Friedrich Junge] (Göttingen, 1984), pp. 687–701. This argument takes the texts rather too much at face value. See further Erik Hornung, *Geist der Pharaonenzeit* (Zurich and Munich: Artemis, 1989), pp. 131–45.

54. Compare Eberhard Otto, *Die biographischen Inschriften der ägyptischen Spätzeit: Ihre geistesgeschichtliche und literarische Bedeutung*, PÄ 2 (1954); *AEL*, 3:13–65.

This high moral status of the elite could be extended into the narrowly religious sphere of the cult. Some biographies of the end of the Old Kingdom and the following period emphasize the protagonist's performance of temple rituals, and a number of grandees bear the title "overseer of priests," which means roughly "chief priest," and "lector priest," that is, priest who performed the rituals.[55] These people vaunted their role in official religion, for it gave them prestige and suggested a concern with the deity. Their claimed role in the cult is analogous to the religious role of the king, who was credited by ideology and the conventions of decorum with performing all cult. As with the king, their claim to perform the cult was probably exaggerated.

No extant evidence fleshes out the elite's claims of participation in rituals with statements that they experienced the deity's action during the rituals. This reticence in the sources may be due in part to decorum. In any case, the elite's display of a religious role implies that that role was an admired privilege to which many people might aspire. They may also have desired such special experiences as this privilege might offer.

How do the biographies of the elite, with their stereotyped literary formulation, compare with the lives of the less fortunate? It is useful to present those lives in a bare, hypothetical outline that relies heavily on analogy with other societies.[56] The regular stages of life that may be drawn into the religious sphere are birth; puberty and the assumption of an adult role in society; marriage; parenthood; and death. All may be interrupted by misfortune, and all represent points of danger and transition. Children may be stillborn or may die soon after birth, for example,

55. Baines, *JEA* 73 (1987): 91; for the succeeding period, see, e.g., Vandier, *Mo'alla* [n. 41], inscription no. 5, pp. 185–98; Wolfgang Schenkel, *Memphis. Herakleopolis. Theben: Die epigraphischen Zeugnisse der 7.–11. Dynastie Ägyptens*, ÄgAbh 12 (1965), texts 43, 45. The title is common also in the Middle Kingdom; see William A. Ward, *Index of Egyptian Administrative and Religious Titles of the Middle Kingdom* (Beirut: American University of Beirut, 1982), pp. 35–38, nos. 259–80; Henry George Fischer, *Egyptian Titles of the Middle Kingdom: A Supplement to Wm. Ward's INDEX* (New York: Metropolitan Museum of Art, 1985), p. 6, nos. 261a–279a. See further Naguib Kanawati, *Governmental Reforms in Old Kingdom Egypt* (Warminster: Aris & Phillips, 1980), p. 130.

A late Old Kingdom royal document reveals that the status of overseer of priests could be institutionalized: chief local administrators are termed "Administrator of New Towns, Sole Companion, Overseer of Priests" (Kurt Sethe, *Urkunden des alten Reichs*, 2d ed., Urk. I:1 [Leipzig: Hinrichs, 1933], p. 131, l. 4; Roccati, *Littérature historique* [n. 47], p. 207). Overseers of priests may be named because they controlled temple storehouses, but the presentation of the titles in a string suggests that this status had become synonymous with high local office, in which case its religious significance could have been reduced.

56. Compare Baines, *JEA* 73 (1987): 83–86.

and very many women, in some archaeologically documented cases a majority, may die in childbirth.[57]

In Egypt, rituals accompanied the birth of a child.[58] The mother was secluded for fourteen days after the birth; there was then a celebration. It appears that many boys were circumcised at puberty. Thereafter, they wore clothes in public. Girls were probably also circumcised, as many have been in more modern times in Egypt and Sudan.[59]

Marriage was the major stage of Egyptian life that seems to have fallen outside the religious context. The institution of marriage existed, and there were sanctions against adultery and sexual misdemeanors, but there is no evidence that rituals or other religious observances were celebrated either at the beginning of a marriage or during its course.[60] Because of the Egyptians' lack of emphasis on marriage and their discreet treatment of sexuality, it is possible to separate sexual morality, which I do not discuss here, from the more general moral conceptions that I do consider. After a marriage began, one hoped to start the biographical cycle again by producing children, who might make one's own name live into a later generation through the names they gave to their children.

Death was the most strongly ritualized of these stages. Whenever possible, tombs, which were people's first destination in the next world, were built in the desert, so that they are often well preserved. For this reason, mortuary beliefs are the best-documented aspect of Egyptian religion. It was vital for the deceased to have had children during life, because the next generation cared for the deceased of the previous one.

Within a culture, the meaning associated with the various stages of a biography and one's ultimate destiny relates to conceptions of the person and the individual's position in the group, of freedom of action, and

57. See, e.g., Jean Leclant, "Fouilles et travaux en Égypte et au Soudan, 1976–1977," *Orientalia* 47 (1978): 271.

58. Wolfhart Westendorf, "Geburt," *LÄ* 2:459–62, with references.

59. Wolfhart Westendorf, "Beschneidung," *LÄ* 1:727–29. For female circumcision, see Thompson, *Memphis under the Ptolemies*, pp. 232–33, with references. The possible dynastic material that Westendorf cites in his n. 12 is very obscure, but the Greek document, which mentions the operation as coming before marriage and being quite expensive, is clear. Since the milieu of the text is Egyptian and such a practice is unknown in the Greek world, it was probably an inherited Egyptian custom, although it is impossible to say how ancient or widespread it was.

60. See in general S. Allam, "Quelques aspects du mariage dans l'Égypte ancienne," *JEA* 67 (1981): 116–35. For adultery, see C. J. Eyre, "Crime and Adultery in Ancient Egypt," *JEA* 70 (1984): 92–105.

of destiny.[61] This sphere of Egyptian belief was very highly developed and can only be alluded to here. Humans and gods, along with sacred animals, shared many aspects of their being. Among these aspects was the potential to take on multiple manifestations, which allowed the dead and deities to move freely between forms.[62] The common features of human and divine even extended to an obscure notion of a god "who is in" people.[63] They may also have related to the belief that gods and mortals shared the predicament of existing in a bounded and threatened cosmos. The idea of a being's multiple manifestations was also important in the cult. A deity was manifest in a cult statue and, if well disposed, received the cult in that form. Yet the deity's being was not exhausted by any one manifestation.

There were numerous and varying concepts of aspects of the person. The most important are the *ka*, approximately the "vital force" that enables the generations to continue and receive offerings in the next life; the *ba* (fig. 32), perhaps the moral essence of a person's motivation and movement, which also enables him or her to be free in the next world; and the *akh*, normally the transfigured spirit in the next world. Most of these aspects came into their own in transition between this world and the next, or between generations, rather than being constant features of people's this-worldly existence and awareness.[64] In this life, the social person was a unity despite this partitioning. The diversity of these as-

61. For Egyptian conceptions of the person, see Jan Assmann, "Persönlichkeitsbegriff und -bewusstsein," *LÄ* 4:963–78. For comparative discussions see Michael Carrithers, Steven Collins, and Steven Lukes, eds., *The Category of the Person: Anthropology, Philosophy, History* (Cambridge: Cambridge University Press, 1985). For destiny, see Siegfried Morenz and Dieter Müller, *Untersuchungen zur Rolle des Schicksals in der ägyptischen Religion*, Abhandlungen der Sächsischen Akademie der Wissenschaften, Philologisch-historische Klasse 52/1 (Berlin [East]: Akademie, 1960); Jan Quaegebeur, *Le dieu égyptien Shaï dans la religion et l'onomastique*, Orientalia Lovaniensia Analecta 2 (Louvain: Leuven University Press, 1975); for free will, see Quaegebeur, pp. 120, 123–25.

62. See, e.g., Hornung, *Conceptions of God*, pp. 135–40; Boyo Ockinga, *Die Gottebenbildlichkeit im Alten Ägypten und im Alten Testament*, Ägypten und Altes Testament 7 (Wiesbaden: Harrassowitz, 1984); John Baines, "*Mswt* 'Manifestation'?" in *Hommages à François Daumas*, vol. 1, Institut d'Égyptologie, Université Paul Valéry (Montpellier: Université de Montpellier, Publication de Recherche, 1986), pp. 43–50.

63. Hans Bonnet, "Der Gott im Menschen," in *Studi in memoria di Ippolito Rosellini nel primo centenario della morte (4 giugno 1843)*, vol. 1, Università degli Studi di Pisa (Pisa: Lischi, 1949), pp. 235–52.

64. See Philippe Derchain, review of Assmann, *König als Sonnenpriester*, in *Chronique d'Égypte* 48, no. 96 (1973): 290–91. The concepts are much discussed; for summaries, see Eberhard Otto, "Ach," *LÄ* 1:49–52; Louis V. Žabkar, "Ba," *LÄ* 1:588–90; Peter Kaplony, "Ka," *LÄ* 3:275–82. See also Gertie Englund, *Akh—une notion religieuse dans l'Égypte pharaonique*, Acta Universitatis Upsaliensis: Boreas 11 (Uppsala, 1978).

pects dramatized questions of motivation, accountability, and freedom, especially those associated with the vital transitions of birth and death. Someone who was successful and/or morally virtuous in this life had access to a multiplicity of forms in the next life. Those forms also empowered the deceased spirit to help those it favored or to take vengeance on attackers.

People were morally accountable for their actions, but their freedom to act was subject to unknown or unknowable influences. Their fate or destiny was fixed at birth, and their death could be in the power of a particular god.[65] Favorable forces, such as "fortune" (*renenet*) (fig. 32) or "the god who is in" a person, could allay an adverse destiny. These ideas were significant for the comprehension of the world and of events in it, because they were sources for answers to the question of why unexpected afflictions or their opposite, episodes of special favor, strike particular people at particular times.

Yet people were also answerable to themselves for what they did and suffered, and in their understanding a balance had to be struck between outside forces and internal motivation. This balance is normally seen most clearly in adversity, but, as a result of the rules of decorum, there is little relevant evidence from early times, because personal religion and motivation were downplayed in public contexts. A complex expression of accountability is found in the Middle Kingdom Story of Sinuhe, whose protagonist appears to exonerate himself for his wrong acts by saying that they were those of a god, not of his own doing.[66] While some later texts similarly present a god as being responsible for a person's actions, Ramesside documents of piety acknowledge faults as having been committed of one's own volition. If people conceded that they had been at fault in an action or event, whether or not they had been aware of it at the time, this recognition was itself a signal of divine favor and allowed them to return to a blessed state.[67] In this area of accountability, concepts of the person and of destiny were crucial to religious change.

65. Compare Baines, *JEA* 73 (1987): 85n30.

66. See Elizabeth J. Sherman, "Djedhor the Saviour Statue Base OI 10589," *JEA* 67 (1981): 100–02; John Baines, "Interpreting *Sinuhe*," *JEA* 68 (1982): 39–42. For a broader study, see Eberhard Otto, "Ägyptische Gedanken zur menschlichen Verantwortung," *Die Welt des Orients* 3 (1964–1966): 19–26.

67. See nn. 165–66, 207 below. For a similar religious cycle, see also, e.g., Lewis, *Ecstatic Religion* [n. 31], pp. 66–70 and passim.

BIOGRAPHY AND RELIGIOUS PRACTICE

If one was lucky and survived to the peak of a career, one began to look to the vital transition of death, for which those who died younger might be less well prepared. Everyone who could afford to do so made elaborate preparations for moving to a world that was, for the blessed, better than this one, even if it was fraught with danger and uncertainty. There the blessed would enjoy the company of the gods or would become gods themselves. For those who were buried according to the full rituals, the long and costly process of mummification had to be provided.[68] The this-worldly aspects of the elite's tomb preparation were also very important. Their tombs were the focus of prestige and competition and presented their status and achievements in a complex artistic form. Tombs endured through generations and provided a continuing cultural focus, whether or not the memory of particular people survived.

People hoped that death would lead them to a desired state in the hereafter, but death did not necessarily end their role in this life. Here the Western view that society consists only of the living blocks comprehension. The Egyptian living and dead were part of the same community, and the dead could intervene positively or negatively among the living. They were an essential factor in the affairs of the living. But memory is short, and very few of the dead survived in esteem or recall beyond a generation or so after their death. So far as general evidence goes, this period could have been shorter still.[69] Even in societies that have no particular beliefs about the role of the dead among the living, short and generally irregular life spans reinforce the importance of death and the dead for human affairs.[70] The Beautiful Festival of the Wadi, in

68. For the social context of mummification, see Thompson's illuminating study in *Memphis under the Ptolemies*, pp. 155–89.

69. Letters to the dead are discussed below; they appear to have been written quite soon after death. Tombs were often built over—or sometimes usurped by other people—fairly quickly after construction and first use. Evidence for long-running cults is strongest for kings and in cases of deification.

70. It has been suggested that the principal inscribed object in many tombs and other monuments, the stela, was invariably dedicated to the cult of the deceased and showed a statue of him: Alan R. Schulman, "Some Observations on the $3\underline{h}$ $\overline{i}kr$ n R^c-Stelae," *Bibliotheca Orientalis* 43 (1986): 302–48, esp. 306–18; see also Friedman, *JEA* 71 (1985): 89, for a similar argument in relation to figures of the deceased in tomb relief. These interpretations are restrictive and oversimplify complex artistic practice and symbolic expression, but if they were correct, the mortuary cult would completely dominate the archaeological record.

which people visited tombs, commemorated their dead, and had meals with them, has a close parallel in modern Egypt.[71]

Although the dead were a potent moral presence for the living and the prospect of death was crucial for the individual, morality should have coherence within this life. Some New Kingdom texts doubt the value of provision for the next life, saying "There is no one who has come back from there"—an obvious insight that is unlikely to have been absent in earlier times.[72] These texts conclude from the uncertainty of destinies in the next life that this life should be enjoyed, an attitude found also in other periods and contexts.[73] The fact that this attitude, which contrasts so strongly with more "conventional" Egyptian views, is found in tomb inscriptions underlines death's potential for keeping people in line. What appears in these texts to be a debate about hedonism concerns on another level the value of quietism and fatalism. The moral significance of questioning the importance of the next life lies in an implied affirmation that one should engage actively in this life.

Within this life, direct participation in the official cult could come at any time during adulthood. Relatively few participated, however, and the purpose of the cult was not private devotion. Public festivals—listed in offering formulas from the early Fourth Dynasty onward[74]—were the chief occasions when ordinary people could come close to the gods and perhaps present to them their own concerns. At festivals the gods were carried out of the temples, almost all of them enclosed in shrines placed on portable barques. The audience could know that the gods were there

71. Erhart Graefe, "Talfest," *LÄ* 6:187–89; Silvia Wiebach, "Die Begegnung von Lebenden und Verstorbenen im Rahmen des thebanischen Talfestes," *SAK* 13 (1986): 263–91. For the modern parallels, see Winifred S. Blackman, *The Fellāḥīn of Upper Egypt* (London: Harrap, 1927), pp. 117–20 (weekly Muslim ritual), 263–67 (annual Christian ritual). For comparable practices in the Roman world, see Hopkins, *Death and Renewal* [n. 25], pp. 201–56.

72. See Jan Assmann, "Fest des Augenblicks—Verheissung der Dauer: Die Kontroverse der ägyptischen Harfnerlieder," in *Fragen an die altägyptische Literatur: Studien zum Gedenken an Eberhard Otto*, ed. Assmann et al. (Wiesbaden: Reichert, 1977), pp. 55–84. For "There is no one . . . ," see Michael V. Fox, *The Song of Songs and the Ancient Egyptian Love Songs* (Madison and London: University of Wisconsin Press, 1985), pp. 346, 379 (ll. 6, 8). A few discreet Middle Kingdom forerunners are known, e.g., Kurt Sethe, *Ägyptische Lesestücke zum Gebrauch im akademischen Unterricht*, 2d ed. (Leipzig: Hinrichs, 1928), no. 27. Overt expression of skepticism is, however, largely absent.

73. E.g., Hermann Kees, "Die Lebensgrundsätze eines Amonspriesters der 22. Dynastie," *ZÄS* 74 (1938): 73–87; see also *AEL* 3:18–24. Similar sentiments are common in biographies of the period.

74. Günther Lapp, *Die Opferformel des Alten Reiches unter Berücksichtigung einiger späterer Formen*, SDAIK 21 (1986), pp. 108–10, with references.

but could not see them. Even to attend some festivals was a privilege to which people aspired in perpetuity.[75]

During festivals or, for the more privileged, during rituals within temples, the god might display a wish, favor, or decision relating to a particular person. This action could be in response to a question, or it could be spontaneous. If provoked by the worshiper, such episodes constitute oracles; if not, they are blessings by the god. Since possibilities for human-divine interaction were limited, even an adverse experience caused by a god, whether outside or within the cult, could be a mark of favor because it was a mark of notice. Oracles are generally held to be New Kingdom innovations, but I see no good reason for this view and prefer to assume that they occurred in all periods.[76] An extension of these practices is seen in the presentation of a personal gift to the god by a worshiper who hoped to secure a benefit. Such gifts were private votive offerings. Evidence for votive offerings is, however, sparse and restricted to a few periods.

The scarcity of evidence for all these practices and spheres of action is a crucial problem for the interpreting of nonroyal religion. Possible explanations for this scarcity include special cultural reasons for the lack of material; the transference of some this-worldly preoccupations from what we might expect to be their focus to other realms, especially that of the dead; and the existence of a great diversity of religious actions, among which interaction with the gods was only one element. Lastly, the pervasive effects of decorum complicate the record in ways that are difficult to assess.

The first two of these possibilities are closely related and can be linked to the character of elite biographies, which supply the only evidence for the attitudes of the nonroyal and nonelite toward participation in religious cult. The royal and semisecular concerns presented by the elite in their descriptions of this life overrode private interests, which in any

75. A prime function of Middle Kingdom Abydos stelae (discussed below) is to obtain this privilege.

76. See Baines, *JEA* 73 (1987): 88–93; Malte Römer, "Ist der Text auf den Blöcken 222/35/184 der Chapelle Rouge ein Zeugnis für eine neue 'Dimension erfährbarer Gottesnähe' (Assmann)?" *Göttinger Miszellen* 99 (1987): 31–34. Jean Leclant, "Éléments pour une étude de la divination dans l'Égypte pharaonique," in *La divination*, Rites et Pratiques Religieuses, ed. André Caquot and Marcel Leibovici (Paris: Presses Universitaires de France, 1968), 1:9, allows for the possibility that the absence of good earlier evidence for oracles is due to the nature of the sources.

case might not have been appropriate for public expression. People's religious aspirations could perhaps be expressed more suitably in relation to the indefinite future of death, for which no secular and biographical aspirations were possible. There are therefore good reasons for connecting the formulation of conceptions of the next world, and people's hopes that they might associate with the gods there, with unspoken or displaced ideas that they held about this world. Although the moral continuity of life and death was not closely connected with temple and cult, the two spheres showed comparable basic concerns, including that for maintaining the fragile created order and community of beings. Seemingly disparate religious actions and responses might thus have similar foci. The wide range of religious practices, which is paralleled in many religions, lessened the centrality of any one practice. Involvement in the official temple cult, for example, need not have been of crucial importance to more than a small minority. A certain number of people participated in the cult as priests, serving one month in four, but before the Late Period the overall proportion involved was probably still small.

The diversity of religious action implies that people's normal religious lives could be conducted away from religious centers. "Irregular" action not related to the official cult and responding to the circumstances of individuals or groups would be more important to people than regular action. It would take place in a private context, among small social groups. Hardly any sources come from such contexts. Thus irregular action may well have been common to all, including the king, but it is largely absent from the public record.

Anxieties, like aspirations, might be displaced onto the next life. Mortuary texts such as the Pyramid and Coffin texts (figs. 1, 30, 52) and the Book of the Dead (figs. 31, 32) present both people's fears and the power of the forces of disorder.[77] These texts were less restricted in content than offering formulas displayed in the public parts of their tombs, partly, no doubt, because they were inscribed in concealed places and served the deceased's destiny in the next life more directly than did the public areas. In mortuary texts the chief response to danger was the use of magic.[78] Other possible modes of action, or justifications for action,

---

77. There are various translations of all three collections; e.g., by Thomas George Allen and R. O. Faulkner into English, Paul Barguet into French, Kurt Sethe and Erik Hornung into German. Several are cited in the Selected Bibliography, the notes to chap. 2, and nn. 113, 116–117 below.

78. Compare Siegfried Morenz, *Gott und Mensch im alten Ägypten*, 2d ed. (Darmstadt: Wissenschaftliche Buchgesellschaft, 1984), pp. 177–87.

are ethical and legal. People might attain the next life by leading a good life on earth. The fullest realization of this conception involves an ethical judgment after death. The date of origin of this idea is disputed and can hardly be resolved on available evidence.[79] Old Kingdom sources are compatible with belief in a judgment, and some details in them are most easily interpreted on the assumption that the idea already existed.[80] Belief in a judgment might therefore have been integral to religion in all accessible periods, and this is the interpretation I prefer. The text that enacts the deceased's successful passage through the judgment, chapter 125 of the Book of the Dead (fig. 32), is not attested before the Eighteenth Dynasty, but there is evidence that some of its underlying ideas may be considerably older.[81]

The judgment was a moral force affecting the individual in this life and in the transition to the next life, but there could also be moral relations between the dead and the living. Tomb inscriptions state that should the dead be wronged, for example by this-worldly assailants who vandalized tombs, the deceased would harm those who had attacked them or would bring a legal case against them.[82] Should the dead win the case (they implied that they always would), the assailant would suffer hideously, either in this life or when attempting the transition to the next. Texts describing sanctions against desecrators and vandals assimilate their treatment to that of sacrificial animals identified with the protagonists of chaos. Some vandals may have been punished in such a

79. For an early date, see, e.g., Siegfried Morenz, "Die Heraufkunft des transzendenten Gottes in Ägypten," in his *Religion und Geschichte des alten Ägypten: Gesammelte Aufsätze*, ed. Elke Blumenthal et al. (Weimar: Hermann Böhlaus Nachfolger, 1975), pp. 86–88. The later date of the First Intermediate Period was proposed by, e.g., Joachim Spiegel, *Die Idee vom Totengericht in der ägyptischen Religion*, Leipziger Ägyptologische Studien 2 (Glückstadt and Hamburg: Augustin, n.d.), pp. 14–15. Neither author presents strong arguments for his view, but the evidence is very sparse. See further Reinhard Grieshammer, *Das Jenseitsgericht in den Sargtexten*, ÄgAbh 20 (1970), esp. pp. 1–2; note, however, that some crucial texts cited there in support of an early date are now generally placed later. What is certain is that allusions to litigation in the hereafter, as opposed to ethical judgment, are common in all mortuary texts.

80. See Baines, *JEA* 73 (1987): 81 with n. 8.

81. See Jean Yoyotte, "Le jugement des morts dans l'Égypte ancienne," in *Le jugement des morts*, Sources Orientales 4 (Paris: Seuil, 1961), pp. 15–80.

82. See Edel, *Mitteilungen des Deutschen Instituts für Ägyptische Altertumskunde in Kairo* 13 (1944): 9–12 (judgment); 12–15 (threats against the violator's person, posterity, and estate). For legal aspects of relations between the dead and the living, see also Hellmut Brunner, "Das rechtliche Fortleben des Toten bei den Ägyptern," *Archiv für Orientforschung* 18 (1957): 52–61; rpt. in Brunner, *Das hörende Herz: Kleine Schriften zur Religions- und Geistesgeschichte Ägyptens*, ed. Wolfgang Röllig, OBO 80 (1988), pp. 299–308.

way, but the prevalence of vandalism and tomb robbery makes plain that these sanctions were largely ineffective. They may have been more important as assertions and gestures than for their direct effect, and it is difficult to see who would have enforced them.[83]

Such claims were pronounced from the point of view of the deceased, who were protecting their rightful interests. The living believed that there were malicious dead people who could haunt them and bring about any number of woes that might seem to the outsider to have natural causes.[84] If a hyena attacked one's animals, a dead person's spirit might be behind it. To put the matter in an outsider's terms, the spirit was invoked both to explain why a particular person had suffered a random loss and on occasions when people experienced direct relations with the dead. Whereas the dead claimed never to be the initial aggressors in cases of disturbance, the living might blame the dead. People do not readily admit that they are themselves to blame.

In order to forestall losses and afflictions at the hands of the dead, people needed to propitiate their spirits with offerings and do nothing to offend them. The identity of the dead spirits is not always clear. Texts describing the damage they caused speak in general terms and do not refer to a small, identifiable group, such as close relatives. Some texts list the "spirits" separately from the "dead," but in these cases the latter are probably the category of the damned in the next world, who were subject to eternal torture and might in turn prey on others like demons. In

83. See Willems, *JEA* 76 (1990): 27–54. This important study, which I have been privileged to read before publication, assembles impressive evidence for ritual killing of people, but only three of the cases cited—the inscription of Senwosret I at Tod, a human sacrifice associated with the execration of enemies at Mirgissa, and events described in the Chronicle of Prince Osorkon—seem to have been enacted. The alternative view, that the issues would be fought in the next world, remains possible, as does the point that afflictions and misfortunes linked this world and the next and could take any form, for which the actions described in the threats would be metaphors or aspirations of the deceased. The brutal nature of the threats is striking testimony to the violence of ancient society and to the sanctions to which it aspired in maintaining the social and cosmic order. See further Anthony Leahy, "Death by Fire in Ancient Egypt," *Journal of the Economic and Social History of the Orient* 27 (1984): 199–206.

84. Georges Posener, "Les '*afarit* dans l'ancienne Égypte," *MDAIK* 37 (1981): 393–401. See also Posener, "Les empreintes magiques de Gizeh et les morts dangereux," *MDAIK* 16 (1958): 252–70, and "Les criminels débaptisés et les morts sans noms," *RdÉ* 5 (1946): 51–56; Yvan Koenig, "Un revenant inconvenant? (Papyrus Deir el-Medineh 37)," *BIFAO* 79 (1979): 103–19. These beliefs are similar to Western beliefs about ghosts, but, because of their relation with the mortuary cult, the Egyptian spirits of the dead have a more significant role. For a superb brief survey of attitudes toward the dead and their spirits, most of them negative, see Posener, "Découverte de l'ancienne Égypte," *Bulletin de la Société Française d'Égyptologie* 112 (1988): 11–18 (no references to sources).

some cases, the dead who were the objects of magical rituals of execration were enemies of the state who were identified by name, including
historically specifiable people who could have conspired to take power
in the country.[85]

Apart from being placated with offerings, the dead could be sent
informative communications or requests, which could be either written
or spoken; in the latter case, no archaeological trace would be left.
Urgent needs could require recourse to the dead outside the set times
when the living went to care for them and to be with them. The most
eloquent text recording such an episode—so eloquent that it has been
suspected of being a work of fiction—comes from Ramesside
Memphis.[86] A widowed husband writes to his wife, who seems to be
about two years dead, about how he cared for her during life and how
he has stayed faithful to her after her death. It is not right that she
should continue to oppress him—in ways he does not specify. He says
twice that he will be judged with her, implying some presiding agency
in the hereafter, but not necessarily the ethical judgment after death.
This judgment could take place while he was still alive or after his death.
It is impossible to tell from the text whether one or both of these possibilities is being referred to.

In a different situation, a request could be made for the dead to assist
the living. Someone who was troubled by affairs in this world and had
no powerfully connected person to turn to for help might appeal to dead
relatives. The finest illustration of this practice and of its wider social
context is in a pair of unrelated Old Kingdom documents dealing with
closely similar cases. One case operates through the largely secular, this-
worldly agency of the courts, while the other involves an appeal to the
spirit of the dead head of a family.

The first document is a papyrus recording a judgment in an inheritance dispute. A man who claims guardianship over the estate and
children of a dead man is opposed by the deceased's son. The son
asserts that the supporting document produced by the claimant is a
forgery.[87] The court decides that if the claimant can produce three reli-
able witnesses to the event recorded in that document, he will have

85. See Georges Posener, *Cinq figurines d'envoûtement*, BdÉ 101 (1987), pp. 55–56.

86. Alan H. Gardiner and Kurt Sethe, *Egyptian Letters to the Dead, Mainly from the Old
and Middle Kingdoms* (London: Egypt Exploration Society, 1928), no. 6; Max Guilmot, "Let-
tre à une épouse défunte (Pap. Leiden I. 371)," *ZÄS* 99 (1973): 94–103.

87. Kurt Sethe, "Ein Prozessurteil aus dem alten Reich," *ZÄS* 61 (1926): 67–79.

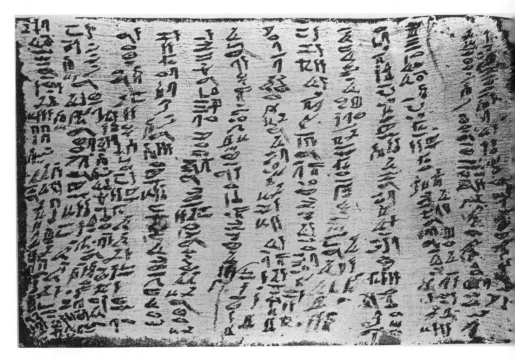

58. Old Kingdom letter from a widow and her son to her deceased husband, written on linen. Egyptian Museum, Cairo, JE 25975. Rephotographed by permission of the Egypt Exploration Society from Alan H. Gardiner and Kurt Sethe, *Egyptian Letters to the Dead, Mainly from the Old and Middle Kingdoms* (London: Egypt Exploration Society, 1928), pl. 1.

won; otherwise, the son should have the management of his father's estate. Except perhaps for an interesting distrust of written documents as evidence, the whole proceeding has many parallels in the modern world.

The second document is a letter written on linen and addressed to the deceased head of a family by his widow and son (fig. 58).[88] Relatives have come and have removed property and servants or slaves from the deceased's house. The widow is especially aggrieved and says that she would rather that she or her son died (it is not quite clear whom she means) than that she should see the son subordinated to the son of the rival woman. At the beginning of the letter, the widow and son cajole the deceased by recalling an occasion when on his deathbed he spoke

88. Gardiner and Sethe, *Letters to the Dead*, no. 1; Battiscombe Gunn, review of *Letters to the Dead* in *JEA* 16 (1930): 148–50; Roccati, *Littérature historique* [n. 47], pp. 295–97.

out against the other side in the case. At the end of the letter they make a similar appeal by quoting aphorisms the deceased pronounced on the importance of inheritance and of solidarity between generations. Both he and his father (who was also perhaps the grandfather of the widow's opponents) are called upon literally to bestir themselves in support of the widow's case. Since the inheritance was not yet settled, the woman's husband must have been fairly recently dead. Perhaps she approached him after failing to get satisfaction in court, or perhaps she thought that her case would not succeed there. The text says nothing of either possibility, but it should not be expected to do so, because such an admission might make her appeal less persuasive to her deceased husband. The gods were not omniscient, and there is no reason to suppose that the dead were either.[89] The fact that the letter was written on linen suggests that, like other such letters, it accompanied an offering. The offering might have helped to make the deceased well disposed toward the petition, or it could have ensured that the letter, which would have formed the wrapping for the offering, would be read as it was removed.

Both these Old Kingdom inheritance disputes took place in the context of extended family groups whose heads may have wielded considerable authority, which could endure in the tomb. Such a social setting was probably widespread. The Heqanakhte letters, a group of early Middle Kingdom private documents, have a revealingly similar social background of an extended family group.[90] Letters to the dead are rare—fewer than twenty are known from a period of about a thousand years—but there is no reason why people should normally have approached the dead in writing rather than addressing them orally. A corresponding oral practice could have been common.

Letters to the dead would have been addressed only to those who could help the writers, or who might be afflicting them. These restrictions might still leave a number of possible recipients. In addition, those who had no one of their own to whom they might turn could have approached a more prominent person who might act as an intermediary in the world of the dead. Although there is no definite evidence for such a practice, there are indications that a closer intermediary among the dead might have been used to transmit a letter to a more remote deceased person.[91]

89. The gods lacked infinite capacity in general; see Hornung, *Conceptions of God,* passim.

90. See James, *Heḳanakhte Papers* [n. 32].

91. See Gardiner and Sethe, *Letters to the Dead,* p. 12.

59. Stela of Ameny and family (Twelfth Dynasty), from Abydos. Ashmolean Museum, Oxford, QL1111. Photo courtesy of the Visitors of the Ashmolean Museum.

Social groups similar to the families in the letters to the dead are prominent in the decoration of thousands of private stelae set up in the Middle Kingdom, in cenotaphs and tombs of varying sizes around the temple of Osiris at Abydos.[92] These stelae were intended to enable everlasting participation in the festivals of Osiris, but functioned also as

92. William Kelly Simpson, *The Terrace of the Great God at Abydos: The Offering Chapels of Dynasties 12 and 13*, Publications of the Pennsylvania-Yale Expedition to Egypt 5 (New Haven: Peabody Museum of Natural History; Philadelphia: University Museum, 1974); David O'Connor, "The 'Cenotaphs' of the Middle Kingdom at Abydos," in *Mélanges Gamal Eddin Mokhtar* 2, BdÉ 97/2 (1985), pp. 161–77.

60. Stela of Dedusobek (Twelfth Dynasty), from Abydos. Ashmolean Museum, Oxford, 1922.143. Photo courtesy of the Visitors of the Ashmolean Museum.

family monuments (figs. 59, 60). Many stelae form pairs or groups of up to fifteen, providing memorials for numerous people associated by kinship or by profession with the principal owner in a group. Abydos was both a regional center for the cult of Osiris and a place where members of the elite who were a little below the highest status could have a memorial.[93] The stelae display features I have posited for lower social groups of the Old and Middle kingdoms: broad religious par-

93. Jean Yoyotte, "Les pèlerinages dans l'Égypte ancienne," in *Les pèlerinages*, Sources Orientales 3 (Paris: Seuil, 1960), pp. 17–74. Yoyotte argues against the application of the term "pilgrimage," with its more recent associations, to ancient Egypt, but, despite the cogent points he makes, there is some evidence against his position. For people at Abydos from Athribis in the Delta, far from the Abydos region, see Helmut Satzinger, "Eine Familie aus dem Athribis des späten Mittleren Reiches," *SAK* 13 (1986): 171–80. For the social groups, see Detlef Franke, *Personendaten aus dem Mittleren Reich (20.–16. Jahrhundert v. Chr.): Dossiers 1–796*, ÄgAbh 41 (1984).

ticipation only at festivals, and the connection between local religious activity and the family. The extreme case of the group of fifteen stelae offers a parallel for the very large groups implied by some Old Kingdom elite tomb complexes. In both contexts, the family group of the chief person commemorated is not so prominently displayed on his monument as are the families on monuments of less prominent people. Presumably the chief person's status and interests were focused more on service to the king than on the family.

The cenotaphs and stelae of Abydos seem to project the ideals of the elite family and of group solidarity past the threshold of death into the next life. There was hardly any presentation on the monuments of the group's religious practices or of its concerns in this life. Thus, these stelae and their architectural context have implications for their owners' personal biographies, cult participation, and tomb decoration, as well as the world of the dead which they aspired to inhabit.

A forum of religious expression that appears to be more narrowly elitist than the stelae of Abydos is found from the Old and Middle kingdoms into later times. A few prominent individuals continued to receive cults past the normal duration of such observances (a generation or so) and became deified to a limited extent.[94] They moved from being ancestors or eminent people whom living people of lesser status might address to being minor gods. Among them were some kings, although in this context a king had scarcely more claim on posterity's attention than anyone else. The best analogy for the cults of the deified dead is the social sphere of the owners of large elite tombs and their subordinates. Some of the cults grew up around such tombs. The adherents to these cults who left monuments were either minor officials, of a rank that the owner of a large tomb might have depicted among his tomb reliefs, or people of slightly higher status. Some of these adherents constructed smaller tombs close to those of their "heroes."

The cults of the deified dead could last for centuries. Some of those worshiped were culture heroes. The extreme case of duration and importance in a continuous tradition is the cult of Heqaib of Aswan, a late Old Kingdom official who was worshiped in the Middle Kingdom by members of the local elite, and by kings.[95] In the course of a very long period, the cults passed over into antiquarianism. In Late Period Memphis they formed part of a commemoration of Egypt's past in which

94. Baines, *JEA* 73 (1987): 87–88 with references.
95. Labib Habachi, *Elephantine IV: The Sanctuary of Heqaib*, 2 vols., AVDAIK 33 (1985). The texts from the site are being studied by Detlef Franke.

both culture heroes and early kings were worshiped.[96] Contemporaries can have had little direct knowledge about either of these groups of remote figures. Some of the royal names could have been taken from lists.

The most important question here is how the cults of the deified dead originated. A good hypothesis would be that the recipients of the cults were dead people who over time acquired a reputation for giving effective help when the living approached them with requests. Such cults could be compared in some respects with the letters to the dead. They seem to have served a rather higher social group than the letters, although the people who approached the deified person could have been socially more diverse than the archaeological evidence suggests. Adherents of lower status might not have left monuments around the cult place. Although those who did not have an intermediary of their own to whom they could turn might have been helped by the deified, there is little evidence for such a possibility. It is better to see these cults not as being in any sense popular but as prolonging into the next life the elite professional and institutional sphere of this life. Subsequently the cults would have achieved some measure of autonomy. In the Heqaib sanctuary at Aswan were family cult places for later high officials, extending group cohesion into the next world and relating that cohesion to a major cult that could have begun in similar fashion.

Some cults of the deified dead also acquired a public association with ethics. Three deified Old Kingdom notables, Hardjedef, Ptahhotep, and Kagemni, later had instruction texts ascribed to them. These three texts, especially The Instruction of Ptahhotep, are fundamental sources for Egyptian ethics.[97] The Third Dynasty culture hero Imhotep was also revered as a sage, but no extant text is ascribed to him, and there probably never was one.[98] In the Late Period he was widely worshiped as a god, partly in association with the antiquarianism of Memphis.[99]

---

96. See Eberhard Otto, "Zwei Bemerkungen zum Königskult der Spätzeit," *MDAIK* 15 (1957): 193–207; Dietrich Wildung, *Egyptian Saints: Deification in Pharaonic Egypt*, Hagop Kevorkian Series on Near Eastern Art and Civilization (New York: New York University Press, 1977).

97. Zbyněk Žába, *Les maximes de Ptaḥḥotep*, Československá Akademie Věd, Sekcě jazyka a literatury (Prague: Československé Akademie Věd, 1956); Gerhard Fecht, *Der Habgierige und die Maat in der Lehre des Ptahhotep (5. und 19. Maxime)*, ADAIK 1 (1958); *AEL* 1:61–80.

98. For a contrary view, see Hellmut Brunner, "Zitate aus Lebenslehren," in *Studien zu altägyptischen Lebenslehren*, ed. Erik Hornung and Othmar Keel, OBO 28 (1979), pp. 111–12, who affirms that such a text certainly existed, but without specific supporting argument.

99. See n. 96 above; Dietrich Wildung, *Imhotep und Amenhotep: Gottwerdung im alten Ägypten*, MÄS 36 (Munich and Berlin: Deutscher Kunstverlag, 1977); Thompson, *Memphis under the Ptolemies*, pp. 24–25, 209–11.

These instruction texts probably date to the Middle Kingdom, when numerous literary texts of other types were written.[100] The Instruction of Ptahhotep, in particular, fuses religion, morality, and general conduct: the god is present even in table manners.[101] In a broad sense, the sentiments of these texts are timeless, and the date of composition says little about the date of origin of their ideas, which have many parallels in Old Kingdom biographies. Society's chief protagonist, the king, seems not to have recorded such ideas in public until the Middle Kingdom, because royal inscriptions comparable with private biographies are not attested from earlier periods and were probably not composed in written form. The first such texts are very roughly contemporary with the literary royal Instruction for Merikare and Instruction of Amenemhat, which present kings as advising their successors.[102]

The fictitious royal authors of these instructions expound general moral principles, which they shared with the elite, of caring for people and promoting the public good, but they also emphasize the social and moral isolation of their role, into which they thus incorporated some of the cosmic implications of cult and mythology. The king was educated with members of the elite, whom he should not later kill, perhaps in recognition of this solidarity (Merikare, ll. 50–51; compare 139–40). But men who acquired large factions or became as wealthy as the king should be killed or driven into exile (ll. 23–27).

The ethical ambivalence of these texts is masked by their literary framing. The Instruction of Amenemhat seems to ascribe the king's alienation to the special circumstances of his having been murdered, while Merikare ends by glorifying the creator's role in founding the world, thereby moving onto a higher plane and dissimulating the harsh implications of what is said earlier in the text.[103] The ambivalence remains important, however, because it distances the king from humanity and

100. For arguments on dating, see *AEL* 1:5–10; Baines, in *Pyramid Studies,* ed. Baines et al., pp. 130–33, with references.

101. Maxim 7; *AEL* 1:65.

102. For Merikare, see works cited in n. 9 above. For Amenemhat, see Wolfgang Helck, *Der Text der "Lehre Amenemhets I. für seinen Sohn,"* Kleine Ägyptische Texte (Wiesbaden: Harrassowitz, 1969; many additional manuscripts); see also John L. Foster, "The Conclusion to *The Testament of Ammenemes, King of Egypt,*" *JEA* 67 (1981): 36–47; Hans Goedicke, *Studies in "The Instructions of King Amenemhet I for His Son,"* 2 vols., Varia Aegyptiaca, suppl. 2, fasc. 1–2 (San Antonio: Van Siclen, 1988); trans.: *AEL* 1:135–39.

103. Amenemhat: *AEL* 1:137; the king mentions an attack and speaks as if from the grave, but he does not indicate the precise circumstances of the conspiracy against him; Merikare: ll. 123–38, *AEL* 1:105–6.

gives some sanction for his bleaker, more pragmatic morality. This morality complements a generally somber attitude that would give any individual king scope to intervene beneficently on behalf of people against a background of anticipated harsher actions.

These instruction texts cannot report fully on royal morality and on the king's presentation of his role to the elite and the rest of the people. They are, however, suggestive in giving a diverse and complex range of possibilities for royal action.[104] Moral "double standards" would allow the ruler to break "human" rules while remaining largely accountable in human terms. This accountability of the king contrasts with his status as some sort of "god."[105] In view of the many constraints on his role, the king's freedom of action could have been less than one might expect, and he would have had a political interest in retaining as much freedom as possible. On another level, the presentation of his divine pretensions in temples and the depiction of his ruthless crushing of foreigners and enemies speak a different language. It would be inappropriate to look for consistency here. Different conventions applied in different contexts and for different audiences. In modern analyses, sources from diverse contexts are often set side by side, and scholars tend to read them too literally. Hardly any ruler's actions and posturings would make a good showing when viewed in this manner.

MORALITY AND THEODICY

I have moved quickly from legal and practical difficulties of ordinary people to moral concerns of the king and how they relate to his role in maintaining the cosmos. Because the ancient evidence is so limited, these domains may seem to us more closely connected than they appeared to be in antiquity, but the parallels among them say two important things about the moral constitution of complex societies. On the

---

104. Royal inscriptions of the early Twelfth Dynasty seem also to have been diverse and complex in expression. For references, see John Baines, "The Stela of Khusobek: Private and Royal Military Narrative and Values," in *Form und Mass: Beiträge zur Literatur, Sprache und Kunst des alten Ägypten: Festschrift für Gerhard Fecht zum 65. Geburtstag am 6. Februar 1987,* ed. Jürgen Osing and Günter Dreyer, Ägypten und Altes Testament 12 (Wiesbaden: Harrassowitz, 1987), pp. 57–59. Although the royal instruction texts must have had royal approval to be disseminated, their presentation should not be assimilated completely with the inscriptions. They are works of literature that were probably not composed by kings.

105. E.g., Hornung, *Conceptions of God,* pp. 135–42.

one hand, a consensus reinforces the cohesion of society as a moral system, whose members share basic concerns to a greater or lesser extent. On the other hand, morality is also about inequality. It responds to and lessens inequality, but it also legitimizes it. A small society can sustain minor inequality in an essentially egalitarian context. Egypt was a highly unequal society, and the position of elite and king was the more strongly dependent on moral legitimation. But such an argument from morality addresses only one aspect of the social order. Elites also maintain themselves through control of political power and coercive force.

In Egypt, official religious practice reinforced the elite's position in society more or less without qualification, but natural morality highlighted inequality. In addition, natural morality separated elite and people from the king, creating overlapping allegiances that helped to bond groups that otherwise had diverging interests—king and elite, elite and the rest. This ambiguity is emphasized on early elite monuments by the absence of royal and, especially, divine motifs such as images of gods. The elite give the appearance of having been nearly as much deprived of central religious symbols as their social inferiors.[106] This is unlikely to have been the true state of affairs, but the appearance may have been valuable for the king, because it reinforced his uniqueness and divinity, and hence legitimized his grosser exactions for his projects. At the time when these rules and conventions for royal and elite monuments were formulated, royal exploitation was on a grander scale than it ever was later. In the First Dynasty retainers were killed so that they could accompany their lord in death, and a couple of centuries later many of the land's people and much of its economic resources were channeled into building the great pyramids.[107]

Ordinary people must have accepted the moralities presented by the king and the elite to some extent. Natural morality could, however, be taken to its ultimate consequences, and it could be asked how such an unequal system was created in the first place. This question is potentially subversive of a society's moral consensus and is not likely to have been raised prominently, but Egyptians did ask it. It is closely related to the still broader problem addressed in theodicy: in a world created by a benevolent deity, what is the source of evil?

106. See Baines, in *State and Society,* ed. Bender et al. [n. 24].

107. For subsidiary burials in early dynastic royal tombs and other installations, see, e.g., Werner Kaiser, "Ein Kultbezirk des Königs Den in Sakkara," *MDAIK* 41 (1985): 52–54, with references.

In any culture, conceptions of evil are bound together with other aspects of the world view. In Egypt, the notion of evil overlapped to a great extent with that of disorder.[108] The fusion of these two ideas would have served the interests of the ruling group by associating publicly sanctioned morality and social subservience with the preservation of the cosmic order. This fusion was also valuable because it integrated "historical" action, principally that of the king, with the general moral order.[109] Such a cosmic superstructure for morality is unlikely to be found in a plural society with divergent and conflicting ideologies. The fusion would hardly benefit the ordinary afflicted person, whose private problems would be too trivial to disturb the cosmic scheme and would therefore not warrant special attention. So far as possible, such minor disorder would always be suppressed or ignored. The heightened commitment to order in Egypt may have reduced the questioning of the composition of society and discouraged the raising of the problem of theodicy, but such issues cannot be banished completely. They were probably raised in all periods, although evidence for them is rare.

The relation between inequality and theodicy is stated explicitly in a Middle Kingdom apologia of the creator god, who distances himself from human wrongdoing, saying: "I made every man like his fellow. I did not ordain that they do wrong (*izfet,* "disorder"). It was their desires that damaged what I had said" (his creative word that brought the world into being?).[110] The Instruction for Merikare takes a still harsher line toward humanity by implicating them in the origin of imperfection in the world. After the creator had brought the cosmos into being and had organized it to suit them, they were nearly destroyed because of their wrongdoing.[111] The creator is not responsible for the origin of evil. He cares so much for people's well-being that "he has built himself a shrine around them; when they weep, he hears" (l. 135). This image of tears relates to the origin of human beings. A wordplay found in the creator's apologia and in other sources says that people arose from the creator's

108. See Reinhard Grieshammer, "Gott und das Negative nach Quellen der ägyptischen Spätzeit," in *Aspekte der spätägyptischen Religion,* ed. Wolfhart Westendorf, Göttinger Orientforschungen, 4th ser.: Ägypten 9 (Wiesbaden: Harrassowitz, 1979), pp. 79–92. See also, in general, David Parkin, ed., *The Anthropology of Evil* (Oxford: Basil Blackwell, 1985).

109. For this conception of history, see Erik Hornung, "Geschichte als Fest," in his *Geist der Pharaonenzeit,* pp. 147–63.

110. Adriaan de Buck, *The Egyptian Coffin Texts,* vol. 7, Oriental Institute Publications 87 (Chicago: University of Chicago Press, 1961), p. 464a–b. Compare the translations of Lesko in chap. 2, p. 101; Lichtheim, *AEL* 1:131–33; Lichtheim's rendering is freer than mine.

111. See references in n. 9 above.

tears—an indirect statement that they are born to suffer.[112] An important idea behind all these statements is that of free will or freedom, for
neither of which the Egyptian language had a single word. People's
freedom to act led to wrongdoing, yet freedom to "follow the heart"
(which also means to have a good time) was a positive value. The
"heart," however, might not follow the wishes of its owner, who might
then fail to control his own actions.[113]

Other texts take a different approach, and place less of the blame for
evil on humanity. The Admonitions of Ipuwer reprove the creator for
present failings in the world, which is going through a catastrophe. The
Dispute of a Man with His *Ba* decries the value of present life, which is
undergoing a social breakdown; in comparison, the next life will be a
sweet release.[114] But even these fragmentary and difficult texts ultimately
bypass the problem of theodicy or affirm the creator's lack of responsibility for evil. These elite literary compositions offer an alternative to the
normal public equation of disorder and evil, in which evil is placed
outside the cosmos. Instead of clear-cut moral certainty, they present
a complex picture in which good and evil blend inextricably. In so doing,
these fictional texts may be nearer to the realities of human experience
than the monumental sources, and they may crystallize widespread
beliefs. But people often prefer moral certainties to complex visions, in
part because of the pragmatic advantages I have mentioned. The linking
of evil and disorder is much more widely attested than their separation.

MAGIC AND DIVINATION

This discussion may seem too abstract and "reasonable" to say
something useful about a society that had hundreds of gods and ex-

112. De Buck, *Egyptian Coffin Texts*, 7:465a. See also Hornung, *Conceptions of God*, pp.
149–50.

113. "Following the heart" is prominent especially in late texts. For a collection of
material (with problematic interpretation), see David Lorton, "The Expression Šms-ỉb,"
JARCE 7 (1968): 41–54, and "A Note on the Expression Šms-ỉb," *JARCE* 8 (1969–70): 55–57.
The imagery of the heart as the seat of freedom is ambivalent in Book of the Dead, chap.
30A, where the heart is enjoined in the hereafter not to betray any guilt of its owner; see,
e.g., Raymond O. Faulkner, *The Ancient Egyptian Book of the Dead*, rev. ed., ed. Carol
Andrews (London: British Museum Publications, 1985), p. 55. See also Baines, *JEA* 68
(1982): 41n.

114. Admonitions: *AEL* 1:149–63; Gerhard Fecht, *Der Vorwurf an Gott in den "Mahnworten
des Ipu-wer,"* Abhandlungen der Heidelberger Akademie der Wissenschaften, Philosophisch-historische Klasse, 1972/1 (Heidelberg: Winter, 1972). Dispute: *AEL* 1:163–69; R. O.
Faulkner, "The Man Who Was Tired of Life," *JEA* 42 (1956): 21–40.

pended a great part of its resources on building temples, providing for the cult, and performing other religious actions (not that such actions are any more irrational than many features of modern society). Yet consideration of theodicy, worship of the gods, and materialistic methods of influencing events that people in some cultures would consider immune to such influence are complementary religious forms. For the Westerner, problems in comprehending the alien and the rationality of religious practices may be posed most acutely by magic.[115] Magic and rationality do not conflict: magic is rational, and its argumentation is often rationalistic. Magical spells and performances exploit many methods of inference and arguments from analogy that have strong logical coherence. These procedures and arguments differ from Western rationality less in their organization and formal properties than in their premises, which often assume different agents and modes of causation from those commonly accepted in the West.

Egyptian magic was a realm of legitimate action and a mode of understanding which, like conceptions of the cosmos, involved all of creation from the highest to the lowest. It was a force that had existed from the beginning and had been essential to the creation of the world. A Middle Kingdom text presents it as the adjunct of the creator god and older than all the gods, that is, as so central to creation that it could not have a temporal position within it.[116] The roughly contemporary Instruction for Merikare says that the creator gave magic to humanity "as a weapon to ward off what may happen." This last phrase may signify misfortune and capricious destiny, and also perhaps the forces of disorder (ll. 137–38).

Magic was a beneficial force, although it could be perverted for antisocial ends. It was widely used in all periods. It invoked the most elemental forces in creation and responded to the capricious elements that threatened the essential sense of order. The earliest attested magical texts are in the royal Pyramid Texts of the late Fifth and Sixth dynasties

115. For syntheses, see Serge Sauneron, "Le monde du magicien égyptien," in *Le monde du sorcier*, Sources Orientales 7 (Paris: Seuil, 1966), pp. 27–65; J. F. Borghouts, "Magie," *LÄ* 3:1137–51; less satisfactory, Wilfried Gutekunst, "Zauber(er) (-Mittel, -Praktiken, -Spruch)," *LÄ* 6:1320–55; see also Hornung, *Conceptions of God*, pp. 207–10. Exhibition catalogue with valuable introduction by László Kákosy, *La magia in Egitto ai tempi dei Faraoni*, Milan 1985 (Modena: Panini, 1985). A useful collection of studies is *La magia in Egitto ai tempi dei Faraoni*, ed. Alessandro Roccati and Alberto Siliotti, Atti convegno internazionale di studi, Milan, Oct. 29–31, 1985 (n.p.: Rassegna Internazionale di Cinematografia Archeologica; Arte e Natura Libri, 1987).

116. Adriaan de Buck, *The Egyptian Coffin Texts*, vol. 3, Oriental Institute Publications 64 (Chicago: University of Chicago Press, 1947), pp. 382–89; trans. in R. O. Faulkner, *The Ancient Egyptian Coffin Texts*, vol. 1, *Spells 1–354* (Warminster: Aris & Phillips, 1973), pp. 199–200.

(fig. 1). Many of these texts may look back to much older oral practice, and they were not all composed for the king.[117] They include numerous spells against snakebite. A contemporary text in nonroyal tombs is directed against crocodiles.[118] Snakes, scorpions, and crocodiles were the chief symbols of the untoward and of moral and divine retribution, such as might result from litigation with forces in the hereafter or from condemnation by a deity.[119] These creatures were named in threats directed at potential violators of tombs, who would be answerable to a god in the hereafter or attacked by the deceased's spirit.[120] There were also rites in the course of which crude figurines of enemies inscribed with lists of mostly foreign names were buried.[121] Some of the conceptions and practices underlying the figurines seem to be royal, but some figurines were found in private tombs, suggesting that they were used for private, perhaps mortuary, purposes.

By the Middle Kingdom, magical texts were included in collections of papyrus texts alongside hymns and other works of literature, of which the most important are the instruction texts mentioned above. One major group of such texts, excavated from a grave in Thebes, was buried with magical objects, including an ivory "wand" and a statuette of a woman with a grotesque mask and two serpents in her hands (fig. 61). It has been proposed that this tomb belonged to a "lector priest and chief."[122] Lector priests were literate members of the elite, but not of its core group. They were reputed to be the principal magicians, and their

117. The texts are translated in R. O. Faulkner, *The Ancient Egyptian Pyramid Texts* (Oxford: Clarendon, 1969). The dating of the texts is problematic, but in written form they must lie between the late Second or Third Dynasty (the earliest time when continuous texts were written) and the date of their inscription. They are not, however, homogeneous and are probably of widely varying dates. Oral forms, whether or not close in wording to later texts, could go back to a date as early as the social contexts in which they were embedded—the Early Dynastic Period or the Old Kingdom. See also Baines, in *Pyramid Studies*, ed. Baines et al., pp. 131–34.

118. J. F. Borghouts, *Ancient Egyptian Magical Texts*, NISABA: Religious Texts Translation Series 9 (Leiden: Brill, 1978), p. 83, no. 122.

119. Compare Chris Eyre, "Fate, Crocodiles and the Judgement of the Dead: Some Mythological Allusions in Egyptian Literature," *SAK* 4 (1976): 103–14.

120. See, e.g., Alexander Scharff, "Die Reliefs des Hausältesten Meni aus dem Alten Reich," *Mitteilungen des Deutschen Instituts für Ägyptische Altertumskunde in Kairo* 8 (1939): 32.

121. See Posener's works cited in nn. 84–85 above. These rites are known from later periods too. The skeleton of a mutilated victim was buried by a deposit of pottery inscribed with execration texts; the case is discussed by Willems, *JEA* 76 (1990): 27–54.

122. Alan H. Gardiner, *The Ramesseum Papyri* (Oxford: Oxford University Press for Griffith Institute, 1955), pp. 1–2; see also, e.g., Wolfgang Helck, "Papyri Ramesseum I," *LÄ* 4:726. For the reading of the title, see Jan Quaegebeur, "La designation *(P3-) ḥry-tp: Phri-tob*," in Osing and Dreyer, *Form und Mass* [n. 104], pp. 368–94.

61. Wooden statuette of a woman with a mask holding serpents in her hands (Thirteenth Dynasty), from a tomb beneath the Ramesseum at Thebes. The Manchester Museum, University of Manchester, England, 1790. Photo courtesy of The Manchester Museum, University of Manchester.

fabulous exploits were recounted in literary texts that used oral folktales as models. Despite the fabulous elements in these texts, they and other evidence point toward the part magic played in the rest of society. Whether the grave in Thebes belonged to a lector priest or not, the find demonstrates that magic was part of high culture. Much of the prestige of magic came from the exclusive access it gave people to special techniques, materials, or knowledge, and it was probably used more fully by the elite than by others. Magic also exploits the strange and exotic.[123]

Magic was a mode of causation invoked through observing the appropriate procedures. People mostly turned to it when normal agencies were ineffective, as in treating many illnesses or relieving the effects of snakebite. It was thus a more individualistic counterpart to such practices as communicating with the dead, and it often had more limited aims. Most people probably used magical techniques in some way or other every day—by wearing amulets, for example. Some statues of kings show an amulet as their principal body ornament.[124] Such everyday magic was prophylactic, an attempt to forestall the untoward, as the Instruction for Merikare expresses it.

In typical Egyptian fashion, the way in which magic was embedded in the established order could be exploited by the practitioner. He might threaten to destroy the present order of the world if the result he was seeking to achieve—usually a worthy one—did not come to pass. In making such a threat, he declared that he was acting in the person of some major deity. He was thus able to sidestep responsibility for the dire potential consequences of a spell's failure by claiming that the god and not he would have caused the cosmic destruction.[125]

Magical performances relied on a mixture of spells, rituals, and prescriptions. The prescriptions employed could include medically efficacious remedies. It is not meaningful to draw a sharp distinction between magic and medicine. Rather, the two are poles on a continuum of approaches to helping the afflicted and bringing about what one desired to happen. Both magic and medicine used exotic and complicated techniques to counter illnesses and afflictions, and their procedures and remedies overlapped to a great extent. For those who could

123. Exotic elements are well known in much ancient and more recent magic. For an example in Egypt, see Yvan Koenig, "La Nubie dans les textes magiques: 'L'inquiétante étrangeté,'" *RdÉ* 38 (1987): 105–10. For the Greco-Roman Period, see works cited in n. 21 above.

124. Common on Middle Kingdom royal statues; see Hans Gerhard Evers, *Staat aus dem Stein: Denkmäler, Geschichte und Bedeutung der ägyptischen Plastik während des Mittleren Reichs* (Munich: Bruckmann, 1929), 1: pls. 36, 39, 69, 77, 81–85, 102, 143; 2:33, sec. 221.

125. See Sauneron, in *Le monde du sorcier* [n. 115], pp. 40–42, and "Aspects et sort d'un thème magique égyptien: Les menaces incluant les dieux," *Bulletin de la Société Française d'Égyptologie* 8 (1951): 11–21.

afford both, the two approaches could complement each other usefully.[126]

Magic could address personal and social problems. However little direct therapeutic effect a magical performance might have, it could improve the patient's confidence and morale or mitigate social tensions. There was an additional and useful ambivalence in the associations of magic. If a performance was successful, the proper order of things was reaffirmed. Should it fail, the evocation of drastic consequences in some spells implies that the failure would be part of a wider, and in practice almost inconceivable, catastrophe. There were many other possible reasons for failure. The existence of this wide range of explanation protected the institution of magic from destructive criticism. It would hardly occur to anyone that the whole system might be insecurely based.[127]

From the late New Kingdom onward, members of the elite occasionally made indirect use of magic to secure for themselves social immortality and permanent prestige as benefactors of humanity. Some private stelae and statues bear magical texts in addition to or in place of biographical texts. King Ramesses III (1187–1156 B.C.E.) and Late Period notables set up in public places fine statues of themselves covered with magical texts. Visitors and priests could pour libations over the statues to produce infusions that constituted magical remedies.[128] Most of these monuments were probably placed in the outer areas of temples and were thus integrated into official religion. The position of the texts on the bodies of the statues suggest that the pouring of the libations was valuable also for the people depicted.

Magical practices seek to correct disorders in personal well-being or social life, but in themselves they leave open the question of which practice should be chosen in any particular case. A response to disturbance and affliction has the best chance of success if the cause is identi-

---

126. As pointed out by Alessandro Roccati, "Les Papyrus de Turin," *Bulletin de la Société Française d'Égyptologie* 99 (1984): 24, who formulates still more skeptically.

127. This is an essential insight of the classic work of E. E. Evans-Pritchard, *Witchcraft, Oracles and Magic among the Azande* (Oxford: Clarendon, 1937). For an Egyptological presentation, see Baines, *Göttinger Miszellen* 76 (1984): 25–54.

128. Pierre Lacau, "Les statues 'guérisseuses' dans l'ancienne Égypte," *Fondation Eugène Piot, Monuments et Mémoires* 25 (1921–22): 189–209; Adolf Klasens, *A Magical Statue Base (Socle Béhague) in the Museum of Antiquities at Leiden* (Leiden: Brill, 1952). For the statue of Ramesses III, see Étienne Drioton, "Une statue prophylactique de Ramsès III," *Annales du Service des Antiquités de l'Égypte* 39 (1939): 57–89; Kenneth A. Kitchen, *Ramesside Inscriptions, Historical and Biographical*, vol. 5 (Oxford: B. H. Blackwell, 1983), pp. 261–62.

fied beforehand. Attempts to discover the cause or significance of an event—they often amount to the same thing—constitute divination, which may be invoked in order to comprehend the present by exploring the past, or in order to inquire about the future. In Egypt it could take the form of prophecy or oracles.[129] Prophecy in which someone is inspired to foretell the future generally lies outside the capacity of someone who does not receive divine guidance. It would have been unwise to depend on it even if it came directly from the gods, because they were less than omniscient. Literary prophecy is known from The Prophecy of Neferti, in which a sage, who was, significantly, also a lector priest, prophesied dire events at the end of the Old Kingdom and a reversal of them by a Middle Kingdom savior—Amenemhat I, who probably inspired the piece.[130] Otherwise, prophecy was not prominent in Egypt, and when the magician in The Prophecy of Neferti offers to tell of the past or the future, this is a literary artifice, not a generally valid pair of alternatives.

Oracles are more limited and practical than prophecy, and are most effective when a question with a simple yes-or-no answer can be posed. An oracle can be asked who has done something or will do something, or what the chances are for achieving a plan. In Egypt, such inquiries were made by all, from kings to peasants, who had access to writing (and so were able to leave archaeological evidence of their activity), and they were probably made by others too. The king used oracles, for example, to confirm a god's approval of military campaigns—only successful oracles and campaigns were recorded—and when making sensitive appointments to religious office. In such cases oracles were integrated into political life. People used oracles to answer many questions, some of them very humdrum, such as whether to cultivate a particular plot of land and with what crop.[131] The normal mechanisms for oracles

129. Leclant, in *La divination*, ed. Caquot and Leibovici [n. 76]; Baines, *JEA* 73 (1987): 85–93. For an essay focusing on the Late Period, see J. D. Ray, "Ancient Egypt," in *Divination and Oracles*, ed. Michael Loewe and Carmen Blacker (London: Allen & Unwin, 1981), pp. 174–90.

130. Wolfgang Helck, *Die Prophezeiung des Nfr.tj*, Kleine Ägyptische Texte (Wiesbaden: Harrassowitz, 1970); *AEL* 1:139–45. On prophecy and instruction texts, see Hellmut Brunner, "Die 'Weisen,' ihre 'Lehren' und 'Prophezeiungen' in altägyptischer Sicht," *ZÄS* 93 (1966): 29–35 (rpt. in Brunner, *Das hörende Herz*, pp. 59–65); Brunner's interesting discussion takes the material rather too literally. Prophecy is widely known in literature of the Greco-Roman Period, but never in an everyday or realistic context. See, e.g., Karl-Theodor Zauzich, "Töpferorakel," *LÄ* 6:621–23; Janet H. Johnson, "The Demotic Chronicle as a Statement of a Theory of Kingship," *Journal of the Society for the Study of Egyptian Antiquities* 13 (1983): 61–72.

were questions addressed in either spoken or written form to a god's statue. When in procession, the god's portable image indicated assent or dissent by moving forward or backward. Like the letters to the dead, oracles were closely involved in legal matters.[132]

Access to hidden agencies could come through dreams. The dead or gods might appear in dreams, or a dream could portray an event that was later interpreted as being either auspicious or inauspicious.[133] In order to interpret a dream or other portentous occurrence, one might consult a specialist, who could be a priest or, in a small community, someone known to have the necessary insight. The elite, who in this context included the scribes of Deir el-Medina, could look up a dream in a dream book and find an interpretation of it, classified into good and bad; the book also contains a spell to ward off inauspicious dreams. This work, which may have been composed in the Middle Kingdom, is, however, more literary than practical.[134] It is not known to what extent such compilations were used in everyday life.

Several late New Kingdom texts, also from Deir el-Medina, refer to "the wise woman"—someone we might term a "seer"—who supplied advice. In one case, she was consulted over what an oracle would say.[135] The seer was yet another source of divinatory enlightenment, who might be consulted in addition to or instead of an oracle.

131. For the priestly appointment, see Kurt Sethe, "Die Berufung eines Hohenpriesters des Amon unter Ramses II.," *ZÄS* 44 (1907–8): 30–35; Kenneth A. Kitchen, *Ramesside Inscriptions, Historical and Biographical*, vol. 3 (Oxford: B. H. Blackwell, 1980), pp. 282–85. For tilling a plot and similar questions, see, e.g., Edda Bresciani, *L'archivio demotico del tempio di Soknopaiu Nesos nel Griffith Institute di Oxford*, vol. 1, Testi e documenti per lo studio dell'antichità 49 (Milan: Cisalpino–La Goliardica, 1975), nos. 1–11; John Baines and Jaromír Málek, *Atlas of Ancient Egypt* (Oxford: Phaidon; New York: Facts on File, 1980), p. 199. For a demotic document that fuses legal processes with the use of divination and oracles, see Françoise de Cenival, "Le Papyrus Dodgson (P. Ashmolean Museum Oxford 1932–1159): Une interrogation aux portes des dieux?" *RdÉ* 38 (1987): 3–11; Edda Bresciani, "Il papiro Dodgson e il *ḥp (n) wpj.t*," *Egitto e Vicino Oriente* 11 (1988): 58–70.

132. See Andrea Griet McDowell, *Jurisdiction in the Workmen's Community of Deir el-Medina*, Egyptologische Uitgaven 10 (Leiden: Nederlands Instituut voor het Nabije Oosten, 1990), pp. 107–41.

133. See in general Serge Sauneron, "Les songes et leur interprétation dans l'Égypte ancienne," in *Les songes et leur intérpretation*, Sources Orientales 2 (Paris: Seuil, 1959), pp. 17–61; Pascal Vernus, "Traum," *LÄ* 6:745–49; see also Baines, *JEA* 73 (1987): 85n27, 87n43. The most important group of dreams from Egypt is that of Hor of Sebennytos, of the second century B.C.E.: J. D. Ray, *The Archive of Ḥor*, Texts from Excavations 2 (London: Egypt Exploration Society, 1976).

134. Alan H. Gardiner, *Hieratic Papyri in the British Museum, Third Series: Chester Beatty Gift* (London: British Museum, 1935), no. 3; the spell is in col. 10, ll. 10–19. See also Baines, *JEA* 73 (1987): 82n10.

135. See Baines, *JEA* 73 (1987): 93.

There were thus many layers of religious practice. One might consult two or three authorities in order to establish the appropriate religious or magical response to an event. Other steps could be taken before one embarked on such a process. For example, there were better and worse days for doing particular things, and some days were generally inauspicious. All these days were listed in calendars.[136] It is easy to imagine that if it was necessary to do something on the wrong day, a special amulet could be worn or a suitable spell could be uttered beforehand.[137] Should the consequences be undesirable despite these precautions, the whole process of turning to oracles, interpretation, subsequent rituals, and so forth might be started in the hope of setting things right again.

This layering of practices had positive aspects in assuring all concerned that everything had been done to meet a problem. It also buttressed the system's integrity. As is the case with magic, such layering was part of the rationality of religion—rather as the multiple stages of modern medical investigations are part of the rationality of medicine. Ancient magic and modern medicine may have different content and different degrees of efficacy, but the strategies they employ are in many ways comparable.[138]

RELIGIOUS EXPERIENCE AND PIETY:
EARLY EVIDENCE

In the practical procedures I have sketched, people had little immediate contact with the gods. Exceptions are two late New Kingdom cases in which the goddess Hathor appeared to people in dreams.[139] Direct personal experience of deities is seldom a religious norm, but it can be a value to which people aspire, as Egyptians did for the next world. In combination with ethical aspects of the leading deity's provi-

136. Compare Emma Brunner-Traut, "Tagewählerei," *LÄ* 6:153–56, and "Mythos im Alltag: Zum Loskalender im Alten Ägypten," in her *Gelebte Mythen: Beiträge zum altägyptischen Mythos* (Darmstadt: Wissenschaftliche Buchgesellschaft, 1981), pp. 18–33.

137. Pierre Montet, *Everyday Life in Egypt in the Days of Ramesses the Great*, trans. A. R. Maxwell-Hyslop and Margaret S. Drower (London: Arnold; Westport, Conn.: Greenwood, 1958), pp. 36–38.

138. For an illuminating analysis of groups of prescriptions in Papyrus Ebers along these lines, see Kent R. Weeks, "Studies of Papyrus Ebers," *Bulletin de l'Institut d'Égypte* 68–69 (1976–1978): 296–97.

139. Baines, *JEA* 73 (1987): 85n27.

sion for the world, this value was prominent in New Kingdom religious developments.

The crisis in these developments came in the mid–New Kingdom, in the time of King Akhenaten (1353–1336 B.C.E.).[140] Egyptologists have often assumed that piety, by which they normally mean direct contact with gods and personal experience of them, was not a feature of religion before the later New Kingdom, and the origin of piety has often been attributed to the aftereffects of Akhenaten's reforms. These interpretations follow the preserved evidence closely, but they do not allow for changes in the character of the documents or for the sparseness of earlier sources, in comparison with which late New Kingdom sources are very abundant.

Before considering Akhenaten's reforms and their aftermath, I review earlier traces of the personal experience of deities. If such experiences can be posited, the picture of earlier religion will be more coherent. Although in all periods relatively few people were directly involved in the cult, the temples and the cult performed in them would have existed in a partial vacuum if they had corresponded with little in the lives of other people. Apart from this general point, several literary texts become more meaningful if it is assumed that contact with the deity, or experience of the deity, was considered possible.

By the Early Dynastic Period, a basic context for interaction between official and personal religion already existed in the form of cults that reached outside the temples during numerous festivals. By the Fourth Dynasty, these festivals were listed in texts in a canonical order.[141] During some festivals, the statues of the gods went out of the temples, which were then relatively modest structures, probably spread throughout the country and through the quarters of larger settlements.[142] Votive offerings, some dating to the beginning of the dynastic period, have been recovered from temples (fig. 62), but they may not provide evidence for the involvement of much of the population in the cult, because most are costly, elite objects (at least one bears a royal name).[143] From

140. For the crisis in general, see Assmann, *Re und Amun.*

141. Lapp, *Opferformel des Alten Reiches* [n. 74].

142. See Baines, in *Pyramid Studies,* ed. Baines et al. The list of Memphite gods, which goes back to the Early Dynastic Period or early Old Kingdom, organizes its gods by quarters of the city. Shrines were presumably scattered correspondingly through the settlement.

143. See material assembled by Günter Dreyer, *Elephantine VIII. Der Tempel der Satet: Die Funde der Frühzeit und des Alten Reiches,* AVDAIK 39 (1986). For the royal name, see Helen Whitehouse, "King Den in Oxford," *Oxford Journal of Archaeology* 6 (1987): 257–62.

62. Group of faience votive figurines of animals (fish, hippopotamus, ibex, baboon), from the "Main Temple Deposit" at Hierakonpolis (First Dynasty?). Ashmolean Museum, Oxford, E.1, E.2, E.3, E.5. Photo courtesy of the Visitors of the Ashmolean Museum.

the beginning, kings were central to provision for the gods and the organization of the cult.

So far, few pre–New Kingdom texts have been identified in which people state that they are devotees of particular deities or make comparable pious declarations.[144] The known examples are in unconven-

144. Pascal Vernus, "Études de philologie et de linguistique (II)," *RdÉ* 34 (1982–83): 115–17. Richard Parkinson has very kindly drawn to my attention two further examples, which he will treat in a forthcoming anthology of Middle Kingdom texts: Sethe, *Ägyptische Lesestücke* [n. 72], pp. 62, 22–63, 3; N. de Garis Davies and Alan H. Gardiner, *The Tomb of Antefoķer, Vizier of Sesostris I, and of His Wife Senet (No. 60),* Theban Tombs Series 2 (London: Allen & Unwin, 1920), p. 24, pl. 29. For an early New Kingdom phrase of personal attachment to a god, see the caption to a figure of the deceased in the tomb of Paheri at el-Kab: ". . . may you do what I say, for I am one of those who adore you": J. J. Tylor and F. Ll. Griffith, *The Tomb of Paheri at el Kab,* Memoir of the Egypt Exploration Fund 11 (London, 1894), pl. 5, bottom right; also translated by Yoyotte, in *Les pèlerinages* [n. 93], p. 31.

tional contexts, being either a small stela of very low artistic quality or a pair of harpist's songs without known parallel. These unusual cases encourage reflection on the significance of the hymns on small Middle Kingdom stelae.[145] The hymns are quite stereotyped and do not by themselves reveal the attitudes of the stela owners. Those from Abydos are addressed to several deities, notably Min, who was not an Abydene god, but had a major cult a day or two's journey away at Akhmim. The choice of which god to address in a hymn could point in some cases to a personal relationship with a deity, but such an interpretation is unlikely to be widely valid. Such a choice could further be compared with maxims about Amun and his worshipers. One such maxim is "There is no refuge for the heart except for Amon(-Re)." These maxims are inscribed on scarabs of the Eighteenth Dynasty and later, but they probably go back to proverbial sentiments.[146] Also relevant to personal relationships with gods are some "pious" phrases in the Cairo Hymn to Amun, a text that is first attested from the Second Intermediate Period.[147]

Further evidence for relationships with deities may be present in three texts that I have interpreted as either referring to oracles or implying divination.[148] The authors of two of them say that the god Horus led them to do something, while the third, The Story of Sinuhe, repeatedly presents Sinuhe's flight abroad from Egypt as having been caused by a god whom he cannot identify. In these three cases a god intervened in human affairs and affected the actions of an individual. The authors of the texts do not say that they themselves experienced this intervention. In the first two cases, the intervention seems to have responded to a request made through an oracle, while in The Story of Sinuhe the pro-

145. Selim Hassan, *Hymnes religieux du Moyen Empire*, Service des Antiquités de l'Égypte (Cairo: Imprimerie de l'Institut français d'Archéologie orientale, 1928); Sethe, *Ägyptische Lesestücke* [n. 72], no. 11. There is no recent study of these hymns.

146. These objects are very difficult to date precisely. They include both generalizing moral statements and specifically pious ones, associating by context two spheres under discussion here. See, e.g., three works by Étienne Drioton: "Amon, refuge du coeur," *ZÄS* 79 (1954): 3–11 (source of the maxim cited in the text here); "Maximes morales sur des scarabées égyptiens," in *Hommages à Waldemar Deonna*, Collection Latomus 28 (Brussels: Berchem, 1957), pp. 197–202; and "Maximes relatives à l'amour pour les dieux," in *Studia Biblica et Orientalia*, vol. 3, *Oriens Antiquus*, Analecta Biblica 12 (Rome: Pontificio Istituto Biblico, 1959), pp. 57–68.

147. Jan Assmann, *Ägyptische Hymnen und Gebete*, Bibliothek der Alten Welt: Der Alte Orient (Zurich and Munich: Artemis, 1975), no. 87. For the pious statements, see Malte Römer, "Der Kairener Hymnus an Amun-Re: Zur Gliederung von pBoulaq 17," in Osing and Dreyer, *Form und Mass* [n. 104], pp. 408 (ll. 29–32), 417–18.

148. Baines, *JEA* 73 (1987): 88–90.

tagonist assumes an intervention in order to explain, long afterward, why he himself took a particular course of action. Oracles must be addressed to specific deities, so they always imply some relationship, if not a direct one, between the deity who gives the oracle and the human recipient. The recipients are specific people or groups of people. These three texts can be compared with the Instruction for Merikare, which extols the creator as one who has an immediate concern for the woes of individual people,[149] but the tone of the text is so lofty and unspecific that an individual's awareness of this concern is probably irrelevant in context. Nonetheless, what is said is compatible with piety and conducive to it.

Personal names of all periods form another crucial but poorly understood body of evidence relating to piety.[150] The majority of the tens of thousands of Egyptian names are meaningful utterances, most of them relating to gods. Continual variation and development in names and the constant appearance of new ones show that their meanings were actively understood and formulated, unlike many names in modern Western society.

Some names make descriptive statements about the gods, that a god is great, strong, enduring, majestic, and so forth. Others relate gods more closely to people by saying that a deity is good or gracious, shows favor, guides perfectly, and so forth. The second of these groups is potentially more relevant for human experience. Both types of name were devised and bestowed in the same situation. In theory, a name was formed from the utterances of the mother or father at a child's birth,[151] but in practice infants were very often named after relatives. It seems that a birth could be conceived of as a sign of a god's favor or as a demonstration of a god's qualities. Birth, the point of transition into the world of creation, was a vital time when the gods might make themselves apparent. It was also very highly ritualized (fig. 63). The other fundamental transition, death, led to a realm in which gods and demons were present everywhere.

Because of the high mortality among infants and mothers, birth was a

149. See *AEL* 1:101–2, 106–7. This orientation is visible principally near the end, in the text's praise of the creator; very different meanings can be seen in some earlier parts.

150. The principal source is Herman Ranke, *Die ägyptischen Personennamen*, 3 vols. (Glückstadt: J. J. Augustin, 1935–1977); this material could probably be doubled. Ranke made valuable thematic collections and analyses of names in vol. 2, pp. 219–27. The only significant later analysis of names in terms of their religious meanings is by Erik Hornung for Early Dynastic names, *Conceptions of God*, pp. 44–49. For demotic names, see Erich Lüddeckens et al., *Demotisches Namenbuch*, fasc. 1– (Wiesbaden: Reichert, 1980–).

151. See Georges Posener, "Sur l'attribution d'un nom à un enfant," *RdÉ* 22 (1970): 204–5.

63. Pottery vase in the form of a squatting figure of a woman, probably a container for mother's milk to be used for amuletic purposes (mid–Eighteenth Dynasty). Ashmolean Museum, Oxford, E.2432. Photo courtesy of the Visitors of the Ashmolean Museum.

time of immediate danger, and this peril is reflected in various types of name. Some New Kingdom names relate a newborn child to a specific god while also addressing the circumstances of birth.[152] Thus

152. A noteworthy feature is that many names do not name a specific god, but use the word *netjer*, "(the) god" (for collection, see Ranke, *Die ägyptischen Personennamen*, 3:80–81). On the interpretation of this phenomenon, see Hornung, *Conceptions of God*, pp. 46–49.

"Ramesses" probably means "Re it is who bore him." Such a name emphatically celebrates the auspicious outcome and gives the credit for it to a particular god.[153] From about 1100 B.C.E. onward, less clearly positive names occur, among which is the type "God *X* said 'He/she will live.'" These names probably refer to an oracular consultation made during the mother's pregnancy, and they would have been given to a child when both the consultation and the birth were successful.[154] Another function of oracular consultations was to authenticate the production of amuletic rolls of spells designed to protect infants against all manner of life's possible dangers, including random accidents. The texts on these rolls are presented as decrees issued by an oracle of one or more deities. The papyri, which date to the period when the name form "God *X* said 'He/she will live'" was popular, were worn round the neck in containers. A third-millennium analogy for the oracular names exists in the name Ankhtify, "One who will live," which presumably records a statement uttered over a newborn baby who was healthier than many others.[155] This name mentions no god. The reason is unknown, but it could be decorum, which was more restrictive then than in later periods.

Thus many people carried throughout life a name that recorded either divine favor and majesty or divine involvement in a particular episode. Such a name would seem incongruous if the god were not very relevant after birth, so it is best to assume that for its holder and his or her kin group the name continued to have meaning throughout life. A name's continuing significance is also suggested by the quite common practice of changing a name. Most changes were not strongly religious, but they nonetheless demonstrate the importance of names to their holders. It would be strange—but not impossible—for people's lives to be so compartmentalized that their names pointed into a religious void. It is more economical to assume that names retained some of their original meaning and value and came to relate to other aspects of their bearers' lives.

153. These names have often been linked with festivals of the gods named, including those of the birth of the gods. A child might have been born on the day of a particular god's festival. Names of the form "God *X* Is in Festival" display such a connection. As with other names, most occurrences after the initial invention of a name commemorated persons in the family holding the same name rather than the specific event characterized by the name's literal meaning.

154. Compare I. E. S. Edwards, *Hieratic Papyri in the British Museum*, 4th ser., *Oracular Amuletic Decrees of the Late New Kingdom* (London: British Museum, 1960), p. xx with n. 1.

155. Ranke, *Die ägyptischen Personennamen*, 1:68, nos. 22–24.

RELIGIOUS EXPERIENCE AND PIETY:
NEW KINGDOM DEVELOPMENTS

The fragmentary early evidence for piety does no more than suggest how deities might have related directly to people, but it is valuable in providing a historical context for New Kingdom evidence. It also raises the possibility that the abundance of evidence from the New Kingdom is due to changes in decorum as well as in underlying belief and practice. Should that be the case, there would have been more continuity between earlier and later times than a narrow reading of the material might suggest. Comparable changes in decorum are visible in other spheres, chiefly in the inclusion of pictures of kings and gods in nonroyal tombs.

This New Kingdom material exhibits important developments, on different levels of belief and practice, in the areas of piety, of discussions of the creator god's character, and of the convergence of morality with piety. These three areas are probably interconnected.

Piety was linked to individual religious action in temples, and the New Kingdom produces evidence for both.[156] The evolution of ideas about the nature of the creator god demonstrates that these ideas were closely connected to practical religion. The most significant episode in this evolution was the religious revolution of Akhenaten, which centered on the problem of polytheism and "monotheism," but also raised questions of theodicy—or rather posed them by ignoring them. Thus, whatever political issues may also have been at stake between the king and the traditional priesthood, the reform provides a key example of the interrelations of religion and society. The convergence of morality with pietistic belief and practice, which is notable in New Kingdom instruction texts and discernible in other sources, was also associated with ideas about theodicy. This fusion of morality and piety related explicitly two spheres that had always been connected but had not previously influenced each other so clearly.[157]

156. For a useful collection of material relating to piety, see Ashraf Iskander Sadek, *Popular Religion in Egypt during the New Kingdom*, Hildesheimer Ägyptologische Beiträge 27 (Hildesheim: Gerstenberg, 1987 [1988]).

157. For the principal texts, see *AEL* 2:135–63. There is no modern edition of The Instruction of Ani, which probably dates to the post-Amarna period, or of that of Amenemope, which may be of the late New Kingdom. For Amenemope, see Irene Grumach, *Untersuchungen zur Lebenslehre des Amenope*, MÄS 23 (Munich and Berlin: Deutscher Kunstverlag, 1972).

Thus concern with the gods and concern with the social person, into which earlier public sources had tended, perhaps misleadingly, to separate religion and morality, appear less distinct during the New Kingdom than before. Two well-documented groups of material provide evidence for the convergence of religious belief and practice: activities around the temples, and discussion among the elite of the nature of deities. Although elite discussion was rarefied, it was probably not confined to the tiny numbers of privileged who created the evidence. It is therefore legitimate to connect the contexts of temple and elite discussion. Nonetheless, it would be wrong to assume that mass movements underlay the changes, because the social order was unequal enough and strong enough to resist unwanted innovation from below.

Piety

Individual action in and around temples must have been either a new development or a vast extension of earlier practice. It could have replaced other, perhaps very different usages, or it could have been an addition to them. In the very long term, by some time in the first millennium B.C.E. temples became the repository of traditional Egyptian culture and the focus of social solidarity. What happened in and around them could therefore have replaced the less homogeneous earlier religious and social focuses of small groups, within which divination and other comparable practices would have taken place. Persuasive detail supports this understanding of the development. But religion is not neatly circumscribed, and for many centuries older and newer habits probably overlapped. Such plurality of practice can be part of the rationality of religious responses to the untoward and attempts to forestall it. By extending the range of possibilities, additional practices afford a better chance of success, or at least a fuller material and psychological context for comprehending failure.

Evidence for individual activity in temples comes from just a few sites, and the main groups of material date to the Eighteenth Dynasty before the reign of Akhenaten. Thousands of votive offerings have been found at shrines of the goddess Hathor, the patroness of women. The most important of these finds were made in western Thebes at Deir el-Bahri (fig. 40), in the adjacent mortuary complexes of the monarchs Nebhepetre Mentuhotep (2010–1960 B.C.E.) (fig. 64) and Hatshepsut (c.

64. Group of small votive offerings (two human female figures and one bovid; mid–Eighteenth Dynasty) from the temple of King Nebhepetre Mentuhotep at Deir el-Bahri, western Thebes. Ashmolean Museum, Oxford, E.864, E.841, E.2714. Photo courtesy of the Visitors of the Ashmolean Museum.

1475–1458 B.C.E.) (fig. 7).[158] Some of the offerings that have the clearest meanings are associated with women's fertility. Where infant mortality is high, women's fertility is always an important concern, especially because premodern medicine could do very little to promote it. Other offerings carry prominently the motif of the deity's ears (fig. 65). Their purpose was evidently to persuade the deity (not always Hathor) to harken to the worshiper's plea.[159] The offerings found have been any-

158. For the material, see Pinch, *New Kingdom Votive Offerings.* I owe to this work the insight that these developments must have depended on royal patronage.

159. For a collection of examples of ears on objects dedicated to many deities, see Sadek, *Popular Religion in Egypt,* pp. 245–68, pls. 1–28.

65. Miniature stela of the New Kingdom showing four ears, from Saq-
qara(?). Ashmolean Museum, Oxford, 1892.1093. Photo courtesy of the
Visitors of the Ashmolean Museum.

thing from beads and other very modest tokens to fine statues of prominent people. Some types of figurine, which represent women with exag-
geratedly large genitals, are probably fertility offerings. They are striking
for not being in normal Egyptian style, and are thus rare instances of
objects used in a public context which are not within the conventions of
the system of decorum.

Hardly any offerings include a statement of why they were offered.
Nonetheless, it is possible in most cases to suggest motives for their
deposition. These motives relate more to practical religion and to magic
than to "pure" worship. Worship of that sort might have been expressed
more fully at festivals outside the temples, although festivals were also
times for "practical" access to a deity.

One of the rare objects with explicit meaning is an inscribed statue
that asks women who come and want various things, such as a "good
(or possibly fertile) husband," to make offerings to it, so that the owner

of the statue will intercede with the goddess on their behalf.[160] This offer of aid in getting the right husband has revealing social implications, as does the fact that the inscription is addressed to women, few of whom would have been able to read. In addition, the object is a significant example of the "intermediary statue," which is a later counterpart of several of the earlier elite practices I have mentioned, including participation in temple cult, aspirations to be present at the festivals at Abydos and to endure in human esteem into the next life,[161] and the deification of private individuals in a status between ordinary humans and the gods.

Intermediary statues, like these other practices, imply that, whatever aspirations most people may have had, only the elite could realistically hope for direct access to the gods. The elite could achieve moral stature in this world and the next by interceding on behalf of their social inferiors. This possibility for the privileged should be seen as devolving from the king, who must have encouraged the whole movement toward piety by granting people access to these temples for the presentation of votive offerings and whatever rituals may have been associated with their presentation. He must also have let members of the elite become intermediaries by giving them permission to set up their statues in appropriate outer parts of temples. Intermediary statues continued to be significant throughout the New Kingdom. Several of the period's most prominent personalities had themselves depicted in this form, some setting up remarkable numbers of statues of various types in different temples (for example, fig. 66).[162]

Votive offerings declined in quantity toward the end of the Eighteenth

---

160. Edouard Naville, *The XI*[th] *Dynasty Temple at Deir el-Bahari,* vol. 3, Egypt Exploration Fund Memoir 32 (London, 1913), pl. 9B. The significance of the "good (or possibly fertile) husband" is uncertain, because in many societies it is not recognized that men may be sterile, but a Late Period offering formula inscribed on behalf of women suggests that such a conception may have existed in Egypt; the idea might also encompass impotence. See Hellmut Brunner, "Fruchtbarkeit," *LÄ* 2:337 with n. 2; Dimitri Meeks, *L'année lexicographique* 1 (1977) (Paris: n.p., 1980), p. 169, no. 77.1835; Georges Daressy, "Notes et remarques," *Recueil de Travaux relatifs à la Philologie et à l'Archéologie égyptiennes et assyriennes* 20 (1898): 74–75, no. CLI (Medinet Habu, chapels of the divine adoratrices).

161. See the valuable discussion of Detlef Franke, "Die Hockerstatue des Sonbso-mei in Leiden und Statuen mit nach oben gerichteten Handflächen," *OMRO* 69 (1988): 65–67.

162. More than twenty statues of Senenmut, the leading personality of the reign of Hatshepsut, are known: Christine Meyer, *Senenmut: Eine prosopographische Untersuchung,* Hamburger Ägyptologische Studien 2 (Hamburg: Borg, 1982), pp. 28–223. See also monuments of Amenhotep son of Hapu of the reign of Amenhotep III: Alexandre Varille, *Inscriptions concernant l'architecte Amenhotep, fils de Hapou,* BdÉ 44 (1968).

66. Quartzite statue of the High Steward Amenhotep (Eighteenth Dynasty, reign of King Amenhotep III), portraying him as a scribe, from Mit Rahina (Memphis). The statue shows signs of wear, demonstrating that it was an object of veneration in antiquity, probably as an intermediary with the gods. Ashmolean Museum, Oxford, 1913.163. Photo courtesy of the Visitors of the Ashmolean Museum.

Dynasty, about the same time as the public display of piety increased and began to extend to a slightly larger social group (fig. 15). It can hardly be a coincidence that these two developments happened at the same time, but the connections between them are not clear. As the offerings decreased—they became very important again in the Late Period—the religion of the less affluent disappeared from view for six hundred years. The best-known late New Kingdom pious monuments are from Ramesside Deir el-Medina, the privileged community of workmen who built the royal tombs.[163]

163. These monuments form the basis of many studies. The most major collection is Mario Tosi and Alessandro Roccati, *Stele e altre epigrafi di Deir el Medina n. 50001–n. 50262,* Catalogo del Museo Egizio di Torino, 2d ser.: Collezioni 1 (Turin: Pozzo, 1972). For a

These people are typical of the social groups that are almost undocumented in earlier material. They were of lower social status than the core elite, but they were still relatively wealthy.[164] They experienced a full range of divine involvement in their lives. The workmen were afflicted by gods for misdemeanors or for failing to acknowledge them and show them respect, and were then rewarded when they realized their errors. Those who had been afflicted in this way later recounted these episodes on stelae that they set up in local shrines. A Theban official of the period dedicated much of his property to the goddess Mut, recounting how he came to do so in a narrative with a literary, almost fictional formulation that is probably meant to assimilate it to the highest models.[165] Another was inspired in a dream by Hathor to build his tomb in a particular place.[166] In the village where the workmen lived, oracles were much used, people consulted seers, and there were various awesome "manifestations" (*bau*) of intervention by gods in human affairs.[167]

Here piety was the most direct of the many ways in which people and gods interacted. A literate person who hoped for direct involvement with cult and deity could still suffer exclusion, and this possibility may throw into relief the importance of access to the gods. In a late

general interpretation, see Battiscombe Gunn, "The Religion of the Poor in Ancient Egypt," *JEA* 3 (1916): 81–94; the people were, however, not poor. For an extensive collection of texts, see Assmann, *Ägyptische Hymnen und Gebete*, nos. 147–200. For a penetrating study of texts preserved in advanced students' exercises, most of which do not seem to come from Deir el-Medina, see Gerhard Fecht, *Literarische Zeugnisse zur "Persönlichen Frömmigkeit" in Ägypten: Analyse der Beispiele aus den ramessidischen Schulpapyri*, Abhandlungen der Heidelberger Akademie der Wissenschaften, Philosophisch-historische Klasse 1965/1 (Heidelberg: Winter, 1965). For some votive offerings, again not of poor people, from Ramesside Memphis, see Alan R. Schulman, "Ex-votos of the Poor," *JARCE* 6 (1967): 153–56. See further Sadek, *Popular Religion in Egypt*.

164. See Jac. J. Janssen, *Commodity Prices from the Ramessid Period* (Leiden: Brill, 1975), pp. 453–66, and "Khaʿemtore, a Well-to-do Workman," *OMRO* 58 (1977): 221–32.

165. John A. Wilson, "The Theban Tomb (No. 409) of Si-Mut, Called Kiki," *JNES* 29 (1970): 187–92; Pascal Vernus, "Littérature et autobiographie: Les inscriptions de *S3-Mwt* surnommé *Kyky*," *RdÉ* 30 (1978): 115–46.

166. Jan Assmann, "Eine Traumoffenbarung der Göttin Hathor," *RdÉ* 30 (1978): 22–50. For a similar but fragmentary text, see Helmut Satzinger, "Zwei Wiener Objekte mit bemerkenswerten Inschriften," in *Mélanges Gamal Eddin Mokhtar*, vol. 2, BdÉ 97/2 (1985), pp. 249–54.

167. See Jaroslav Černý, "Egyptian Oracles," in Richard A. Parker, *A Saite Oracle Papyrus from Thebes in The Brooklyn Museum*, Brown Egyptological Studies 4 (Providence, R.I.: Brown University Press, 1962), pp. 35–48, and "Troisième série de questions addressées aux oracles," *BIFAO* 72 (1972): 49–69; Baines, *JEA* 73 (1987): 93 (seers); J. F. Borghouts, "Divine Intervention in Ancient Egypt and Its Manifestation (*b3w*)," in *Gleanings from Deir el Medîna*, ed. R. J. Demarée and Jac. J. Janssen, Egyptologische Uitgaven 1 (Leiden: Nederlands Institut voor het Nabije Oosten, 1982), pp. 1–70.

Ramesside letter to a god, the sender complains that the god has not processed out from his chapel to judge an oracle on a public matter. This letter is perhaps the bluntest reproach to a god extant, but, as its modern editor observed, the intended audience was probably more the priests who would have presented it in the chapel than the god himself.[168] Thus it may say little about underlying religious attitudes, except that some proprieties were less important than might be expected.

Discussions of the Creator God's Character

Alternative conceptions of the creator can be traced back to a list that organizes a statement of his beneficence to living beings. This list was incorporated into a Middle Kingdom Coffin Text, but it is probably older. Attitudes like those implied by the list may be pursued further back, to Old Kingdom solar temples (fig. 53), where reliefs showing the fullness of nature seem, on the basis of their context, to praise the god.[169] In these sources, the essential idea is that the creator, who here is always the sun god, is vastly more significant than other deities, is responsible for all living beings, and created an order that is essentially good. This view does not fit well with more widely attested conceptions of the sun god, in which he plays the principal role in cosmic processes but depends on the participation of many other beings to maintain the order of things.[170] The divergence between these conceptions raises problems for the sun god's relation with the rest of the pantheon, but the more and less well-documented views seem to have coexisted from as early as either of them was recorded on the monuments.

The sunny presentation of the alternative view seems to ignore the problem of evil. It is as if the question simply should not arise. The origin of evil in human volition, which is stated in the creator's apologia and in the Instruction for Merikare, seems out of place here. Apart from its beliefs about forms of disorder outside the cosmos, traditional polytheism almost requires tension and disorder within the pantheon and in the cosmos.[171] Polytheism thus accepts two possible locations of evil, so

---

168. John Barns, "The Nevill Papyrus: A Late Ramesside Letter to an Oracle," *JEA* 35 (1949): 69–71.

169. See Siegfried Morenz, "Eine 'Naturlehre' in den Sargtexten," in his *Religion und Geschichte*, pp. 319–27; Assmann, *Ägypten*, pp. 214–15.

170. For the opposing traditions, see Assmann, *Re und Amun*, pp. 54–95.

171. Principally embodied in the god Seth; compare Herman te Velde, *Seth, God of Confusion*, 2d ed., PÄ 6 (1977).

that the existence of evil is not deeply problematic because nothing is truly perfect. All these points are well known from the religion of classical Greece, and they apply to mainstream Egyptian polytheism.[172] By contrast, when a single god dominates the cosmos in a henotheistic system, and that system has the optimism of the alternative Egyptian view, the question of theodicy arises in more acute form.[173]

The later, New Kingdom sources for the alternative view simply turn away from this question. Their bland approach may appear surprising, but it may be in keeping with the "idealistic" tradition of the solar temple and the list in the Coffin Texts. The Cairo Hymn to Amun, which is first attested from the Second Intermediate Period, a little before the New Kingdom, asserts that the creator is a being of a different order from all others, including the other gods, and that he created everything, down to the insects.[174] These ideas lead into a "new solar religion,"[175] for which the clearest evidence dates to the reign of Amenhotep III (1390–1353 B.C.E.), Akhenaten's predecessor. Unlike the Cairo Hymn, the hymns of the new solar religion completely remove the middle tier of traditional beliefs; the rest of the gods are not mentioned. In his beneficence the creator brought the world into being and floods it with light, whose rays are apparently his essential manifestation. All beings give praise to him, both by their very existence and in their acclamations. When the god is absent at night, the world is "as if dead"—and Akhenaten's hymn adds that "wild beasts maraud and insects bite." But the god's presence is so miraculous that even babies stop crying.[176] The other gods are absent from the presentation of the new solar religion. Both before and after the time of Akhenaten, a multitude of beings was depicted and described as accompanying and opposing

172. See, e.g., Walter Burkert, *Greek Religion: Archaic and Classical*, trans. John Raffan (Oxford: Basil Blackwell; Cambridge: Harvard University Press, 1985), pp. 182–89. It is not clear to me why Burkert terms Egypt a special case (p. 182).

173. Compare Hornung, *Conceptions of God*, pp. 230–37.

174. See n. 147 above; Assmann, *Re und Amun*, pp. 170–78.

175. The concept is Assmann's (*Re und Amun*, pp. 96–143), but he terms the phenomenon a *"neue Sonnentheologie."* The word "theology" is, however, problematic for Egyptian thought (see Baines, *Göttinger Miszellen* 76 (1984): 47–48), and I prefer the more neutral "religion." The principal texts are nos. 54, 76, 113, 151, 161, 253, in Jan Assmann, *Sonnenhymnen in thebanischen Gräbern*, Theben 1 (Mainz: von Zabern, 1983), and I. E. S. Edwards, *Hieroglyphic Texts from Egyptian Stelae etc.*, vol. 8 (London: British Museum, 1939), pl. 21 = Wolfgang Helck, *Urkunden der 18. Dynastie*, Urk. 4/21 (Berlin [East]: Akademie, 1958), pp. 1943–49.

176. "As if dead": Helck, *Urkunden der 18. Dynastie*, p. 1945, l. 1. For the other citations, see Maj Sandman, *Texts from the Time of Akhenaten*, BiAe 8 (1938), p. 94, ll. 1–3, 11–12.

the sun's course.[177] These beings who symbolized the struggle of the cosmos against the forces of disorder are absent from Akhenaten's religion.

In its pre-Akhenaten form, the new solar religion did not amount to monotheism. The latest of Akhenaten's formulations of his beliefs may have made that final transition. This is uncertain, however, because it is not known whether the traditional gods were believed not to exist or whether they were only excluded from mention.[178]

A second new style of hymn seeks to unify the idea of a single dominant creator with polytheism. These texts use a model in which the gods and the world are ultimately manifestations of a distant creator, whose intermediate form is a group consisting of Amun, Re, and Ptah.[179] Seth, the god of disorder within the cosmos, was later sometimes added to this trio. The vision of these hymns is that of an organized, hierarchical henotheism, in which the ultimate unity of the divine is strongly present and is emphasized. The texts have normally been dated to the end of the Eighteenth Dynasty and seen as part of the reaction to the reforms of Akhenaten, but the identification of the Leiden Hymn to Amun in a tomb from the reign of Amenhotep III[180] suggests that they form part of a discussion that had as its starting point the general position reflected in the Cairo Hymn to Amun. Part of the thrust of these hymns is toward a unified conception of the pantheon, but they also integrate a dominant and caring creator with the plurality of local manifestations in traditional religion.

In terms of morality, both the new solar religion and the henotheistic hymns definitively extended the sphere of being and of the creator's care

177. See Jan Assmann, "Die 'Häresie' des Echnaton: Aspekte der Amarna-Religion," *Saeculum* 23 (1972): 109–26, and *Re und Amun*, pp. 96–143. See also Donald B. Redford, *Akhenaten: The Heretic King* (Princeton: Princeton University Press, 1984), pp. 157–81.

178. See Hornung, *Conceptions of God*, pp. 244–50, and "Die Anfänge von Monotheismus und Trinität in Ägypten," in *Der eine Gott und der dreieine Gott: Das Gottesverständnis bei Christen, Juden und Muslimen*, ed. Karl Rahner (Munich and Zurich: Schnell & Steiner, 1983), pp. 48–66.

179. See Hornung, *Conceptions of God*, pp. 219–21; Jan Assmann, "Primat und Transzendenz: Struktur und Genese der ägyptischen Vorstellung eines 'Höchsten Wesens,'" in *Aspekte der spätägyptischen Religion*, ed. Westendorf, pp. 7–42, and *Re und Amun*, pp. 179–286.

180. Jan Zandee, "Ein doppelt überlieferter Text eines ägyptischen Hymnus an die Nachtsonne aus dem Neuen Reich: Hieratischer Papyrus Leiden I 344 vso. IV, 1–5 und thebanisches Grab des Cheriûf, Nr. 192," *Jaarbericht van het Vooraziatisch-Egyptisch Genootschap Ex Oriente Lux* 27 (1981–82 [1983]): 3–22; Zandee, review of Jan Assmann, *Sonnenhymnen*, in *Bibliotheca Orientalis* 44 (1987): 127.

to encompass all the known world, including plants. (The inanimate world was never a focus of strong attention, perhaps because of associations with the desert and disorder.) The expansive conception of the creator god's care did not lead to political pacifism and seldom involved a wider personal quietism. The extreme exponent of the new solar religion, Akhenaten, was not a pacifist.[181] His universalism was, however, a precursor of other religions and, in encompassing all of humanity, it was in theory as broad as strands of thought in later world religions. Yet the new solar religion's pointed ignoring of evil and misfortune and of all the traditional responses to them made it incomplete. It is as if those in the later Eighteenth Dynasty who elaborated this universalism were persuaded by the sweetness and light of Egyptian decorum to believe that the world really was like that. This coincidence is especially paradoxical, because Akhenaten explicitly rejected existing decorum.

The new solar religion did not confront moral issues in any significant way. In the intolerant form propounded by Akhenaten, it centered on the ruler, taking to the limit the idea of the king as the sole performer of the cult and emphasizing his divinity.[182] An individual had no access to the god, only to the king. Thus the god's universalism and benevolence could have had only a very restricted impact. In effect, the new religion was addressed to the few, and it seems to have been adhered to by few.

The official religion at the new capital of Akhetaten (modern el-ʿAmarna) has left no trace of magic, that extra effective force in the constitution and manipulation of the world which had always been available to everyone. However, amulets and other objects related to magic and traditional beliefs have been found at el-ʿAmarna outside the elite quarters.[183] The elite who accepted the new beliefs may have abandoned magic along with traditional religion, but others did not.

Another very important omission from the monuments at Akhetaten was mention of the world of the dead. Akhenaten and his courtiers built large tombs at the site, and in doing so they superficially continued earlier practices and aspirations. But the nonroyal tombs lack scenes relating to the hereafter, and the royal tomb, which contains mourning

181. Wolfgang Helck, "Ein 'Feldzug' unter Amenophis IV. gegen Nubien," *SAK* 8 (1980): 117–26.
182. See, e.g., Assmann, *SAK* 8 (1980): 1–31.
183. T. Eric Peet and C. Leonard Woolley, *The City of Akhenaten*, vol. 1, *Excavations of 1921 and 1922 at el-ʿAmarneh*, Egypt Exploration Society Memoir 38 (London, 1923), pp. 65–66; Barry J. Kemp, "The Amarna Workmen's Village in Retrospect," *JEA* 73 (1987): 30–36.

scenes commemorating the death of one of Akhenaten's daughters, includes nothing that points to a specific destiny in the next world.[184] The only evidence for beliefs about life after death is found in texts mentioning the hope that the deceased will receive gifts of unguents and aromatics and will emerge as a *ba* to view the sun and to move freely among the "lords of 'eternity'" (possibly the transfigured spirits of the dead).[185] The offering formula of traditional religion, according to which the king gave gifts so that the deceased would be able to receive benefits in the next life, was retained, as befits Akhenaten's emphatic placing of himself at the center of the new religion. There is no evidence for an ethical judgment after death, and the realm of the dead is only vaguely alluded to. Because so much of moral discourse and social competition had traditionally been conducted in terms of the next life, a whole area of meaning, which was crucial for this life as well as the next, must have seemed to be lost. A legitimate context for the indirect expression of anxieties and doubts had disappeared, and the blandness and optimism of Akhenaten's religion could be no substitute.

Despite the new religion's universalism, its ignoring of suffering was narrowly elitist. Insofar as social morality legitimizes inequality and addresses problems that arise from it, the new religion had no morality. It replaced possible moral interaction among social groups and the redressing of wrong with the assertion that wrong did not exist—and hence there was no need for the sort of practical religion that had previously been normal. The contrast in the hymns between positive day and negative night could conceivably have developed into a formulation of theodicy, but the form of this contrast derived more from the traditional conception of the created and uncreated worlds than from less

184. Nonroyal tombs: Norman de Garis Davies, *The Rock Tombs of El Amarna*, 6 vols., Archaeological Survey of Egypt 13–18 (London: Egypt Exploration Fund, 1903–1908); royal tomb: Geoffrey Thorndike Martin, *The Royal Tomb at el-Amarna: The Rock Tombs of el 'Amarna, Part VII*, vol. 2, *The Reliefs, Inscriptions and Architecture*, Archaeological Survey of Egypt 39 (London: Egypt Exploration Society, 1989), pls. 26–28, 58–78. In other contexts, the hymns from before and after the central Amarna Period are juxtaposed in context with traditional funerary material; some of these pieces may date within the reign of Akhenaten. There is a complete contradiction between the negation of darkness and death in the hymns of the new solar religion and conventional mortuary beliefs.

185. The summary of Adolf Erman has not been superseded: *Die Religion der Ägypter: Ihr Werden und Vergehen in vier Jahrtausenden* (Berlin and Leipzig: de Gruyter, 1934), pp. 124–26. See also Étienne Drioton, "Trois documents d'époque amarnienne," *Annales du Service des Antiquités de l'Égypte* 43 (1943): 15–43; Rolf Krauss, "Der Oberbildhauer Bak und sein Denkstein in Berlin," *Jahrbuch der Berliner Museen* 28 (1986): 35–38; Geoffrey T. Martin, "Shabtis of Private Persons of the Amarna Period," *MDAIK* 42 (1986): 109–29.

global ideas of evil and disturbance within the world. Here and in other respects, the new religion did not have time to develop and to meet the problems of suffering and loss. Jan Assmann has observed that because Akhenaten's religion excluded personal relations with the deity, it negated piety by channeling human-divine relations through the king.[186] In its ignoring of broader social relations and of deprivation and loss, it also negated morality. These aspects of the reforms did not long survive the death of Akhenaten, whereas the presentation of the creator's nature, which was not so closely tied to the king and formed part of an ongoing debate, exerted a continuing influence. As often happens, aspects of religion which relate to social concerns proved more resistant to change than abstract ones.

As king, Akhenaten retained the power structures and international relations of the day. At the same time he attempted to transform both general religious practice and, at least by omission, the form of the cosmos within which society existed and had its meaning. The essence of his solar beliefs had been elaborated before his reign, so his attacks on religious practice and his denial of the traditional cosmology were the more revolutionary aspects of his rule. But whereas alternative solar beliefs and the new solar religion had previously stood alongside other beliefs in a tolerant religious pluralism, Akhenaten made them intolerant. He also extended his privileged understanding of his beliefs' implications to many other cultural areas, of which the most immediately striking is representational art. He excluded images of his god in human form—a phenomenon paralleled in other religious traditions—and introduced a radically new artistic style (figs. 47, 48, 51). His religious vision, which, the texts state, was shared fully with no other person, is an example of a religious reform whose chief thrust was to purify belief and practice. In most societies, religion resists such rapid and reductive transformations as he attempted, and Egypt was no exception.

In the aftermath of Akhenaten's reforms, kings abandoned the conception of a single deity. Rather like him, however, they claimed a special relationship with the principal gods, developing this conception in new directions. Whereas Akhenaten had almost fused himself with the creator god, the subsequent presentation of the king's nature makes him into the divine essence of that which is human. His access to the god was now modeled on more general human piety, while the creator's

186. *SAK* 8 (1980): 29.

responses to the king showed that he had a special concern for his beloved royal son. It is uncertain to what extent it was the kings themselves who introduced this piety. If, as I argue, piety had existed for many centuries, the change is more likely to have taken up and developed widespread contemporary attitudes than to have introduced new ones. As the king formulated his position, it nevertheless tended toward exclusivism, although of a type different from Akhenaten's.[187] At various other points in Egyptian history, kings similarly restricted to themselves practices or ideas that had previously been more widespread.

The reforms of Akhenaten were abandoned under the child-king Tutankhamun (1332–1322 B.C.E.) (fig. 45), whose restoration stela marks the return to more traditional religion. The text of the stela states that during the previous period the gods had not answered when prayers were addressed to them.[188] Such a dialogue between worshiper and deity is a fundamental characteristic of piety. The notion that the king should have a direct or pious relationship with the gods had been formulated since the time of the Instruction for Merikare (ll. 63–68). In a formal sense, there had always been a reciprocity between the king and the gods: the king performed the cult for the gods, and they gave him prosperity and success.[189] This is the crucial context of Tutankhamun's text, whose vision hardly extends beyond the king and so does not strongly imply the existence of piety in society as a whole.

A thematic descendant of this text is the narrative of the Battle of Qadesh, composed under King Ramesses II (1279–1213 B.C.E.). In this text, the king reproaches Amun for failing him on the distant Syrian battlefield. In faraway Thebes, Amun hears the king and grants him supernatural strength to defeat the enemy, who are attacking him on all sides.[190] This royal dramatization of pious relations, personal loss, suf-

187. The first study to point to the existence of typical later pious formulas before the time of Akhenaten was Georges Posener, "La piété personnelle avant l'âge amarnien," *RdÉ* 27 (1975): 195–210. I have cited a variety of additional evidence and arguments in preceding sections.

188. See n. 10.

189. For the more general context, see Hornung, *Conceptions of God*, pp. 197–207, with references.

190. Kenneth A. Kitchen, *Ramesside Inscriptions, Historical and Biographical*, vol. 2 (Oxford: B. H. Blackwell, 1979), pp. 32–48; *AEL* 2:65–66. For a study, see Scott Morschauser, "Observations on the Speeches of Ramesses II in the Literary Record of the Battle of Kadesh," in *Perspectives on the Battle of Kadesh*, ed. Hans Goedicke (Baltimore: Halgo, 1985), pp. 123–206.

fering, and divine succor may seem rather exaggerated. The presentation could have been intended in part to show that the king, like his subjects, must experience suffering—a point that had been formulated in a very different way in Middle Kingdom royal instructions. The Qadesh text belongs to the period when people displayed their piety on their monuments. This public elite piety, with its rhetorical royal forms, appears less "practical" than earlier religious usage, and some scholars have considered it more truly religious.[191] Such a value judgment may impede understanding.

It is possible to relate the royal display of piety to developments in the status of the king. From the time of Amenhotep III or earlier, kings had sought to emphasize their own divinity and had set up colossal statues of themselves which served in part as deified intermediaries between people and gods and in part as cult objects in their own right. Akhenaten's claim to an exclusive knowledge of his deity fits this emphasis well. The practice of setting up such colossal statues began about the time the deposition of votive offerings in the temples of Deir el-Bahri went into decline, and the practice paralleled and surpassed the nonroyal dedication of intermediary statues of conventional scale. In the reign of Ramesses II, formal cults arose around colossal statues of him at his Delta capital.[192] The king may have attempted in this way to channel through himself the increasing tendencies toward piety in the wider society. There is no way of knowing whether the attempt succeeded among the people as a whole, from whom no evidence is preserved, but the cult of such statues, which was tied to the identity of particular kings, was relatively short-lived. Within a century or so, these cults had disappeared, while the gods and their cults continued to increase in significance, both as the chief foci of religious action and in their economic and political positions in the country. The exaltation of the king's position may have been a deliberate manipulation of religion, in which kings attempted to take control of a tendency toward piety that origi-

191. In different ways, this attitude permeates Adolf Erman's *Religion der Ägypter* and James Henry Breasted's *Development of Religion and Thought in Ancient Egypt* (New York: Scribner's, 1912; rpt. Harper & Row, 1959), which terms the Ramesside Period the "age of personal piety." There are echoes of it in Morenz, *Ägyptische Religion = Egyptian Religion;* see, e.g., pp. 85–87 = 81–83.

192. See, e.g., Labib Habachi, *Features of the Deification of Ramesses II,* ADAIK 5 (1969); Dietrich Wildung, "Göttlichkeitsstufen des Pharao," *Orientalistische Literaturzeitung* 68 (1973): 549–65; Sadek, *Popular Religion in Egypt,* pp. 11–16, noting the probability that the cults were under royal patronage.

nated elsewhere and to master it for royal purposes. The reason for the failure of this attempt was probably in part religious and in part political.[193]

Thus the evidence from the late New Kingdom displays reactions against Akhenaten, but it also exhibits continuing reflection on doctrinal and moral issues raised during his reign. The hymns of the new solar religion continued to be inscribed for some decades, during which the henotheistic style of religious discourse, which accepted polytheism fully, also developed greatly. Henotheistic discourse accorded well with public forms of piety, but the extent to which it integrated the more diverse forms of practical religion is unknown. In any event, the structure of religious practices proved resistant to royal intervention both during and after the time of Akhenaten.

The Convergence of Morality with Pietistic Belief and Practice

Late New Kingdom instruction texts fuse piety and general moral and worldly advice in a more overtly religious manner than their forerunners. The principal text, The Instruction of Amenemope, emphasizes again and again that what happens is what god ordains. It develops the widespread Egyptian ideal of the "truly silent man," which is also prominent in hymns and prayers. This ideal implies a belief that although the gods created order and uphold it, they are free to act by their own lights and may appear to be capricious. There is thus a source of possibly random affliction that is not attested in the same form from earlier times.[194] The morality of these instruction texts focuses as much on

193. Compare the conclusions of Nicolas-Christophe Grimal, *Les termes de la propagande royale égyptienne de la XIXᵉ dynastie à la conquête d'Alexandre*, Mémoires de l'Académie des Inscriptions et Belles-Lettres n.s. 6 (Paris: Imprimerie National–Boccard, 1986), pp. 556–57. For an illuminating discussion of historical developments in a similar light, see Maurice Bloch, *From Blessing to Violence: History and Ideology in the Circumcision Ritual of the Merina of Madagascar*, Cambridge Studies in Social Anthropology 61 (Cambridge: Cambridge University Press, 1986).

194. For Amenemope, see n. 157; *AEL* 2:146–63. On the "truly silent man," see Fecht, *Literarische Zeugnisse* [n. 163], p. 123. For the idea of divine free will and human resignation in the face of it, see Hellmut Brunner, "Der freie Wille Gottes in der ägyptischen Weisheit," in *Les sagesses du Proche-Orient ancien*, Travaux du Centre d'Études supérieures specialisé d'Histoire des Religions de Strasbourg (Paris: Presses Universitaires de France, 1963), pp. 103–20 (including conference discussion). This idea is not in itself new; various passages in Middle Kingdom instruction texts emphasize that what happens is what the god plans and not what people intend. See, e.g., John W. B. Barns, *Five Ramesseum Papyri* (Oxford:

accepting and enduring events as on making them happen. This morality is concerned with being reconciled to what may come one's way rather than with giving in order to improve others' fortunes, which had been the essential thrust of moralizing in earlier biographies.

This New Kingdom development elaborates a strand of thought identifiable in the earlier instruction texts, which are addressed to people at the beginning of their official careers. In those texts, self-effacement and the acceptance of what may happen are presented in a secular context, as being pragmatically advantageous. The later texts take the ideas much further and reformulate them in overtly religious terms. The new version creates a more "democratic" ideal, one better suited to people who are rather lower down the social scale than the upper-elite audience of the principal earlier works, but also more individualistic and less focused on social cohesion.

The passive ideal of the later instruction texts seems to represent a major religious transformation and is in harmony with other evidence, such as a greeting formula in late Ramesside letters, in which the writer asks after the health of the addressee and then continues: "I am alive; tomorrow is in the god's hands."[195] With important variations, much writing of the Late Period is also characterized by quietism and by resignation to the divine will.

The late New Kingdom instruction texts and the wide range of practices attested from that period combine to produce a varied picture of religious belief and action encompassing everyone from the inner elite to the lowest social groups visible in the sources. The proportion of the textual and archaeological record that is religious rather than secular seems significantly greater than in earlier times. From the first millennium B.C.E., this proportion is greater still.[196] Late New Kingdom evidence seems also to show that some old practices that had been sited within social groups were replaced by new ones related to the gods and focused on large or small temples. Thus the latest known letters to the

---

University Press for Griffith Institute, 1956), pl. 1 col. A18, pl. 2 col. B1, 11; p. 4 no. 18. For relevant examples in the Instruction of Ptahhotep, see Žába, *Les maximes de Ptahhotep* [n. 97], p. 40, col. 11, ll. 2–4; p. 25, col. 6, ll. 9–10; *AEL* 1:65 (maxim 6), 69 (maxim 22).

195. See Edward F. Wente, *Late Ramesside Letters*, Studies in Ancient Oriental Civilization 33 (Chicago: University of Chicago Press, 1967), nos. 1, 17. Egyptian texts in Jaroslav Černý, *Late Ramesside Letters*, BiAe 9 (1939), to which Wente gives precise references.

196. For theoretical discussion of this "sacralization," see Baines, *Göttinger Miszellen* 76 (1984): 47–50.

dead date to the Ramesside Period and are contemporary with the earliest letters to gods.[197]

This abundance of material evidence may reflect well the existence of a great number of religious observances. At New Year, for example, there was a host of practices inside and outside the temples, including formalized and religiously motivated gift exchange.[198] If letter formulas are to be believed, people would go to local shrines three times in a ten-day week, or even daily, to inquire about the well-being of absent relatives and to pray in their behalf. They would also go up to three times a week to make libations. The absent relatives wrote and asked that those at home perform these rituals in their behalf while they carried out similar rituals in the temples of the gods of the region they were visiting.[199]

In a striking change in religious style which took place in the late New Kingdom, "secular" scenes nearly disappeared from tomb decoration.[200] Most of the new tomb scenes have other-worldly subjects and would aid the deceased's existence in the hereafter, but the decoration also includes increased numbers of this-worldly hymns to the gods. These changes parallel the display of piety on nonmortuary monuments. All these developments could be due in part to changes in decorum rather than to changes in religious belief and practice. If this was so, ideas and practices that first come into view during this period should be posited for earlier times as well. But even if this hypothesis is correct, the system of decorum was so ancient and so vital to public life and display that alterations in it were serious matters, and should not be seen as isolated or superficial alterations. The introduction of the open display of piety on monuments was, by any reckoning, a development of substance, whether or not piety had been displayed earlier in personal names, attitudes, and actions. This increase in public and monumental religion formed part of an overall increase in religious activity and concern.

Another development that seems to have spanned the time of Akhenaten and came into its own many centuries afterward, in the Late

197. See Baines, *JEA* 73 (1987): 97 with n. 90.

198. See J. F. Borghouts, *Nieuwjaar in het oude Egypte,* inaugural lecture (Leiden: Rijksuniversiteit te Leiden, 1986).

199. E.g., Wente, *Late Ramesside Letters,* nos. 1, 4, 9, 16, 45.

200. The interpretation that this change shows an intensified focus on religion is not the only one possible. Religious material could have been presented in tombs as a matter of prestige, so that people took advantage of a privilege that had become available through the weakening of centrally influenced decorum. If this latter interpretation should be correct, the change would have been a "democratization." This alternative is probably valid in part, and it does not contradict the argument I propose in the text.

Period, was a great expansion in religious practices related to animals.[201] Sacred animals were, among other things, manifestations of deities, and they were more approachable than the cult images in temples. They could also be objects of piety.[202] For worshipers, the animals' relation to deities was comparable to that of living and deceased human intermediaries.[203] Some sacred animals gave oracles. Although an individual could dedicate burials of animals, the animals were not personal but communal religious property. While alive, they were kept in temple complexes, and they were normally buried in vaults or catacombs filled with the mummies of other animals of various species. Thus the increase in animal worship was in keeping with the general movement toward community practices in later Egyptian religion.

The picture of late New Kingdom religious practices that can be sketched is more closely integrated than that of any earlier time, and the intensity of ritual activity is striking. Separate strands of earlier official cult and of practical and perhaps devotional religion appear to have come together into a single complex to an extent to which they had not done earlier. A lessening of the constraints of decorum may have affected the way people acted and thought, as well as the evidence available to us. The components of this change were probably both narrowly religious and more broadly social.

Religion concentrated increasingly on the temples and on the living, whereas in earlier times the personal aspirations of the elite had been recorded in tombs that were individualistic in focus and could include no direct religious expression about the gods. Most members of the elite for whom evidence is preserved now held priestly office and administered the vast wealth that the temples had accumulated.[204] The con-

201. On these practices, see Hans Bonnet, *Reallexikon der ägyptischen Religionsgeschichte* (Berlin: de Gruyter, 1952), pp. 812–24; Dieter Kessler, "Tierkult," *LÄ* 6:571–87, and *Die heiligen Tiere und der König*, vol. 1, *Beiträge zu Organisation, Kult und Theologie der spätzeitlichen Tierfriedhöfe*, Ägypten und Altes Testament 16 (Wiesbaden: Harrassowitz, 1989). Kessler's interpretations would revise traditional understanding of animal cults very radically, but much in them seems problematic to me. For a good presentation on the basis of everyday documents, see Thompson, *Memphis under the Ptolemies*, esp. pp. 190–265.

202. Siegfried Morenz, "Ein neues Dokument zur Tierbestattung," in his *Religion und Geschichte*, pp. 304–12.

203. See Herman te Velde, "Mittler," *LÄ* 4:161–63.

204. See Hermann Kees, *Das Priestertum im ägyptischen Staat vom Neuen Reich bis zur Spätzeit*, PÄ 1 (1953; *Indices und Nachträge*, 1958); Serge Sauneron, *The Priests of Ancient Egypt*, trans. Ann Morrissett (New York: Grove, 1960). For the late New Kingdom, the picture of an elite dominated by holders of priestly office may be skewed by the lack of

struction and decoration of large tombs did not cease, but the practice became less important. In the aftermath of the New Kingdom, provision for the next life was focused on elaborate coffins, whose decoration reached a peak of excellence at that time, as did the mummification of the bodies interred in them. The proportion of people who could aspire to a burial with mummification seems to have declined gradually in the Third Intermediate Period.

In the late New Kingdom and its aftermath, the king's power and his influence on religion declined, although his central position in temple iconography remained largely unchanged. The reality outside the temple was different. One late Ramesside text asks whose master the king is, implying that he is no one's.[205] Another presents him expressly as a man in contrast to the god Amun, something that would probably have been unthinkable a couple of centuries earlier.[206]

By the Late Period, the civil administration of the country seems to have been conducted by people whose temple statues—their principal monuments—displayed titles that were almost exclusively religious. Dreams with religious significance now occurred in temples, rather than being personal experiences that took place outside the temples. Such changes may have contributed to the increased integration of local communities, which were larger than they had been in earlier times. People traveled less about the country for reasons of state, and the central state intervened less in local affairs. Society was becoming more urban, and the "manorial" or partly manorial ideals of the earlier elite were in decline.

This picture applies principally to the Late Period. Nonetheless, the piety of the late New Kingdom—which is by no means its only religious manifestation—fits such a social context well.[207] Although piety looked to local centers, it was an individual matter, and the extended family was not so much a focus of display as it had been.

---

evidence from the north; it is unlikely to be fully valid for the Ramesside capital. During the Late Period, almost all officials had priesthoods.

205. Wente, *Late Ramesside Letters* [n. 195], no. 21.

206. Alan H. Gardiner, *Late-Egyptian Stories*, BiAe 1 (1932), p. 72, ll. 9–10; *AEL* 2:228. The person referred to, Kha'emwese, is probably King Ramesses IX and not a vizier of the same period. The former reading is supported by parallels in the diplomatic correspondence of the Amarna letters. If the latter were assumed, the statement would be robbed of much of its point.

207. On piety, see in general Morenz, *Ägyptische Religion* = *Egyptian Religion*, pp. 85–116 = 81–104; Hellmut Brunner, "Persönliche Frömmigkeit," *LÄ* 4:951–63. For a different approach, see Assmann, *Ägypten*.

CONCLUSION

From the vast span of time I have surveyed, the evidence for everyday religious beliefs and practice is sparse and fragmentary, and its organization may defy analysis. Because of this paucity of evidence, it is often necessary to combine material from widely differing periods and contexts in order to suggest a meaningful interpretation. A consequence of these difficulties is that the problem of how to interpret the sources is in the background of all study. The sources were not created and then almost randomly preserved or destroyed to supply us with a balanced picture of Egyptian religion. Gaps in the available sources may point to genuine characteristics and emphases of religious culture, such as decorum, or to distortions of the record caused by the pattern of preservation of archaeological sites and of modern investigation.

If one is to compensate for these difficulties in the sources, it is necessary to construct a framework within which evidence can be evaluated. Such a framework is both conceptual, relating to the organization of religious and other beliefs, and sociological, relating to the organization of society. I have viewed developments in religious forms both as conceptions that have their own rationale and acquire their own momentum and as practices that take place in a social context. In so doing, I have often used arguments from analogy or silence. This procedure has many drawbacks, but it has the crucial advantage of helping us to see Egyptian beliefs and practices as rich variations on universal human forms and conceptions, rather than as unique and alien phenomena.

Societies construct shared worlds that give meaning to successes and failures and to their effects on groups and individuals. In these worlds, connections between social, religious, and moral concerns are particularly important. The Egyptians created an attractive but in a sense superficial public ideology and iconography that concentrated on positive experiences and ignored the darker side of life or pushed it to the margins of the cosmos. The public image, which I have hardly discussed, has tended to convince modern people, perhaps more than it convinced the Egyptians themselves, that Egyptian life had a charmed quality. I have attempted to show that that public image was complemented by more nuanced views and actions that accepted the reality of adversity and responded to it. Only traces of these views and actions are preserved.

Despite the diversity of the beliefs and practices I have reviewed, they are coherent, both in their conceptual organization and in their response to human need. But coherence is not the same as rigid logic, and religious life should be allowed an appropriate degree of nonrationality. Our own beliefs and practices are not always rational, and ancient ones should not be evaluated by standards stricter than those we apply to ourselves. These complex areas of life and belief, of morals and loss, are never straightforward, any more than gods are, but they are vital both to society and to religion. Although the Egyptians very often disguised this fact, they were well aware of it.

DYNASTIC CHRONOLOGY

with Names of Rulers and Periods Mentioned in the Text

Dates are approximate, with a margin of error rising to more than a century for the early third millennium B.C.E. An alternative date for the beginning of the First Dynasty is 3100 B.C.E. For 2000–664 B.C.E., the margin of error is up to thirty years, after which most dates are exact to within one year. Overlapping dates indicate competing dynasties.

PREDYNASTIC PERIOD		c. 5000–2950
EARLY DYNASTIC PERIOD (1st–3d dynasties)		c. 2950–2600
1st Dynasty	*c. 2950–2800*	
Narmer (Menes?)		
Aha (Menes?)		
Den		
Semerkhet		
2d Dynasty	*c. 2800–2675*	
Peribsen		
3d Dynasty	*c. 2675–2600*	
Djoser		
OLD KINGDOM (4th–8th dynasties)		c. 2600–2150
4th Dynasty	*c. 2600–2480*	
Khufu		
Khafre		
Menkaure		
5th Dynasty	*c. 2480–2340*	
Niuserre		
6th Dynasty	*c. 2340–2180*	
Pepy I		
Merenre		
Pepy II		

Chronology supplied by John Baines, following Rolf Krauss, *Sothis- und Monddaten: Studien zur astronomischen und technischen Chronologie Altägyptens*, Hildesheimer Ägyptologische Beiträge 20 (Hildesheim: Gerstenberg, 1985).

FIRST INTERMEDIATE PERIOD (9th–11th dynasties)		*c.* 2150–1970
10th Dynasty	*c. 2090–1970*	
Akhtoy		
Merikare		
11th Dynasty	*c. 2081–1939*	

MIDDLE KINGDOM (11th–13th dynasties)		*c.* 1970–1640
11th Dynasty (all Egypt)	*c. 1970–1939*	
Nebhepetre Mentu-		
hotep	c. 2010–1960	
12th Dynasty	*1938–c. 1756*	
Amenemhat I	1938–1908	
Senwosret I	1918–1875	
Senwosret III	1836–1818	
13th Dynasty	*c. 1756–1630*	

SECOND INTERMEDIATE PERIOD (15th–17th dynasties)		1640–1520
HYKSOS PERIOD (15th–16th dynasties)		

NEW KINGDOM (18th–20th dynasties)		1539–c. 1075
18th Dynasty	*1539–1292*	
Ahmose	1539–1514	
Amenhotep I	1514–1493	
Thutmoside Period		
Thutmose III	1479–c. 1426	
Hatshepsut	c. 1475–1458	
Amenhotep II	c. 1426–1400	
Thutmose IV	1400–1390	
Amenhotep III	1390–1353	
Amarna Period		
Amenhotep IV/		
Akhenaten	1353–1336	
Semenkhkare	1335–1332	
Tutankhamun	1332–1322	
Ay	1322–1319	
Horemhab	1319–1292	
RAMESSIDE PERIOD (19th–20th dynasties)		
19th Dynasty	*1292–1190*	
Ramesses I	1292–1290	
Sety I	1290–1279	
Ramesses II	1279–1213	
Merneptah	1213–1204	
20th Dynasty	*1190–c. 1075*	
Sethnakht	1190–1187	
Ramesses III	1187–1156	
Ramesses IV	1156–1150	
Ramesses IX	1126–1108	

THIRD INTERMEDIATE PERIOD (21st–25th dynasties)		c. 1075–718
21st Dynasty	*c. 1075–945*	
22d Dynasty	*c. 945–718*	
25th Dynasty	*c. 770–656*	
Piye (formerly read		
Piankhy)	c. 750–718	

LATE PERIOD (25th–30th dynasties)   c. 718–332

25th Dynasty (cont.)	*c.*	*718–656*
Shabaka	c. 718–703	
26th (Saite) Dynasty		*664–525*

GRECO-ROMAN PERIOD   332 B.C.E.–395 C.E.

Macedonian Dynasty	*332–305*
Ptolemaic Dynasty	*305–30*
Roman Period	*30* B.C.E.–*395* C.E.

SELECTED BIBLIOGRAPHY

Allen, Thomas George. *The Book of the Dead, or Going Forth by Day.* Studies in Ancient Oriental Civilization 37. Chicago: University of Chicago Press, 1974.

Assmann, Jan. *Ägypten: Theologie und Frömmigkeit einer frühen Hochkultur.* Stuttgart: Kohlhammer, 1984.

———. *Ägyptische Hymnen und Gebete.* Bibliothek der Alten Welt: Der Alte Orient. Zurich and Munich: Artemis, 1975.

———. "Die 'Häresie' des Echnaton: Aspekte der Amarna-Religion." *Saeculum* 23 (1972): 109–26.

———. *Der König als Sonnenpriester: Ein kosmographischer Begleittext zur kultischen Sonnenhymnik.* ADAIK 7, 1970.

———. *Liturgische Lieder an den Sonnengott: Untersuchungen zur altägyptischen Hymnik, I.* MÄS 19. Berlin: Hessling, 1969.

———. "Die 'loyalistische Lehre' Echnatons." *SAK* 8 (1980): 1–32.

———. *Re und Amun: Die Krise des polytheistischen Weltbilds im Ägypten der 18.–20. Dynastie.* OBO 51, 1983.

———. *Sonnenhymnen in thebanischen Gräbern.* Theben 1. Mainz: von Zabern, 1983.

Baines, John. "Interpretations of Religion: Logic, Discourse, Rationality." *Göttinger Miszellen* 76 (1984): 25–54.

———. "Practical Religion and Piety." *JEA* 73 (1987): 79–98.

——— and Jaromír Málek. *Atlas of Ancient Egypt.* Oxford: Phaidon; New York: Facts on File, 1980.

——— et al., eds. *Pyramid Studies and Other Essays Presented to I. E. S. Edwards.* Occasional Publications 7. London: Egypt Exploration Society, 1988.

Bonnet, Hans. *Reallexikon der ägyptischen Religionsgeschichte.* Berlin: de Gruyter, 1952.

Brunner, Hellmut. *Das hörende Herz: Kleine Schriften zur Religions- und Geistesgeschichte Ägyptens.* Ed. Wolfgang Röllig. OBO 80, 1988.

Černý, Jaroslav. *Ancient Egyptian Religion.* Westport, Conn.: Greenwood, 1979.

Egypt's Golden Age: The Art of Living in the New Kingdom, 1558–1085 B.C. Boston: Museum of Fine Arts, 1982.

Englund, Gertie, ed. *The Religion of the Ancient Egyptians: Cognitive Structures and Popular Expressions*. Proceedings of Symposia in Uppsala and Bergen, 1987 and 1988. Acta Universitatis Upsaliensis: Boreas 20. Uppsala, 1989.

Faulkner, R. O. *The Ancient Egyptian Book of the Dead*. Rev. ed. Ed. Carol Andrews. London: British Museum; New York: Macmillan, 1985.

——. *The Ancient Egyptian Coffin Texts*. 3 vols. Warminster: Aris & Phillips, 1973–1978.

——. *The Ancient Egyptian Pyramid Texts*. Oxford: Clarendon, 1969.

Frankfort, Henri. *Kingship and the Gods: A Study of Ancient Near Eastern Religion as the Integration of Society and Nature*. Chicago: University of Chicago Press, 1948.

—— et al. *The Intellectual Adventure of Ancient Man*. Chicago: University of Chicago Press, 1946. Also published without the essay on ancient Israel as *Before Philosophy*. Harmondsworth and Baltimore: Penguin, 1949.

Gardiner, Sir Alan. *Egypt of the Pharaohs: An Introduction*. Oxford: Clarendon, 1961.

Helck, Wolfgang, Eberhard Otto, and Wolfhart Westendorf, eds. *Lexikon der Ägyptologie*. 7 vols. Wiesbaden: Harrassowitz, 1972–.

Hornung, Erik. *Ägyptische Unterweltsbücher*. 2d ed. Bibliothek der Alten Welt: Der Alte Orient. Zurich and Munich: Artemis, 1984.

——. *Altägyptische Höllenvorstellungen*. Abhandlungen der Sächsischen Akademie der Wissenschaften, Philologisch-historische Klasse 59/3. Berlin (East): Akademie, 1968.

——. "Die Anfänge von Monotheismus und Trinität in Ägypten." In *Der eine Gott und der dreieine Gott: Das Gottesverständnis bei Christen, Juden und Muslimen*, ed. Karl Rahner, pp. 48–66. Munich and Zurich: Schnell & Steiner, 1983.

——. *Conceptions of God in Ancient Egypt: The One and the Many*. Trans. John Baines. Ithaca: Cornell University Press, 1982; London: Routledge & Kegan Paul, 1983. First published as *Der Eine und die Vielen: Ägyptische Gottesvorstellungen*. Darmstadt: Wissenschaftliche Buchgesellschaft, 1971.

——. *Geist der Pharaonenzeit*. Zurich and Munich: Artemis, 1989.

—— et al. *Der ägyptische Mythos von der Himmelskuh: Eine Ätiologie des Unvollkommenen*. OBO 46, 1982.

Kemp, Barry J. *Ancient Egypt: Anatomy of a Civilization*. London: Routledge; New York: Routledge Chapman & Hall, 1989.

Lesko, Leonard H. *The Ancient Egyptian Book of Two Ways*. Near Eastern Studies 17. Berkeley: University of California Press, 1972.

Lichtheim, Miriam. *Ancient Egyptian Literature*. 3 vols. Berkeley: University of California Press, 1973–1980.

Morenz, Siegfried. *Egyptian Religion*. Trans. Ann E. Keep. London: Methuen; Ithaca: Cornell University Press, 1973. First published as *Ägyptische Religion*. Religionen der Menschheit 8. Stuttgart: Kohlhammer, 1960.

——. *Gott und Mensch im alten Ägypten*. 2d ed. Darmstadt: Wissenschaftliche Buchgesellschaft; Zurich: Artemis, 1984.

——. *Religion und Geschichte des alten Ägypten: Gesammelte Aufsätze*. Ed. Elke Blumenthal et al. Weimar: Hermann Böhlaus Nachfolger, 1975.

O'Connor, David, and David P. Silverman, eds. *Ancient Egyptian Kingship: New Investigations*. Cambridge: Harvard University Press, forthcoming.

Otto, Eberhard. *Ancient Egyptian Art: The Cults of Osiris and Amon*. Trans. Kate Bosse Griffiths. New York: Abrams, 1967. Published in England as *Egyptian Art and the Cults of Osiris and Amon*. London: Thames & Hudson, 1968. First published as *Osiris und Amun: Kult und heilige Stätten*. Munich: Hirmer, 1966.

Pinch, Geraldine. *New Kingdom Votive Offerings to Hathor.* Oxford: Griffith Institute, forthcoming.

Posener, Georges. *De la divinité du pharaon.* Cahiers de la Société Asiatique 15. Paris: Imprimerie Nationale, 1960.

Pritchard, James B., ed. *Ancient Near Eastern Texts Relating to the Old Testament.* 3d ed. with supplement. Princeton: Princeton University Press, 1969.

Redford, Donald B. *Akhenaten: The Heretic King.* Princeton: Princeton University Press, 1984.

Sadek, Ashraf Iskander. *Popular Religion in Egypt during the New Kingdom.* Hildesheimer Ägyptologische Beiträge 27. Hildesheim: Gerstenberg, 1987 (1988).

Sauneron, Serge. *The Priests of Ancient Egypt.* Trans. from 1st French ed. by Ann Morrissett. New York: Grove, 1960. Available in a revised French edition as *Les prêtres de l'ancienne Égypte,* 2d ed. Paris: Persea, 1988.

Simpson, William Kelly. *Religion and Philosophy in Ancient Egypt.* Yale Egyptological Studies 3. New Haven: Yale Egyptological Seminar, Department of Near Eastern Languages and Civilizations, Yale University, 1989.

———, ed. *The Literature of Ancient Egypt.* New Haven: Yale University Press, 1972.

Thompson, Dorothy J. *Memphis under the Ptolemies.* Princeton: Princeton University Press, 1988.

Trigger, B. G., et al. *Ancient Egypt: A Social History.* Cambridge: Cambridge University Press, 1983.

Velde, Herman te. *Seth, God of Confusion.* 2d ed. PÄ 6, 1977.

Westendorf, Wolfhart, ed. *Aspekte der spätägyptischen Religion.* Göttinger Orientforschungen, 4th ser., Ägypten 9. Wiesbaden: Harrassowitz, 1979.

Wildung, Dietrich. *Egyptian Saints: Deification in Pharaonic Egypt.* Hagop Kevorkian Series on Near Eastern Art and Civilization. New York: New York University Press, 1977.

Willems, Harco. "Crime, Cult and Capital Punishment (Mo'alla Inscription 8)." *JEA* 76 (1990): 27–54.

INDEX